Advance Praise for

All the Scary Little Gods

"I'd endorse this book for the prologue alone. Our stories are important. Natalie's story will help people who are looking for an empathetic witness, needing to find their voice, seeking to gain an understanding of the emotional and spiritual abuse they are under, and asking who will rescue them. Others need to ask what about Natalie's story disrupts their own? Ultimately, the reader will be faced with this question: Why is the Church full of anemic lovers?"

—**Aimee Byrd,** Author of *The Hope in Our Scars* and *Recovering from Biblical Manhood and Womanhood*

"During an epidemic of spiritual trauma and abuse, many women are noticing the impact and taking steps toward healing and growth. Natalie Hoffman offers an authentic and informative approach through her journey of trauma and working out her faith with vulnerability and genuineness. She openly and bravely sits with the pain and internal struggle while offering hope and support through the deconstruction process with the desire to come alongside other women to help them fly free in their journey with God. I recommend this book for those who are longing for camaraderie and support in the excruciating journey of healing from spiritual abuse and trauma through holding an empathetic witness to each other's experiences."

—**Naomi Norton,** PhD, LCMFT, LMFT

"Natalie's story is not for the critics; it is for the prisoners. Sadly, the critics don't know that they are also prisoners. So, for those who know they are prisoners, please, please read her book!

"Natalie has one of the clearest and most powerful voices in the world of helping people find freedom. While many people who have labored under spiritual abuse turn away from the trappings of religion, Natalie ran toward the Life-Giver and His ways of giving life. In the process, she has made a way for others to do the same. I met Natalie because of her voice, her integrity, and her love for finding life and truth in the Scriptures. She has become a colleague and an ally for all those same reasons. If you have lived in fear, shame, or the pressure to perform to make a mad God happy, then you will find a new way to think and live in these pages!"

—**Bob Hamp,** LMFT Therapist, Author, Teacher at Think Differently Counseling | Think Differently Academy

"For every woman whose voice has been silenced, Natalie Hoffman wants to let them ROAR! In this poignant memoir, Natalie gives voice to the little girl who was told again and again that she had to be smaller, less than, and not take up so much space. She gives voice to the young woman desperately trying to follow Jesus and do the right thing, yet at the same time feeling used, neglected, and abused by those who were supposed to be her protectors and advocates. For those hurt by parents or spouses and having that hurt compounded by churches and counselors, Natalie shows how you can rise above your programming and learn that you have a voice. That you matter. And, most of all, that you are truly, deeply loved by the One who sees every time you are silenced—and who wants to give you back your voice."

—**Sheila Wray Gregoire,** Author of *The Great Sex Rescue*, Founder of BareMarriage.com

"As a fellow survivor of legalism and false narratives in the Church, I found *All the Scary Little Gods* to be wholly relatable, compelling, and full of truth. Natalie's prose is both powerful and vulnerable, weaving her past experience of emotional and spiritual abuse with her current hard-won wisdom and insight in a captivating chronicle of inner strength, redemption, and love. Fellow victims and survivors of covert abuse, as well as those who struggle with reconciling a good God with marital and parenting struggles, will find an empathetic witness and sound assurance in Natalie's words. If you read one memoir this year, make it this one."

—BETH LOTTIG, Editor, Founder of Inspire Books

"Natalie is gifted with a thought-provoking ability to be candid and relevant in her storytelling about her own life, beginning in early childhood. Her insights and discoveries will help any reader—victim, survivor, people helper, family, and friend—to best understand the necessity to question and change our entrenched beliefs and programming if we are to find the path to self-acceptance and healthy love for self and others. This book provides the road map to healing for all those who have been harmed, and I truly hope every therapist will read this life-changing work."

—ANNETTE OLTMANS, Founder of The Mend Project

"With vulnerability and insightful reflection, Natalie shares her journey of healing from a fundamentalist culture fueled by toxic theology. *All the Scary Little Gods* is a memoir that gives voice to those who have felt isolated by spiritual abuse. Natalie reminds readers that there is a path forward toward authentic faith and that our grief-filled steps toward God sometimes lead us away from communities and traditions of our youth."

—STACEY BYINGTON WYNN, PCC, MDIV, Founder of ClarityUnleashed.com

"*All the Scary Little Gods* is an achingly beautiful and wonderfully creative glimpse into a healing self-awareness where we meet with our earlier selves in empathy and converse with them in kindness."

—Rick Pidcock, Religion Writer at *Baptist News Global*

"Natalie offers the reader a uniquely personal window into the world of a survivor's heart who has done years of exceptionally difficult and detailed inner-healing work. Natalie not only shares with us a clear understanding of her past trauma in poignant and sometimes even humorous vignettes, but she then brilliantly pairs those alongside her present view of God in a safe, inviting, and therapeutic method; this book is like a therapy session in a memoir."

—Emily Elizabeth Anderson, Founder of Thriving Forward

"What a journey. Thank you, Natalie, for taking us readers on such a heartbreaking liberation journey. Truly, the words in this book come from a bruised and wise sage who has lived through hell to speak to such heaven. *All the Scary Little Gods* helps me believe more deeply in the truth of the gospel."

—Dr. Andrew J. Bauman, Founder & Director of the Christian Counseling Center for Sexual Health & Trauma, Author of *SAFE CHURCH: How to Guard Against Sexism & Abuse in Christian Communities*

One girl's quest to find
TRUTH and LOVE
in a Maze of Religious Abuse

NATALIE HOFFMAN

Copyright © 2023
All the Scary Little Gods: A Memoir
Natalie Hoffman

All rights reserved. No part of this publication may be reproduced, distributed, or transmitted in any form or by any means, including photocopying, recording, or other electronic or mechanical methods, without the prior written permission of the publisher, except in the case of brief quotations embodied in reviews and certain other non-commercial uses permitted by copyright law.

FLYING FREE
M·E·D·I·A

Flying Free Media
PO Box 128
3050 145th Street
Rosemount, MN 55068
FlyingFreeNow.com

ISBN: 978-1-7328943-3-4 (print), 978-1-7328943-4-1 (epub)

Ordering Information:
Special discounts are available on quantity purchases by corporations, associations, and others. For details, contact the publisher at the address above.

Publishing and Design Services: MartinPublishingServices.com
Editor: Tiffany Yecke Brooks, Kelly Wiggains
Author Photo: Lollipop Media

Unless otherwise noted, Scripture quotations taken from the Berean Standard Bible (BSB). The Holy Bible, Berean Standard Bible, BSB is produced in cooperation with Bible Hub, Discovery Bible, OpenBible.com, and the Berean Bible Translation Committee. This text of God's Word has been dedicated to the public domain.

Scripture quotations marked (NIV) are taken from the Holy Bible, New International Version®, NIV®. Copyright © 1973, 1978, 1984, 2011 by Biblica, Inc.™ Used by permission of Zondervan. All rights reserved worldwide. www.zondervan.com The "NIV" and "New International Version" are trademarks registered in the United States Patent and Trademark Office by Biblica, Inc.™

For the nine loves of my life.

You didn't know it,
but you were the angels
who led me Home.

Contents

Preface 1

Foreword 3

Prologue 7

Part One 9

1. Bawl Baby 13
2. The Get-Out-of-Hell-Free Card 18
3. All the Pretty Little Ponies 21
4. Devoted 24
5. The Birds and the Bees 27
6. Thief in the Night 30
7. Lunch Lady 33
8. Converts 36
9. Apple of God's Eye 39
10. I Found It! 44
11. Missions 47
12. Beats 50
13. My Utmost for His Highest 53
14. Sweet Sixteen 57
15. The Theater 60
16. Rebellion Is as the Sin of Witchcraft 63
17. Satan's Children 67
18. First Kiss 70
19. Girl Crush 74
20. Nanny 79

21	Saddle Up Your Horses!	82
22	Clicking	87
23	Dating Jesus	91
24	Baby Girl	94
25	Bedrest	98
26	A Reason to Live	101
27	Enough Faith	106
28	Sex at the Beach	110
29	Even If It Kills Me	113

Part Two 119

30	Trust God	127
31	A Crucified Life	132
32	I Am a Sheep	136
33	Forks	140
34	Y2K	144
35	Red Heifer	148
36	Crying Out	152
37	Epidurals	158
38	Dodgeball	161
39	Standards and Convictions	166
40	Death and Life	170
41	Tongues and Quilts	174
42	Marriage Conferences	178
43	Visionary Woman	181
44	The Letter	187
45	Soap	192
46	The Fool	195
47	Road Trip	198
48	The Hotel Room	203

Part Three 207

49 Shifting 209
50 First Domino 213
51 Marriage Intensive 218
52 Detach 224
53 The Table 229
54 A Little Note from Rosie 231
55 Flying Free 234
56 A Record of Wrongs 240
57 Goo 248
58 Bible Counseling 250
59 Balls 258
60 Separation 263
61 BRAVE 266
62 My Voice 268
63 George 271
64 Confrontation 275
65 Hoops and Masks 278
66 Burn the Ships 282
67 Mental Health 284
68 Another Hotel Room 287

Part Four 289

69 You Don't Know God 291
70 Drugs and Therapy 294
71 Stalkers 298
72 Redemption Stories 300
73 Love Just Is 306
74 Connecting the Dots 308
75 Wedding Day 311

76	Soap and Vodka	312
77	Funerals	314
78	Flying Away	317
79	Dad	322
80	Tsunami	330
81	Mom	334
82	Letting Go	339
83	The Art of Grief	345
84	What a Son Needs	350
85	COVID	353
86	Sin	358
87	Church and Bible	363
88	Prayer	370
89	Surprise	376

Epilogue 379
Dear Reader 380

Preface

This story isn't just my story. It belongs to all the little girls who grew up in hyper-conservative homes and were terrorized and threatened, not necessarily by physical violence but by ideas about their origins, their identities, and the God who created them. The danger in writing and releasing our stories to the public is that we bump up against the privacy of other people we care about. In order to mitigate some of the fallout from that, I've chosen to change the names of almost everyone in my story.

This story is also not the *whole* story. It's just the part that has to do with my programming about God, how and why it all unraveled, and what my relationship with God looks like today. I suppose some people will disagree with my experiences, and that's okay. They are still my experiences. I lived them, after all. Someone else may have been in the room with me at any given time and have a completely different perspective about what happened and why. That's okay, too. That is their story, and it belongs to them. But I have learned that contrary to what I was taught, just because someone else has their own story about what happened doesn't make my perspective imaginary or irrelevant.

My story matters just as much as anyone's, and I have a compelling reason to tell my story. *I believe women should be free.* Free to think for themselves. Free to question long-held religious traditions. Free to doubt. Free to grieve. Free to explore. Free to lead. Free to make mistakes. Free to set boundaries. Free to find safety. Free to speak out. Free to be authentically who they were created to be—and to love and enjoy who that unique person is. I believe women have deep within them a *Great and Safe Love*. My story is about finding that Love and changing the world with it.

xoxo

Natalie Hoffman

Foreword

I first met Natalie a few years ago when she graciously invited me onto her podcast to talk about one of my books on recovering from religious trauma. Natalie is from Minnesota, as is my entire extended family, so we immediately bonded over a hilarious conversation on the simultaneously charming and absolutely bonkers culture of the North Star State.

What really stood out to me, however, was her tremendous wisdom and perspective when we transitioned to the much heavier topic of damage wrought by toxic religious teachings. Natalie was clearly a woman with a deep and battle-worn faith who refused to accept pat answers, lazy theology, or abusive practices; what was more, I could see how wholeheartedly she empowered others to demand better, as well.

This is why, when Natalie told me she was working on a memoir about her own experiences deprogramming herself from the harmful religious teachings that had imprisoned her in a life of devastating anxiety, silent suffering, and submissive abuse, I knew that it was going to be powerful—not only as a story but also as a tool for others facing similar challenges.

A memoir is not a self-help book, but it can be incredibly empowering. The most important question a memoir can answer is "How?" Of course, the five Ws—*Who, What, When, Where, Why*—are all important as well. But no matter how engaging the narration, what really makes a memoir dynamic is when it transcends its inward focus on the narrator's journey and turns outward to inspire readers toward new growth and deeper wisdom themselves.

After nearly twenty years as an author, professor, writing coach, and editor, I have learned that "How?" is, ultimately, a question of agency and empowerment. I have also learned that the best gifts a memoir can offer to its readers are answers to the questions it poses.

How did the author end up in those circumstances?

How did they feel?

How did they change?

How did they find their voice?

How did they move forward?

This is what Natalie gives to her readers in *All the Scary Little Gods*. It is so much more than simply an account of her story (though every person's story is important and worthy of being heard). It describes her struggle to free herself from the damaging programming that controlled her for most of her life—and, in doing so, provides readers with a real-life example of how they can do the same.

Her writing is vibrant and deeply intimate. The innocence, honesty, and humor (seriously, she is *so funny* sometimes) that Natalie breathes into her storytelling make *All the Scary Little Gods* both deeply personal and remarkably universal. Readers will recognize themselves at many points in Natalie's story, which functions almost like vicarious therapy for parsing and interrogating the ways that toxic church cultures can swallow people whole. (But also, still go to *actual* therapy, too, if you can.)

If you have struggled with reconciling the harmful ways that twisted theology has entrapped you while simultaneously struggling to embrace the beautiful and freeing parts of your faith, this book will give you guidance.

Foreword

If you feel isolated, ignored, or abandoned in your quest to reclaim your own body, mind, and soul from the scary little gods of your own life, this book will stand beside you as an empathetic witness.

If you are frustrated with how long it took to open your eyes to the damage being perpetrated by narcissists masquerading as people of God, this book will offer compassion.

If you are angry at the systems that protect abusers, silence victims, and perpetuate their own twisted version of truth—systems that feed and nurture all the scary little gods in your own world—this book will show you how to fight back to liberate yourself. In fact, the Greek word usually translated "salvation" in the Bible is *sōtēria*, which literally means "liberation," "deliverance," or "freedom."

All the Scary Little Gods delivers a message of salvation—of liberation and deliverance—for anyone who feels trapped in a controlling, manipulative, or abusive culture. For anyone imprisoned by their own scary little gods.

You deserve more. You are worthy of respect, dignity, and love. You deserve to be free.

—Tiffany Yecke Brooks, PhD,
Author of *Gaslighted by God: Reconstructing a Disillusioned Faith*

Prologue

"You don't know God," the church elder said, his eyes locked and loaded on me from across the conference table. "He's absent from your narrative."

The room went woozy, and I struggled to bring my brain back online, managing to sputter, "God is the *center* of my narrative!"

But he wasn't listening. He already had his story about me.

Here's mine.

Part One

*"Trauma is not what happens to us,
but what we hold inside
in the absence of an empathetic witness."*

—Peter A. Lavine, *In an Unspoken Voice*

Every human being needs to be seen and known by another. An "empathetic witness," as Peter Lavine puts it. This is how we experience love, connection, and healing. When a person experiences life alone without anyone to witness what she has gone through—or even worse, when she is told her experience is all in her head or that she is making a big deal out of nothing or that she deserves it—she will experience trauma. That trauma will permeate and impact every area of her life unless she is able to metabolize it with an empathetic witness both within herself and outside of herself.

I've invited my younger self to tell Part One of my story from her perspective. In asking little Natalie to do this, I'm giving her space to share her experiences, and I am offering to be her adult empathetic witness. While her life seemed to be wholesome and full of love to the average outsider, she was missing an empathetic witness for many of her childhood experiences. Her body held that trauma inside, influencing her thinking and impacting her relationships in profound and confusing ways.

*Please excuse me. I'm so sorry for interrupting, but I **did** have an empathetic witness. I don't remember a time when I wasn't aware of a Big Presence inside of me. Like Someone was watching me. That Presence was my empathetic witness, and I loved it, even though I didn't know what it was. That Presence kept me fighting to find the Truth in the middle of a lot of liars, liars, pants on fires. I just want to make sure you know that. I don't mean to ruin your book or anything.*

xoxo

Little Natalie

Oh, darling girl. This is *your* book. You are welcome to jump in any time. I value your voice.

Dear Reader, she's right. Little Natalie usually is. All these years and experiences later, I have come to see that for me, the One who created the universe, the quark, and little girls and boys has been the empathetic witness I've needed to process trauma and weave those experiences into something transcendent. Isn't that what Jesus promised when He said, "*It is for your benefit that I am going away. Unless I go away, the Advocate will not come to you; but if I go, I will send Him to you*" (John 16:7)?

For me, the journey has been about discovering that empathetic witness in the tangled maze of religious programming that taught me how to worship and fawn after scary little gods. Gods that included authority figures, pet religious beliefs, my own confused and conflicted shadow parts, and a powerless, petty god made in the image of all the abusers I had ever known: a god who gaslighted, manipulated, and terrified humans for his glory and pleasure.

Part One

I offer this book to the many survivors of emotional and spiritual abuse who never had an empathetic witness and desperately needed one. Here's mine. To me, He is capital-L Love. Christ. Creator. Source. God. My Friend. This Spirit is in me, and this Spirit is in you whether you have ever experienced it or not. What if we can clear away the clouds of fear and shame, even just a bit, so we might catch a glimpse of this Loving, Empathetic Witness right there inside of you? I promise, Love is watching you from within.

I also offer this book to those readers who know and love humans. Your destiny is to continue the work of the Great Empathetic Witness by offering your own eyes, ears, and heart as an empathetic witness for others. This is Love in action. This is how we heal ourselves and others.

And this, dear friend, *is how we change the world.*

1
Bawl Baby

I'm a bawl baby. I bawl when I have to get dressed. I bawl when I have to wipe the dishes. I bawl when my youngest sister, Alice, jumps extra spaces in Sorry!, and I tattletale on her, and Mom gets mad and reminds me that I'm five years older than Alice, which makes me old enough to be good. Alice isn't old enough to not skip spaces yet. I bawl when I have to take a nap. I stare at the flower patterns in the sheets until the flowers rearrange themselves into eyeballs and noses and mouths, and then I bawl. I'm not scared. I'm bored. The good news is that I don't bawl as much as my other little sister, Marcy. She gets first place in the bawl baby contest. It's comforting to know I'm not the worst bawler. That's got to count for something.

I take ballet lessons, and my mom makes me a silky red ballet costume. There are twinkling sequins on the skirt, and I feel like a princess when I wear it. I want to take tap dance lessons like my friend Paula down the street. She has her very own pair of shiny black patent leather tap shoes, which she lets me use, and I get to try out a tap lesson after my ballet class. I learn to shuffle ball, ball change. Over and over. Shuffle ball, ball change. The clicky-clicks are so satisfying, and I try to make them fall into the kinds of musical patterns Shirley Temple's tap shoes make, but mine sound like a clumsy elephant. If I could keep taking dance lessons, I might be able to dance like Shirley. I love dance lessons, but Mom says I bawl too much, and I don't deserve dance lessons. I'm trying to figure out the trick for how to make things turn out happy, but I always end up bawling.

I bawl when I have bad dreams—like the one about Alice falling into the seal pool at the zoo and getting eaten by seals. I bawl when I think about Mom dying. I bawl when I think about how our house could burn down. You never know about the future, and there are so many bad things that can happen. It's like there's a part of me that thinks if I bawl about it, the bad things won't happen. Mom says I even bawled a lot as a baby. She would walk the floor with me all night long just to stop me from bawling. Alice doesn't bawl. She cries in a sad sort of way that makes your heart break. When she cries, my mom scoops her up and loves her until she's happy again. She's just a cute little thing and has good reasons to cry. But I am a Great Big Ugly Thing, and I have no good reasons to bawl.

"Shut up, or I'll give you something to bawl about," Mom sometimes reminds me, so I try to keep the bawling quiet, but bad noises just keep coming out like a volcano. I'm kind of gross that way. I go to my room and shut the door and try to bawl into my pillow so Mom won't know. I imagine what it would be like if she came in and hugged me when I'm bawling. My mom's hugs fill me with all the good feelings, and I love when she sings "Daddy's Little Girl" and tickles my arm. But when I'm bawling, she stays away. I have bad breath and snot coming out of my nose, and who would want to be around someone like that?

My aunts and uncles and cousins all come over for Thanksgiving, and I argue with Mom about something. She tells me I'm rude. My stomach gets heavy rocks in it, and my face burns. I want to disappear. If I disappear, I will not bother everyone anymore. If I disappear, maybe people will miss me. I don't want to be rude; I want to be missed, so I decide to run away to the garage. I pack a few things in a box, and on my way through the kitchen to the garage, I notice one of my aunts roll her eyes and smile at my mom in a secret sort of way. They don't notice that I notice. Then I go out to the garage to sit and hope someone wonders where I am and comes to find me. It's cold and quiet in the garage, and this is where a Big Ugly Naughty Girl belongs. She doesn't belong in a house full of pumpkin pie, laughter, and hugs.

After a while, I feel cold, and nobody comes. I quietly slip back into the warm house and shyly look around at my relatives from the corner of my eye to see if anyone misses me, but they just keep talking and laughing like I'm not there. Like they never knew I left. I go to my room and bawl. I make sure to do all my disgusting bawling on the floor behind my bed in case anyone walks in. How embarrassing.

Another day I wipe dishes with Mom, and I bawl about it again. I hate wiping dishes. I never get them totally dry, even though I try hard to get the towel in the cracks of the Tupperware lids so they won't get moldy. Suddenly, I feel my face smash into the countertop, and everything is swirly. I slowly raise my head to look at Mom, confused and wondering if she knows what just happened. Her face looks mad and surprised and sorry at the same time. My mouth tastes like metal, and my tongue feels around for my front tooth. Most of it is missing, and what's left is sharp and snaggly. I open my mouth to show Mom.

"Damn," she whispers.

That word punches me in my stomach like that counter punched me in the face. My mom can yell like nobody's business, and she does. But she never swears because she is a Christian. I know it's my fault she swore. I'm sad and scared. Why am I so naughty? It will cost my dad a lot of money to fix this bawl baby's tooth. My dad works hard every day, and he is quiet and funny and good. He never yells or gets mad. He doesn't deserve to have a daughter like me. I need to try harder to be good.

I think about what it would be like to be dead. Sometimes I imagine myself on the ground with my mouth gaping open and my eyeballs rolled back. I imagine my mom finding my poor dead body and picking me up and rocking me back and forth, so sad and sorry to see me gone. She would cry and cry, and I would feel her rocking, rocking, rocking me in my deep, dead sleep. I would like that. If I were dead, I would not be rude and ugly and bawling all the time. I would be quiet and easy to love, and I would only cry when I had a very, very good reason, and it would just break your heart. Once, I asked my mom if she would feel sad if I died, but she said thinking about one's own death was selfish and dramatic.

Damn.

Bawl Baby

Little Natalie, I read these words and feel so much affection for you. Every single tear was like a little jewel, rich with meaning. Feeling deep emotions and crying are both a part of being human, and you were entering into the fullness of your own humanity. I'm so proud of how you showed up for your life! I admire how you jumped all the way in. Splash! And by the way, thinking about your own death is not selfish or dramatic. It's human. Hey, you are HUMAN! And that's all you need to be.

2
The Get-Out-of-Hell-Free Card

I'm walking down the hall of an old church in white patent leather shoes and a hand-crocheted jumper. This building is not like the little neighborhood church my family walks to on Sunday mornings with the sun streaming in the big windows and the little nursery full of chubby babies. St. Timothy's. I never met St. Timothy, but I liked his church.

This is Kerrie's church, and it's called Soul's Harbor. Kinda weird. Kerrie is the neighborhood girl my mom babysits, and the grown-ups drop us off in a room full of kids I've never seen before. They're not from my school, and I have butterflies in my stomach. Kerrie and I find seats in the middle row and sit down. I briefly consider crawling under my chair to hide, but I know the pretty teacher will get mad at me if I don't sit up straight and listen, and I want her to like me. She starts talking, so I settle in. This is church, and I know what to do in church. I will show her how good I am.

The teacher tells us about heaven and hell and how Jesus loves the whole wide world and has the whole thing in his hands. I can feel the kids fidgeting around me, all of us wishing we were home eating bologna sandwiches with lots of butter. But when she announces that everyone is *going to hell to burn forever-and-ever-amen in the everlasting fires with the demons because God is so holy that He can't look at any of us wretched sinners*, my ears perk up. This is important information. *Pay attention.*

Her face suddenly brightens as she tells us that there is *Good News*! Jesus loved the whole wide world so much that He died and went to hell *so we wouldn't have to*. And then three days later, *up from the grave he arose, with a mighty triumph o'er his foes*. He beat the devil at his own game, and now, if people will just invite Him into their hearts, they can go to heaven instead of hell.

That's it? All I have to do is pray a prayer? Sign me up! And as if the teacher is reading my mind, she says, "Would anyone like to pray this prayer with me and invite Jesus into your heart?"

I immediately raise my hand. This is a no-brainer. I can tell the teacher is happy when she sees my hand in the air. We walk out the door to the hallway, and I wonder why I'm the only one taking her up on the offer of a ticket to heaven. The rest must have already invited Jesus into their hearts. Makes sense. They are used to the Soul's Harbor way, and I'm not. Nobody at St. Timothy's told us this important information, so I didn't know about the get-out-of-hell-free card, but thank God I do now. Let's do this.

The teacher prays a prayer while I bow my head and close my eyes and fold my hands to make double-certain-sure it will work. Prayer is serious business. When she's done, she gives me a tiny white Bible with some verses in big letters. I hold it in awe, thinking about how my dolls will love it. This is a big day. I know something important has just happened, and now Jesus lives in my heart. Plus, a pretty teacher likes me. Plus, I'm not going to hell. Plus, I have a new dolly book. It's a *miracle*.

I will never forget this day as long as I live.

Little Natalie, that little prayer and little white Bible are sweet. Yes. But I've got a little secret. Those things were not your first encounter with God. God was with you when you were being formed in your mother's womb, and God is embedded in your DNA. You are made in the image of your Creator, and nothing can ever separate you from that love, precious one.

3
All the Pretty Little Ponies

I anxiously lick a salty mustache of sweat on my lip. My stuffed animals are lined up on both sides of my bed to protect me from the scary horse that chases me at night. During the day, my pretty little pony lives in the basement, and I love to rock it back and forth and feel like I'm flying. But at night, he turns into a scary horse who comes upstairs to get me. He can't get past my stuffed animals, so as long as there are no breaks in the line, I'm good to go. "Hush-a-bye, don't you cry. Go to sleep, you little baby." But as soon as I fall asleep, a loud voice starts counting backward. "TEN. NINE. EIGHT." Like that. If I don't get the Sam-heck-outta-there before the voice says "ONE," the scary horse will get me. I blink my eyes hard to wake myself up, and then I try not to fall asleep again. *Please, dear Jesus, don't let me have scary dreams. Please, dear Jesus, don't let me have scary dreams.*

Now that I have Jesus living in my heart, maybe He will help me if I'm good. I try hard to be good during the day, so when I need Him at night, He will answer my prayers with a "yes" instead of a "no" or "maybe." "*Please, dear Jesus, don't let me have scary dreams.*" If I say it enough and believe hard enough, and if I've been good enough, He will help me.

When I get to sleep without any scary dreams, I let Him know I'm *most extremely* grateful. If I am thankful enough, He might help me again the next night. I'll make Him *so, so* happy and *so, so* pleased He has helped me that He'll want to offer a repeat performance of His miracles the next night. He needs to know He can count on a thankful heart from this girl *for sure*.

When I do have scary dreams, I know it's not Jesus' fault. It's mine. Either 1) I wasn't a good girl that day; or 2) I didn't pray hard enough; or 3) I didn't have enough faith. He probably had to allow the scary dreams because I got mad at Marcy the day before. Or maybe I didn't like something at dinner and said so. I'm a very ungrateful girl, and also, I bawl. Also, I'm lazy. I'd rather die than wipe dishes.

I try and try to be a good girl, but I don't like naps and hockey puck hamburgers that have no flavor. Sometimes, I want something super bad, like my own banana seat bicycle. It's definitely not God's fault if I'm selfish and naughty and get chased by scary horses, and I would never in a million years think it was because He might give me worse dreams to teach me a lesson. Learning lessons is important and helps me grow up to be a good girl. There is nothing wrong with God Almighty, no sirree. But there is something wrong with me. Tonight, I will say I'm sorry and pray extra hard for the scary horses to leave me alone.

You live in a chaotic world, sweet girl, and it's hard to make sense of it. You feel alone and afraid at night. You don't know this yet, but love is right there within you. You are a little girl doing everything you can think of to keep yourself safe. You are brave and creative, and I am proud of how you are growing.

4
Devoted

If I could pick one word to describe my mom, it would be *devoted*. She is devoted to being a stay-at-home mother, devoted to her daughters, devoted to her husband, devoted to her church, devoted to her God, devoted to her clean home, and devoted to what is right and true.

Mom and I get born again within a few days of each other. I know because she starts talking a lot about Jesus and the Bible. She reads her big Scofield Study Bible and listens to hymns and sermons on the radio every day. She loves Jesus, and He loves her right back and tells her everything there is to know.

She gives me a Bible that belonged to my great-grandma. It smells old and has pages so thin I think they might dissolve when I turn them. What if I accidentally wreck a Holy Bible? I especially like the indentation marks where each new book starts so I can easily find the different books, which comes in handy in Sunday school or Pioneer Girls when we are asked to look up Bible verses in a speedy way. I wonder if this is cheating, but nobody says anything.

Mom has me read a chapter from my Bible every day, as well as a chapter from a book with short stories about people who obey God. This is called Daily Devotionals, and she says this is like putting on my spiritual perfume. I always remember to put on my spiritual perfume because I definitely want to smell like Jesus. This is how other people will get their ticket out of hell. The more I smell like Jesus, the more they will want to ask Jesus into their hearts, so they can do devotionals and smell like Jesus, too. One day, the whole world will smell beautiful. I'll do my part.

We move into a new house my mom keeps neat as a pin, and this means we had to leave St. Timothy's behind us. We are now going to a cute little Evangelical Free church, but it's not totally free. They still take a collection every Sunday morning and Sunday night, but even though it's not free, it's still friendly, and it feels like family. My mom digs right in and gets involved singing, teaching Pioneer Girls, and doing Bible studies, where she learns a bunch of wisdom. She doesn't keep all that wisdom to herself. She generously shares it with everyone else who loves wisdom. She studies and prays and thinks about wise things every day while I'm in school, and when I get home, she serves me up some Blueberry Cha Cha and teaches me what she learns. She is the voice of God in our family and church because He talks straight to her, and she listens and obeys. I don't know anyone else as devoted to God as my mom is, and I hope I will be as devoted to God as she is when I grow up. Because of my mom, our family is special, and God is extra close to us.

Even though my dad drinks beer.

Little Natalie, I am devoted to you, now and forever. Your devotion will wax and wane, and that's okay. It is your Creator's love and never-failing devotion that will hold you close. No matter what.

5
The Birds and the Bees

Matt lives directly across the street from me, plus he sits directly across the desk from me in second grade. He's a skinny little boy, and I feel like a big white beluga whale standing next to him. I don't think he notices, though, because he has a big mouth and swaggers like a spindly cowboy, taking up a lot of space for being so little. Plus, he knows stuff I don't know.

One day I find out exactly what he knows. With a wee little smirk on his wee little face, he tells me sex means a boy putting his penis in a girl's vagina. One minute I'm learning about how to write a haiku, and the next I'm learning about . . . *that*.

When I get home from school, I break the news to Mom. Does *she* know about this? She does, and she's mad. She tells me this is "God's plan for people who get married, so they can have babies" and that I wasn't supposed to know about The Plan until I was older.

Wait. *That* was *God's* idea? No way. We keep our bottoms to ourselves, thank you very much. But now I can't stop thinking about it. I worry about it when I'm around anyone with a penis. I worry they are also thinking about *sex*. I feel like a bad girl for thinking bad thoughts about people with penises, but thoughts pop into my head the same way words pop out of my mouth. There is something wrong with me, and I hope the blood of Jesus is strong enough to save even a sinner such as I.

I love singing hymns at church, and I sing with all my heart because Jesus will have mercy on me if I have a strong and mighty faith. I'm hoping my devotion and faithfulness will weigh more than the weight of my sins because I do more than *think* about sex. Sometimes, when I'm playing with my Barbies, I make Ken and Barbie kiss and put their bodies together. Ken doesn't have a penis. Why would they give Ken a girl bottom if he's a boy? *Weird.* Anyway, after they have sex, they have a baby. I like playing Barbies by myself because they can have all the sex they need in order to have all the babies they want. They *love* babies like I do. When I'm with my little sisters, I have to pretend they can have babies without the sex part because my little sisters don't know about sex yet.

There are mostly boys in my neighborhood, and I've tried making friends with them. I try to show them how to play Gunzilla (I can't say Godzilla because that would be taking the Lord's name in vain), but none of the boys want to play with me—except the boy who lives next door. One day, he and his older sister invite me over to his house with two other girls. We all go into their basement for something they call a "show." I love shows. I sit on the couch, and one of the girls comes out of the bedroom and into the living room totally naked. I stare at her body. Her skin is white and curvy in the dim light. I'm embarrassed. I don't like this show. Plus, what if the boy is next? I don't want to see a real, live penis. I tell my new friends I have to go, and they scowl as I leave.

I take my pillow that night and imagine it's a cute boy's face and kiss it. I'm a naughty girl. I hope nobody ever finds out just how naughty I am. Thank goodness Jesus died for naughty girls like me. I will pray the prayer again. Just in case.

The Birds and the Bees

Little Natalie, I'm sorry you learned about sex this way. You are <u>not naughty, only incredibly curious</u> and full of heart, which is exactly how God created you to be. I adore you and all the other children who are trying to figure out life without a compass. Your Creator has every last one of you in a Great Heart of love, safely known and held.

6

Thief in the Night

Every Sunday, our family goes to church and Sunday school in the morning and even more church in the evening. Every Wednesday night, we go to Pioneer Girls. I love church most of the time. Tonight is different because we get to watch a movie in church. I hardly ever get to see movies because they cost money, so I'm excited. But this movie is scary. Some of the people in this movie didn't ask Jesus to come into their hearts in time, and Jesus came like a thief in the night and took all the Christians out of the world in a big event called the rapture. Everyone who wasn't a Christian got left behind. They had to get the Mark of the Beast, which is like a tattoo on their body, or be hunted down and killed. If they got the Mark of the Beast, they would go straight to hell, but if they didn't get the Mark of the Beast, as soon as they got killed by the government, they would go to heaven with the others that got out of Dodge earlier. So, I'm secretly hoping they will get shot by the government and be done with it, but in the movie, they just run and run and run.

A woman sings a creepy song called "I Wish We'd All Been Ready," and the church is dark and sad. Am I choking? My throat is closing up. I swallow hard so I won't bawl. Bawling in church is embarrassing. What if all my prayers to invite Jesus into my heart still haven't worked? Then, I will be left behind when the Rapture comes, and I'll have to decide between getting shot or going to hell. I don't like those choices. When the movie ends and the organ plays the song "Just as I Am," the pastor invites everyone to come forward who doesn't want bad things to happen to them. *This is a no-brainer.* I walk up that aisle before anyone else. I can't understand why my dad doesn't run up the aisle with me to give up beer and ask Jesus into his heart, too. Does he want to be left behind?

    I pray the prayer and believe as hard as I can. I hope my prayer sticks this time.

Oh, little Natalie, every prayer is heard with so much love. Love's Presence holds you near when other frightened children bleed their fears into you. They just want to be safe, and they don't know how, so they are doing the best they can with the limited understanding they have. One day you will never need to be afraid again because perfect love is coming for you.

7
Lunch Lady

We have two lunch ladies at our school—the fat one and the skinny one. They're both meaner than the German Shepherd that lived across the street in my old neighborhood. I've never seen either lunch lady smile. I keep quiet in the lunchroom because if any of the kids notice me, they'll make fun of me. I sit by Lori, and we mind our own beeswax. Lori's last name is Sletton, which sounds like Slutton, so that's what they call her. I'm Jesus Freak, and she's Slutton. Sometimes Slut, for short. Anyway, some of the kids are saying swear words, and the skinny lunch lady comes over with a scowl on her face. "What am I hearing over here?" I shrink. I get scared when grown-ups get mad.

One of the boys points in my direction and says, "She took God's name in vain."

I look around in horror. Who took God's name in vain? I didn't hear anyone doing that. I heard some other swear words, but not that one. Who was he talking about? Then, I see the skinny lunch lady's black beady eyes narrow in on me. ME! She thinks *I* took the good Lord's name in vain? That's impossible! I'd never be the apple of God's eye if I did that! My mom would have a heart attack. I don't even say "Gosh" or "Golly" for fear of sliding down the slippery slope.

I swallow nervously and croak out, "I didn't say that."

She must not have heard me because she barks, "TAKE YOUR LUNCH BOX TO THE WALL. FACE THE WALL AND EAT YOUR LUNCH THERE. AND NO MORE SWEARING!"

My body burns with shame. I take my Waltons lunchbox to the cement wall and practice my skills at not bawling. I'm getting better. Hot tears threaten to tumble out, but I hold my breath in my chokie throat and muster all my muscles to keep them in. I hear the kids laughing.

That night, I tell my mom what happened. She teaches me that when people do mean things, we should show love back. That's the Christian way. So, I draw and color a picture for the skinny lunch lady and write: "I am sorry for being bad. I hope you have a nice day."

When I give the picture to her the next day, that crabby, skinny lunch lady smiles! It's a wonderful thing to spread love to crabby people. Be nice and make them smile. The Christian way works.

Oh. And don't forget to say you're sorry, no matter what.

Lunch Lady

It hurts to be accused of something you didn't do, little Natalie. I feel your pain of rejection and betrayal. I hold your reality and your truth close to my heart where it will always and forever matter. You did your best to offer forgiveness to the other children and love to a lunch lady. One day you will grow up and offer forgiveness and healing love to yourself as well.

8

Converts

I'm in third grade. The most interesting part about school is my teacher. Last year, Mrs. Hilla had short, curly, white hair, and she made satisfying slurpy noises when she sucked on cough drops and read chapters of *Pippi Longstocking*. I loved to watch her mouth wobble excitedly and her eyes dart about dramatically as she read out loud.

But this year is different. Mrs. Lebens is younger and prettier than Mrs. Hilla, but she's crabby. I suspect it's because she's married to Mr. Lebens, the tall, crabby gym teacher. I've always hated gym, but I'd rather eat five of Mom's burnt hockey puck hamburgers than endure one hour of gym class with Mr. Lebens. He doesn't like girls who can't throw or catch, which means he doesn't like me. Maybe Mrs. Lebens isn't good at throwing and catching, either. She's a crab, but her eyes are sad. Part of me feels sorry for her because she has to go home with Mr. Lebens every day. She has bad breath, and I hate when I have to get my paper corrected at her desk. Maybe Mr. Lebens would be nicer to her if she sucked on a minty cough drop like Mrs. Hilla.

When we have free time, I tell all my classmates how to invite Jesus into their hearts. It only takes a minute, and it's easy, but some of them are not sure they can pray on their own. I tell them I will help them after school. "Meet me by Door C," I say. I'm excited. I'm like a real missionary telling lost souls about Jesus, and I wish all day to see kids waiting at Door C after school. When school is over, I rush to the door and see kids standing around in their winter coats and boots, waiting for my instructions. I also see my carpool lady's car huffing and puffing exhaust into the winter air as it waits for me, but this is more important. I turn to the kids and tell them to bow their heads and close their eyes, and I will pray the prayer out loud. If they pray the prayer in their hearts at the same time, Jesus will come into their hearts, and they will go to heaven when they die.

I know how to pray this prayer because I've prayed it myself so many times to make sure I don't go to hell. "Dear Jesus, I do bad things and deserve to go to hell when I die, but You died on the cross for my sins. Please come into my heart to be my personal Savior so I can live forever in heaven with you. In Jesus' Name, Amen."

After we pray, I instruct my new converts to go tell someone they know as soon as possible. That's the glue that makes the whole thing stick. Pray the prayer and then tell someone—*bam*—they are born again. I say their next job is to read the Bible and pray every day, and they'll grow, grow, grow. And now, they can save someone else. This is called evangelism. My mom taught me how to do evangelism. She has hundreds of little books telling the Good News, and she passes them out everywhere we go. She's even got scary ones called Chick tracts. Some of them show pictures of demons and Catholic priests torturing people on racks. I think they are supposed to scare people to heaven, but as long as they get there, that's all that matters.

When I finish spreading the Good News, I slog through the snow over to the carpool lady's car as fast as I can in my big boots. I must have scored major points with God—almost an entire class worth. I feel happy until I get in the car and see the carpool lady's scrunched-up face looking back at me. She lives in the house behind us and yells at her husband so loudly we can hear it from our backyard. Now she yells at me for making everyone wait. I'm scared and embarrassed. I don't want to be naughty. I want to be good. I thought I was doing a good thing, but now I'm not so sure. Is this persecution?

If it is, then it's okay. My points just doubled.

My serious and ambitious little flower, you have always had an infinite number of points with love. No hoops to jump through. No words to say correctly. No converts to collect. Love is powerful and holds you safe without requiring anything from you. Love is always here. Let's clear away the clouds of fear and shame so you can experience love and find peace.

9
Apple of God's Eye

I love the story of David. He was one of the Israelites, God's chosen people, and on top of that, he was *the apple of God's eye*. That means he was God's favorite. But he wasn't everyone else's favorite. King Saul was jealous and chased him all over the place. I'm in fourth grade this year, and the kids in my class don't like me anymore, but it's not because they are jealous. I wear glasses and clothes that aren't cool, and I talk about Jesus. Last year, everyone wanted to hear about it. This year, they don't, so they throw snowballs, mud, and names at me. *Goody-Goody Two-Shoes. Four Eyes. Religious Freak.* The snowballs and mud aren't so bad because they usually miss. The words hit every time.

The carpool lady's daughter doesn't like me because I told her about hell, and she tries to drown me in her wading pool. Sometimes I do wish I was dead, but when Jane holds my head under the water with her long, bony arms, I change my mind about that. I miss breathing. Plus, how embarrassing to drown in a wading pool at the hands of a skinny, mean girl. Another day, a boy chases me down the street waving a jackknife. I am on a bike going faster than he is, but I am sure I'll get sliced and diced. And then one day, a group of boys drag me into a house down the street and throw me on the floor. I don't know what they are saying. Their voices swim in my ears, and I feel like I am back in the wading pool with Jane holding my head under the water. I am afraid I might throw up on their mother's floor, and she'll get mad at me, so I pray, and you know what? They let me go.

They laugh while I run out of the house and down the street back home. Embarrassing.

God comes through for me again while I am walking home from my friend's house alone. I see a bunch of boys up ahead making snowballs. I know they will pelt me as I walk by, but in the nick of time, I remember watching a movie called *The Hiding Place*. Corrie and Betsy Ten Boom prayed the guards would not see the Bible they were hiding, and God hid their Bible from the guards. If God could hide a Bible, can He hide me? I am bigger than a Bible, but I try it. I pray with as much holiness as I can muster: "Please, dear God, hide me from these boys!" I walk right past them. Nobody even looks at me—a modern-day miracle. I'm pretty sure I *am* an apple in God's eye, just like David and Corrie and Betsy.

I read a book called *Light From Heaven* about a dad who hurts his wife and beats his son. He's a good Christian man at church, and everyone admires him, but he is not good at home. His godly wife honors her husband and never tells a soul except God. She prays and forgives, and she teaches her kids to pray and forgive, too. That mean old dad keeps hurting everyone until they all grow up, and the obedient and godly mother dies a noble death. I wish I could be like that mom and love, pray, and forgive no matter what anyone does to me, but I am not a good person like she is. I keep thinking she should fight back and get out of there, but she is godlier than I am. When she watches her four-year-old get beat up, she completely puts her hope in God. I know she did what was right, but I feel sadness in every corner of my body when I think about that little boy. I read this book many times, hoping I will understand how this kind of forgiveness works, but it only confuses me more. It just goes to show how much I have to grow in this area of longsuffering because there is something rebellious inside of me that wants to fight back.

Like the day I am minding my own beeswax at my desk and Tom Hoffman (the eighth boy on my "Boys I Like" list for the year) comes up behind me and starts poking my back. I freeze and wait for him to stop. He doesn't, and that's when it happens. The rude monster that lives inside of me roars awake. I swirl around, grab his shirt, and pull hard. POP! A button rolls away on the floor, and the monster slams into Tom. His hand comes down hard on the top of my head. I stand up, shocked, and run out of the room. My teacher, Mr. Belrose, doesn't do anything about it because he's afraid of the boys in my class. He's even scared of some of the girls, and I don't blame him.

One time, someone steals something off Mr. Belrose's desk, and he wants to know who it is. I feel guilty even though I have no idea what he is talking about. I feel like I made the crime happen somehow. Part of me is worried he might blame me since he's scared of everyone else. If he blames me, I'd still be nice to him, and the problem would be solved. Then, everyone would feel better except me. And that's why I think God's all I've got. My parents can't do anything. The teachers can't do anything. The old bus driver man can't do anything. He's even more scared of the bullies than Mr. Belrose is. When I have to ride the bus, I sit in the front seat because the mean kids usually sit in the back, but sometimes they come up to the front, cracking jokes and squishing me against the window. I stare out the window and concentrate on the trees and houses going by and say a mantra in my mind, "The joy of the Lord is my strength. The joy of the Lord is my strength."

But you know what? I am gladly chased by my enemies, just like David, as long as I can be the apple of God's eye, just like David. My original goal was to stay out of hell, but now I want more. I want to be God's favorite. I'm a greedy gut. If I were Jewish, like the new boy down the street, I would have a better chance. I think he's going to be number nine on my list of boys I like for this year. Josh is cute and quiet. He's not like the other boys in my neighborhood. If I married him, would I be a Jew? He's lucky. He doesn't even have to try to be the apple of God's eye. He's an automatic shoo-in just for being one of God's chosen people. I'm a big, ugly, white Norwegian whale with stringy yellow hair. There are no Norwegians in the Bible. I'll have to love God harder to make up for it. Plus, when I get persecuted for God, I have a better chance of being His favorite. At least that's how it was with David in the Bible.

Dear apple of my eye, you are a delight to my heart. The Creator loves the people of this world, each one a rare jewel in love's sight. I love how you continue to look for God. You are relentless in your search. Love is your North Star, and you know this, deep inside, where love's code was embedded within you at your creation. Keep looking. One day you will discover that you are already Home.

10
I Found It!

Something exciting is happening. People are wearing pins that say, "I found it!" Freeway billboards say it, too. It's like a game. People are supposed to stop and ask, "What did you find?" And then you tell them about Jesus and how He'll give them a ticket out of hell if they invite Him into their hearts.

People can call a phone number and ask, "What is everyone finding?" And volunteers, like my mom, answer their questions about Jesus. The world is getting Born Again because of a pin. I want to do my part to save the world, starting with my dad and my grandparents because they're heading straight to eternal damnation. My dad drinks a can of beer a couple times a week, and my grandma smokes, although she tries to hide it when we come over, which is the same thing as lying. My mom is smart, and she can tell.

So, every night, my mom and sisters and I pray that God will save my dad, my grandparents, and my Catholic relatives. It seems like a big ask, but God is a big God, and He can do anything. Mom tells us stories of people who stop drinking beer, smoking cigarettes, and dancing when Jesus comes into their hearts. It's like the beer, cigarettes, and Jesus can't be in the same space, but when Jesus takes the wheel of your car, a miracle happens.

My grandparents on my mom's side go to a little white Episcopal church in the country. My grandparents on my dad's side go to a little red brick Lutheran church in Hawley, Minnesota. And my favorite Catholic cousins go to something called a mass every week. I went

I Found It!

with them once when I stayed overnight with my cousin, and it was embarrassing because they stood up and knelt down and chanted stuff, but I didn't know any of the words. I tried to keep up and mumble along, but I felt stupid.

All my relatives go to their favorite church places on Sunday, but they are all still going to hell because, sadly, they are not Christians. When I ask them if they want to invite Jesus into their hearts and become a Christian, they say they *are* Christians.

But Mom says *nope*. They are not. They think praying to Mary and doing good deeds gets you into heaven, so they go to church to collect points from God or Mary. But they will never collect enough points from anyone to make it into eternity. To get to heaven, you only have to pray that one prayer and believe with all your heart that Jesus will come into your heart. That's it. If you think good deeds will cut it, that just means you're a prideful person who thinks you can be good enough for a holy God. Nope. You can't. You will go straight into the fiery furnace because all your good deeds are like filthy rags.

I wonder why anyone would do a good deed then? Are good deeds bad? I don't get it, but God knows. My poor relatives are all trying to do their best. They make delicious food for the holidays and summer picnics, and they say nice things and laugh all the time. They are jolly people. But little do they know they are going to hell. I'm scared about that. I love them. Every night, I pray for their souls so we can be together after we die.

People are creative and inventive as they search for ways to soothe their fears and solve the puzzle of their shame. Your young heart, little Natalie, is eager to jump into the arena and engage in the game of life, and this makes me smile, even laugh, with deep delight and joy. Do you know where you got that love for all the people in your circle? It comes from a fountain of life within you. A fountain that originates in love. Keep drinking from that fountain.

II

Missions

My sisters and I are allowed to watch *Little House on the Prairie*, *The Waltons*, and two hours of Saturday morning cartoons each week. My mom pops popcorn with lots of melted butter, and sometimes we each get a small glass of Pepsi. I take tiny sips in between tastes of salty popcorn to make it last. Sometimes my dad makes his famous chocolate malts with real malt powder. Once in a while, a special series will be on TV, and if it's educational, my mom lets me watch it. I love these specials because there is a new episode every night for a whole week, and I get to stay up late with my mom and dad because I'm the oldest.

One of the TV specials I get to watch is called *Roots*, and it's about Black people. The other one is called *Holocaust*, and it's about God's chosen people. Sometimes I still bawl into my pillow when I think about Kizzy getting stolen from her mom and dad. At Christmas, I ask for a Black Mattel Happy Family and a Black Barbie and a Black Ken. Sadly, there are no Jewish Happy Families, Barbies, or Kens, but I do already have Black baby dolls. Isabel and Elizabeth are the apples of my eye. Now that I have all my new Black dolls, my sister Marcy and I play "generations" with them. I relive the stories I watched in *Roots* over and over, humming sad songs and making Marcy bawl. I feel good to see her bawl. Someone *should* cry for the Black people. I hate people who kidnap and rape and gas. I hope they all burn in hell forever and ever. Why didn't people see what was happening and help? Why did so many people ignore what was happening? Sometimes I think about Corrie Ten Boom from *The Hiding Place* movie, and I wonder if God will ever call on me to risk my life to help people who are lied about and kicked out of their communities and killed. I pray that God will help me to be brave and do whatever He wants me to do. I vow to think about *Roots*, *Holocaust*, and Corrie Ten Boom for the rest of my life. I promise to God I will never forget.

One year, we have a missions conference at church, and we host a missionary couple in our house. Maybe God wants *me* to be a missionary? In my imagination, I can see Africa, where Kunta Kinte came from; and Germany, where the Jews were gassed; and Holland, where Corrie lived; and Norway, where my great-grandma was born. What would God want me to do in a faraway land like that? Maybe I can be a teacher since I like to talk. Some people want to have regular jobs and a regular life, but I won't be like that. I want to give up my regular life to help people. During the mission's conference, I rededicate my life to God. I let Him know I will gladly go anywhere He wants me to go and do anything He wants me to do. I want to be 100 percent committed to Him.

If I'm a missionary, maybe that will make up for the fact that I'm not Jewish.

I love how your heart is expanding to hold space for all of God's beautiful children. Keep feeding it. This love will grow. It is inevitable. Sometimes it will show up like justice. And sometimes it will show up like mercy. And sometimes it will show up like silence. And sometimes it will show up like speaking out. Always know that I am 100 percent committed to you, little Natalie. I've got your back, and you will have the backs of others. And one day all the children will be free.

12

Beats

My mom is beautiful. She was the homecoming queen in high school and looks like an angel in her picture. She also sings. She could have been a real singer, but then she got married and had my sisters and me, and this is the job she wanted most of all: to be a mom with three little girls. She got her wish!

But she still sings. She sings in the church choir, and she also sings solos. Everyone loves to hear her sing. I watch her singing up in the front of our church, and I can hardly believe she is my mom. She is the prettiest mom at church, and I want to be exactly like her. I worry all the time that God will take her away from me. I couldn't live without her.

While we're in school, Mom makes crafts and cleans our house and bakes. When we come home, the house is warm with sunshine, the smell of chocolate cookies, and the sounds of hymns on the radio. We have a Christian home. This is the best kind of home to grow up in, and I feel lucky. The Christian word for what I feel is "blessed." I feel blessed, better than lucky. Luck is all the non-Christians have.

Every year when the weather gets warm, people with long hair and colorful, flowy clothes come to our house selling Christian records with cartoons on them. My mom always buys one, and suddenly the whole world is exciting. I belt the song lyrics to "Bullfrogs and Butterflies" at the top of my lungs. We also have records by Evie Tornquist and the Bill Gaither Trio. I love the way the different voices sound together. Mom calls this "harmony," and one day in the car, she teaches me how to find the pitch underneath the melody. I practice every day until I sound like I'm right on the album, and nobody can tell the difference between my voice and the other voices. It's called blending, and I'm good at it. There's not much else to do in life other than homework, reading, and blending. So, I blend.

My sisters and I are only allowed to listen to Christian music that doesn't have a beat because beats bring the evil spirits into your home. There are some exceptions to this rule. For example, we have a record called *Dumb Ditties,* which has a bunch of old songs on it like "Monster Mash," "Pink Shoelaces," and "Yummy, Yummy, Yummy." They have beats. I guess because they are old there are no demons attached to them. They are safe, thank goodness, because I love them with all my heart, and I would hate to love demon music. We also have the *Sound of Music* record, and I love to pretend I am Maria. Dancing is a sin, but tap dancing, ballet, and the kind of dancing Maria does on the hills that are alive with the sound of music are safe. So, I sing and dance like Maria and sometimes feel that my own heart will *burst open* because it is so full of the sound of music.

One of my favorite records, *He Lived the Good Life,* is a Catholic record from my Catholic aunt. I'm surprised Mom lets me play it since Catholics are going to hell for praying to Mary and torturing the Protestants, and Mom says Jesus did not *only* live a good life. He was *God.* The only song I'm personally worried about is the one called "Sinnin' Woman." It sounds kind of sinful, even though it has zero beats and is the most boring song on the record. But I guess that makes sense since it's about sin. I need to be careful. Very, very careful.

I love that you are discovering the gift of music, little Natalie! Music is another universe all its own, and you will come in and out of that magical place, teeming with its own colors, sensations, and creations, a million times in your life on the earth. First you will tiptoe carefully, afraid to dive in. But one day you'll enter into the Song and enjoy it with childlike abandon. Because love is there. Because love is the Song. And you never need to be careful with love.

13

My Utmost for His Highest

My dad finally gets saved and gives up beer (but not hunting), and we find out that Mom is a prophet. But don't get too excited. She can't tell the future. A modern-day prophet simply knows what is right and wrong, so Mom uses her gift on the way home from church by telling us who is doing things right at church and who is doing things wrong. Margaret, for example, is doing things wrong. Her husband has died, and she needs to be loved so badly that she settles for marrying a *divorced* man. God hates divorce, and if you get remarried after divorce, you're an adulterer.

As it turns out, not many people at church are doing things right. A narrow road leads to righteousness, after all. I worry I am also doing things wrong, but I feel better when I focus on other folks and their mistakes instead of mine. A prophet is especially supposed to tell leaders if they are doing something wrong because if leaders get it wrong, then what hope is there? Mom has to talk to our youth pastor often because he listens to Christian rock, but he never listens to her. Nobody listened to the prophets in the Bible, either. Eventually, the youth pastor gets seduced by a couple of the girls in my youth group. I guess satanic beats will do that to a person.

Mom's Bible, books, and notepads are spread out on the table, and she studies hard. I'm pretty sure she has a direct line to God Himself. The carpool lady who lives behind us calls Mom a "hostile hypocrite." Their family is obviously heading straight to hell unless they repent.

But like the Israelites, they also refuse to listen to the prophets, so I guess they'll find out what happens to stiff-necked people who harden their hearts.

Speaking of hell, maybe I deserve to go there, too. I waffle back and forth on this. On the one hand, I love Jesus and would lay down my life for Him. I read the Bible and even sing solos in church for the glory of God, making sure not to focus on me but to get out of the way so people can concentrate on God. But on the other hand, I get jealous of my little sister, Alice, and I'm annoyed that Marcy doesn't care about trying to make herself look nice by wearing makeup. And she bawls too much about dumb stuff. I know. I'm a hypocrite, and I've got what Mom calls "a bad case of premenstrual syndrome." PMS ruins my spirituality. I hate that.

But there is one thing I love. Boys. They're fascinating. I love Cowboy-Boot-Billy and Megan's flirty, rebellious brother, Bob, and cute little Shawn, who is the size of a third grader even though we're going into high school together next year, and about every other boy in between. I want to scoop them all up and marry every single one. I'm boy-crazy and fickle as a puppy in a yard full of squirrels. Again, not very spiritual.

And then there's my rudeness. My poor prophetic mom is exhausted trying to get me to stop being rude. "You are SO RUDE!" she regularly reminds me. Sometimes she has to spank the rudeness out of me, and I lose the privilege of being with my friends. That's when I get overwhelmed with self-pity, which is of the devil. I chafe under the house rules that hang on the back of my bedroom door and often wish myself older and freer. I would never in a million trillion years run around and smoke and do drugs. I only want to put on lipstick in my bedroom and voice my own thoughts and find someone who enjoys hearing them—preferably an adorable and mischievous boy. Still, I'm glad God gave me a prophetic mom because Lord knows I need all the help I can get.

Oh honey. You make me smile. That's all

14
Sweet Sixteen

There are two significant things about turning sixteen for me. First of all, my mom is still alive, which is an answer to a prayer I've been praying for as long as I can remember. "Please don't let my mom die until AFTER I'm sixteen." It seemed like a reasonable request that wouldn't alter God's plan too drastically. Once I turned sixteen, which I figured would never happen anyway, what with the imminent rapture and all, I'd be old enough to handle my mother's death.

The second significant thing about turning sixteen is that I get to date. I'm not seeing a line out the door for requests, but at least now it's a real possibility. I have loved a hundred, maybe a thousand, boys since I was in kindergarten, but I was never allowed to go with any of them. My mom used to ask, "Go where?" And since I didn't have a logical answer for her, dating was off the table. But now, I can actually go somewhere with a boy by myself.

As long as he is a Christian.

And drives.

My mom throws me an amazing surprise birthday party and invites all the new friends I've made since starting high school. Now I know I'm not actually ready for her to die, and turning sixteen hasn't solved anything about overcoming my fears or my obsessions with boys or my selfishness or my rudeness or my rebellion, which is, according to the Bible, "as the sin of witchcraft."

Maybe when I'm twenty-five.

In the meantime, I'm looking for opportunities to go places with Christian boys. First, I survey the social landscape at my high school and discover there are not many prospects. As a new fish swimming in a pond of about two thousand, the main difficulty lies in the fact I can't always tell if someone else is a Christian or not. I haven't quite figured out if casual Christians or undercover Christians count for dating purposes. Where are the lines? I'm forever wondering.

Because of my problem with loving every boy I lay my eyes on, my mom gives me a solid antidote in the form of a book called *Passion and Purity* by Elisabeth Elliot. I read it many times and earmark several pages and underline sentence after sentence. I want to be patient, pure, and passionate like Elisabeth and Jim, the godly missionary man she loved. So far, I have not met anyone like Jim, but when I graduate from my ungodly public school and go to a Christian college, I will likely meet several Jims, and one of them will be mine. We'll have an eternal, pure, and holy love followed by many little Jimmy-babies. Sigh. Then I will finally be everything I know God wants me to be. He will love me, and Jim will love me, and my cute babies will love me, and I will be happy.

I can't wait to grow up.

Look how you continue to search for Truth, little Natalie. You don't give up. You keep fighting to know the answers. One day you will discover life was never about having all the answers. It was only ever about you and love joining together as One. Love is the answer, and there are no edges. Love is already in your Grown-Up. And We are brilliant there.

15

The Theater

I love the theater, and I have always wanted to be in a play. This summer, I'm in our community theater production of *The Music Man*, and it is magical. I meet new and interesting people and fall madly in love with my friend Megan's older brother, Sean, who plays the role of Tommy. I had hoped to get the role of Zaneeta, who is secretly dating Tommy, but I end up with the role of a townsperson. I have a blast anyway, and I use my imagination to pretend a town girl could still win Tommy's heart if she tries hard enough. Sean certainly knows how to flirt with me, and I don't think that's in my imagination.

I sometimes think God doesn't look too kindly on the theater because when you are in a play, you step on stage to be noticed. You make yourself big and offer a performance. The best actors exude confidence and strut their stuff. Theater people have sex with each other and drink and maybe even do drugs. (I heard that somewhere.) I notice couples kissing backstage, so maybe the rumors are true. I think God wants Christians to be humble and unassuming and pure, so I feel guilty about being in the theater. But don't theater people need to hear the gospel? How else are they going to find out about Jesus unless we Christians get in there, like undercover agents, and do friendship evangelism?

Well, after the summer, school starts again at my high school, and I really, *really* want to be in the theater. Auditions for the fall play, *Look Homeward Angel*, are coming up, and I want to audition. I get my script, bring it home, and start reading.

The play has the word "angel" in the title, which seems promising to me, being a Christian and all, but I read swear words in the script. One of the characters takes the name of the Lord in vain. I'm torn. I wonder if the directors would let me say a different word. Gosh? Golly? Jeepers? Would even this be considered a compromise for me as a Christian? I hate not knowing where the lines are.

The next day in school, I inquire about the possibility of saying "Gosh" instead of "God," and I'm told that, no, the script will not be tampered with. The name of the Lord *will* be taken in vain. You'd think this would be a no-brainer for me, but alas, my heart is wavering, and I'm sorely tempted. Should I be a lukewarm, compromising Christian whom God has to spit out of His mouth? Or should I star in the fall play?

I choose to be a star in the fall play. May God have mercy on my soul.

But then I get a letter from my mom. I know she is serious, concerned, and scared when she writes me a letter instead of just sitting down in the kitchen to tell me what's on her mind. I must also consider her prophet status and realize that God will speak to me through her if I choose to be humble and teachable. I solemnly read the letter. Mom writes about how my junior high cousin, Jordan, was beat up last month. (Something to do with pot.) She writes how he forgets to talk to God about his problems and how he has gone down the slippery slope of complacency, and she is afraid this will be my fate as well. She warns that the temptation toward complacency is subtle and deceptive. I may be on the brink of a decision that marks the beginning of the end of my serious walk with God. Is the thrill of stardom worth that?

Well. When she puts it that way.

I join the choir.

All the Scary Little Gods

I see inside your heart, little Natalie. In there, if God said "Jump," you would jump. Right now, you have God all mixed up with your mom's ideas of what is right. That creates distorted ideas for you. But in time, love will unravel this within and for you.

16
Rebellion Is as the Sin of Witchcraft

Every year I go to the Bill Gothard Seminar with my parents. It's a week-long seminar held in the Twin Cities where an older, single man named Bill Gothard teaches families how to be the best families in the world. We get a big red book and a workbook, and we sit through hours and hours of lectures. I love it because my friend Melissa's family goes too, and I get to see her. I love it because Mr. Gothard tells interesting stories with chalk. I love it because the lessons he teaches have easy-to-understand steps, and if you do them, you'll please God and make everyone happy with you. I wish I would have known about these steps when I was younger. Maybe my family would like me better.

But there is something seriously wrong with me. I try and try, but I am rebellious, and "rebellion is as the sin of witchcraft." I'm terrified of being a witch, but luckily, we go to hear Bill Gothard every year, so I get reminded of the easy-to-understand steps and have a fresh start at being obedient, submissive, and good. Mr. Gothard teaches us that God set up an umbrella system in the family where the dad protects his family by obeying God, and then the mom protects the kids by obeying the dad, and then the kids protect themselves when they obey their parents. If you get out from under the umbrella, you're toast. I imagine the demons standing out in the rain, ready to grab anyone who would dare step out from under the umbrella.

Here's the problem: I'm *very* obedient on the outside. I get mostly straight As. Never wear things to show off my chest, which is easy because I don't even have one. I'm concave. I never lie, cheat, smoke, drink, do drugs, or have sex. And, of course, I love God with all my heart, mind, and soul. But I get angry when someone is mean or tells a lie or cheats or doesn't listen or care. I have a hard time laying down my rights, which is the Christian way. I obey but do not always respect all of Mom's rules—like the one about making sure the bathroom towel is lined up perfectly, corner to corner, after using it. I don't respect my dad because when *he* doesn't line up the corners perfectly, and Mom yells at him for the millionth time about it, he never stands up for himself. He just meekly takes her yelling and apologizes. I guess Jesus was meek and mild, so I should be proud of my dad for giving up his rights to hang the towel however he wants to, but I'm too depraved.

One of the ways Mom helps me practice staying under the umbrella is by not talking to me until I have examined my ways and repented. I hate the silent treatment, but she explains that when we sin, we break fellowship with the one we sinned against. The way to mend that broken relationship is to fully repent, and this requires a couple of things. First of all, we must recognize how our actions hurt the other person. We need to actually *feel* the pain of the other person. Then, when we are in a place where we feel super sad for their pain, we look at how our actions caused that pain for them. Then, we go to that person and tell them we are sorry. We must not just say, "I'm sorry," though. We need to say, "I'm sorry for . . ." and then specifically list everything we can think of that we may have done to hurt their feelings. When we are done with that, we ask them if they will forgive us. We can't *expect* them to forgive us. They may not be ready to forgive us, but if we give them time and space, they may come to a place where they can forgive us, and when they do, we will once again have fellowship with them. Mom's silence is a sign that I have sinned and not repented and made things right with her yet, so I get lots and lots of practice repenting.

What stumps me is that Mom has never been sad or sorry for the ways she has hurt me. But then maybe she didn't do anything offensive. Maybe, like she says, I make up things in my head, and she is God's prophet and knows much more than I do. When I have doubts like this, I try not to think about them, and I also feel, deep down, my confusion has something to do with the Big Thing wrong about me. This Big Thing I can't explain but I'm worried I will have to live with for the rest of my life. No matter how pretty I try to make the cup look on the outside, an ugly little monster lives inside.

One day I have the audacity to confront my mom. We are having a heated argument, and I'm already too mad to care if she yells at me, so I say out loud what I'm genuinely curious about. "I just want to know; do you believe you are *always* right? That you can't *ever* be wrong about *anything*?"

I look at her rebelliously. Like a little witch. She holds my gaze with a parental defiance that strikes me as a little witchy, too, and she replies so slowly and coldly I can feel her words in my bones. "Yes. I'm always right. I'm your mother."

My next thought is *very* rebellious, so I do not dare speak it: "*That's insane.*"

And I know in that moment I'm the one who is right.

So much energy and will in God's passionate daughters! Love only requires three things because they are the doorway to peace for all of us: Act justly. Love mercy. And walk with God in humility. When you move toward these beautiful ways to live, you will experience increasing wisdom, insight, direction, joy, peace, and love. Together, in these ways, you will change the world.

17
Satan's Children

It's weird. Theater is the playground of the devil, but singing jazz love songs and dancing in our school jazz group, Freestyle, is wholesome and good? I would try to figure it out, but I'm afraid I would get convicted about it and then have to quit Freestyle. And I love Freestyle with every fiber of my being. I love the harmonies, the friendships, the teamwork, the practices, the traveling, the excitement of performing, the way our performances make the audience feel, and the way all of it makes me feel. How can it be wrong when it feels so right?

So, I won't think too hard about it. Just like I don't want to think too hard about entering the Junior Miss contest. My mom is excited for me to compete, and she makes me a gorgeous dress. My mom can make absolutely anything—clothing, crafts, drapes, blankets—*anything*. She's my biggest cheerleader, and I don't know what I would do without her.

I worry throughout the entire contest, though, because it's all about *me*, *me*, *me*. To win, I must be confident. I must look pretty. I must be smart. I must be physically fit. The whole pageant process is self-centered. Growing up, I was taught that even looking in the mirror too long is vain and selfish, and now here I am, competing with a bunch of other high school seniors to be chosen as *the best*. And I loathe myself for feeling this way, but I want to win desperately. My mom writes a letter to me, and I read it before the big night. She says I have the best figure, the best gown, the best personality, and the most exciting smile. She says I have the loveliest voice and the best talent and the most creative mom. (She's the most hilarious mom, too.) Then, she tells me to get out there and get what's mine. She says there are a lot of Satan's children trying to win this pageant, but I should do my best for the heavenly Father. Don't let Him down. Be the light.

I want to be the light. If I win, my life will be worth something. I'm a failure at being humble, not arguing, not being rude, not disagreeing, not having an opinion, and not rebelling. But if I could prove that I can be someone special and important. Someone who matters. Then, I will deserve to exist. Then, I will be loved.

I get third place.

The embarrassing thing is that I bawl on stage about it. Everyone thinks I'm bawling because I'm happy to have won a trophy, but nope. I'm bawling because I lost. I am not the light. I am not the best. I am an "almost, but not quite" kind of person. If self-pity is of the devil, I'm officially possessed.

But college is right around the corner, and I'll work extra hard to make the best use of my privileges and opportunities and bring glory to God with my life. My senior class votes me "Most Likely to Become a Nun," but I'm going to a Christian college where I hope to find my Christian husband. Maybe life will be easier when I'm not surrounded by so many of Satan's children.

I adore you, little Natalie. The light of love will shine in you and through you the more you see God's love for all humans, from the ones who are the most lost in darkness to the ones who are walking in the freedom of love's light. Where they are in their journey is precisely where love is because love is everywhere. As you grow in your awareness of love, you will find your own heart expanding towards them because the adversary doesn't ultimately win anyone or anything. Love does. Just wait and see.

18
First Kiss

I'm officially an adult living away from home in the dorms of a Christian college, and there are a million opportunities here. Gone are the days of languishing in boredom. Here, I can sing in the choir, act in the theater, volunteer, DJ a late-night campus radio show, date as many boys as I want to, become a resident assistant, go roller-skating until two in the morning, and learn interesting things in my classes.

I am finally free to make my own choices without anyone judging me for listening to Amy Grant sing "Old Man's Rubble." I rebelliously listen to Michael W. Smith, the Imperials, White Heart, DeGarmo and Key, Glad, Farrell and Farrell, and my favorite, Steven Curtis Chapman. All with super fun satanic beats. I'm secretly worried about myself, but I'm also sick of the Bill Gaither Trio and Evie Tornquist, and nobody around me seems possessed by demons for all their listening.

In fact, most of my friends listen to *secular* radio! Now, *there* is a line I see clearly. I try to help them see how this is putting sexual thoughts inside their heads and making them want to be married, but they only laugh at me and crack jokes about how I will marry a pastor and be the perfect pastor's wife. I'm not so sure because now I have to admit I secretly love listening to the radio with them. They weren't kidding about that slippery slope. If I'm honest, I have had sexual thoughts and wanted to be married even before I listened to Debbie Gibson, Phil Collins, Billy Joel, and Whitney Houston. I guess I just gave up. I mean, not on virginity. I'd never give up on that.

First Kiss

My first college crush is on the president of the student body, Kyle. Go for the top dog because, well, why not? He is tall, hilariously funny, and plays basketball. My roommate, Melissa, and I bring him muffins in hopes of winning his heart. It works. For Melissa. I forgive her because that's what Christians do, and then I promptly fall in love with Ted. Ted is not funny like Kyle, nor is he destined to be a pastor, but he is interesting to talk with. He likes books and music, and he ends up being the first boy to kiss me.

Well, that's not technically true. I play the role of Ruth in the spring comedy, *Dear Ruth,* and in that production, I kiss two boys on stage. But does that count? I don't think so. It's like kissing your puppy. I feel nothing except mild repulsion, but since those stage kisses are, officially, my first, I never hear the end of it from my friends. But I always think of my first real kiss as being with Ted. We are taking a walk on campus one night, and he politely asks if he can kiss me. I politely say yes, and he bends into my face and sticks his tongue in my mouth. I step back in horror. "WHAT ARE YOU DOING?!"

"That's called a French kiss." He explains in his philosophical voice.

"Oh." How was I supposed to know? Besides my acting gig, I have never kissed anyone, French or otherwise. I guess Ted could be my teacher. He teaches me for a couple of minutes, and then we both get bored and finish our walk.

We have some great conversations, but we also have a couple of uncomfortable arguments about music and alcohol. He believes all music is fine, and the idea that beats are satanic is ludicrous to him. He also thinks it's silly to believe drinking is a sin. Jesus turned the water into wine, for crying out loud. I point out that this was actually grape juice, but he doesn't buy it.

In the end, he writes me the sweetest letter telling me that he really likes me, but he cannot see himself with anyone who has such antiquated views on music and alcohol. He says I have a prohibitive conscience. He is sorry to break up with me for these reasons, as they seem insignificant in the grand scheme of things, but he's afraid we may not see eye to eye on other things in the future as well. I'm crushed, but I have to admit, he's right. I figure he's on the slippery slope to becoming an alcoholic who might hole up in a dark place listening to satanic head-banging music until he shrivels up and dies of demon possession. I don't want to be part of that.

It's a shame, too, because he's such a smart guy otherwise.

First Kiss

You fill my heart with so much joy, little Natalie. I love to experience your journey of discovery with you, and love covers you and your college friends and this college boy you enjoyed getting to know for a time. Here's a little secret. That boy won't end up languishing in dark places in drunken stupors but will one day marry another precious girl, and together they will raise a family in love. You will choose a different path, but both paths lead inevitably in wider concentric circles to a Greater love and Knowing. And this is why I experience and accept all your choices with joy.

19
Girl Crush

I grew up spending one week every summer at Camp Cherith in Minnesota, and I loved it. During free time, I walked through the woods alone if I wanted to. I drank pop and wore the same clothes every day, and nobody noticed or cared. I took horsemanship, and when I got old enough, I was a corral aide and got up with the sun to muck stalls and brush horses and get them saddled and bridled for classes. Sometimes, when I was picking out rocks from their shoes, I got kicked. It was thrilling. But the best part was hearing the sounds of the breeze, tree frogs, loons, and singing girls all mixed together in a blend I can't put into words. I felt close to God at camp. So close I wondered if this was where He hung out most of the time. I never wanted to leave.

When the opportunity comes to be a camp counselor for junior high girls at Camp Cherith in Wisconsin this summer, I jump at the chance. The first week, I get to know the rest of the summer staff while preparing the camp for the arrival of the first campers, and I'm magnetically drawn to one of the staffers in particular, the horse director, Debbie. One of my millions of dreams is to live on a horse ranch and ride horses every day, but having millions of dreams does not translate into having millions of dollars, so I figure the closest I'm going to get to that dream is to befriend a camp horse director. I spot her for the first time as she stands in a circle with all of the other new staffers around the flagpole. She's short, stocky, and athletic. She looks at me from across the circle, and her whole face lights up in a smile with the energy of the sun. It takes me by surprise. What does she see in me, a stranger, that makes her smile like that? Something inside me ignites, and I like her instantly. We become friends and go horseback riding together a few times on the weekends during our breaks between campers.

I love being a camp counselor. I love bantering with the girls in my cabin each week. I love sharing Jesus with them. I can see how many of them feel like I do: misunderstood, unseen, unheard, disrespected. I want to create a safe place for them to experience belonging when they are in my care. I feel God moving and breathing Love through me, and it's deeply satisfying.

On the weekends, Debbie and I go into town to do laundry and eat hamburgers at a local drive-in. She has a motorcycle that terrifies me, and she knows about bad stuff I've never heard of. She was sexually abused throughout her childhood, and camp is her safe place. The trouble is that once camp is over, she has to go back to her other life. When I talk about college, she wistfully listens, and my heart breaks for her. She doesn't have the privileges I have, and I feel the injustice of this. I write a letter to the president of my college, sharing Debbie's situation and asking him if he might allow her to come to college on a scholarship. To my surprise he writes back and says that if she's willing to work hard for one year and save all her money, he will consider offering her a scholarship for the rest.

As the summer progresses, I find myself wanting to spend every waking minute with Debbie, and when she isn't around, she's all I can think about. There is a terrifying thought on the edge of my brain that I push down every time it bubbles to the surface. I'm not sure what the thought is until one day I let it come all the way up and intentionally stare at it in horror. It's this: "I'm crushing on Debbie like I crush on boys." And I feel my insides exploding like a detonated bomb. I know one thing: I can't ever tell anyone. I believe God put me in Debbie's life for a reason. I'm supposed to help her. I'm supposed to rescue her from her past and her family. But here I am, allowing a terrible thought to get in the way. *Why, oh why am I so bad?*

When the camping season is over, the summer staff all moves to the staff house for one final week to clean up and shut down the camp for the season. Of course, Debbie and I stay in a room together. Everyone knows we are best friends. I change clothes in the bathroom where I can have privacy because I'm terrified that Debbie is crushing on me like I'm crushing on her, and it's embarrassing.

One night I wake up, and Debbie is lying next to me in my bed looking at me. I stare at her silently while my heart pounds in my chest, and I can feel her finger tracing a line on my stomach. I hold my breath, contemplating, thinking about what it would be like to kiss her. And then I turn away, horrified. What is wrong with me?

She comes home with me on her way back to Chicago to meet my parents. My mom immediately dislikes her and tells me she's been suspecting something satanic was happening to me all summer. God told her I was in grave danger, so my mom rescued me through her prayers. Debbie leaves for home, and after a couple of final vacation weeks with my parents, I eagerly move back into the college dorms.

I'm a resident assistant my sophomore year, so instead of sharing a room with two other students, I get to share a room with only one student of my choosing. Of course, I choose my best friend, Melissa, again. She surprises me on my birthday with a visit from Debbie because that's the kind of friend she is. But for some reason, seeing Debbie in my school setting is jolting, and I feel repulsed by both her and me. I try to be polite, but Debbie can tell I am not the same girl I was last summer. I have transformed into a privileged snob. I loathe myself on so many levels when I imagine myself through her eyes, and it's a relief when she leaves. I don't answer any of her letters, and I try to push the whole ordeal out of my mind like it never happened.

For a while, I date a guy who wants to be a missionary to the Muslims. Peter sings in the men's choir, studies missions, and hangs out at Hamline University playing basketball with Muslim students in hopes of introducing them to Jesus. Of everyone I've met at college so far, Peter is the most like Elisabeth Elliot's Jim. He doesn't even kiss me for the longest time, and everyone teases us until one night in the car, the temptation is too much, and we kiss. It is a very good kiss, unlike the French fiasco with Ted from the year before, so we do it some more. And some more. And pretty soon we are taking long walks on campus at night to find little nooks and crannies to kiss in. So much for being like Elisabeth and Jim.

The sad thing is, I'm such a brat I end up breaking it off with him because I keep thinking he is too heavenly to be of any earthly good. How could I think such a horrid thought about an incredibly kind and godly man who is also a great kisser? *Who am I?* I don't deserve him. Maybe I don't deserve anyone.

You wondered for years what these experiences were about. What was God's message in them? Did you navigate them successfully, or did you "fail" in your mission? In later years, when these things come up in others you love, you will discover why love brought you to a place that jolted your world for a time. You will find another layer to love. One that is hard for many to accept or understand, but you'll see it because of these experiences, and love will hold you and all the people, regardless of their ability to see or feel it, safely in the palm of God's hand.

20
Nanny

Summer break comes around again, and this time I'm living with one of my professors, Mrs. Wilder, who recently had a baby and is writing her dissertation. Mrs. Wilder needs a live-in nanny, and I need an excuse not to go home for another summer. I watch her three-year-old daughter, Rita, who has the deepest, most adorable dimples, and her itty-bitty newborn brother, Jordan, during the day, and at night they let me drive their Honda Civic to Perkins where I have a serving job. Mrs. Wilder also supervises a couple of self-study literature classes I take to catch up on my degree since I decided to switch from journalism to English Education in my second year. I stay busy, and I love it.

I'm concerned about Mrs. Wilder being a working mom. Shouldn't mothers stay home to raise their children? That's what I grew up learning, but Mr. and Mrs. Wilder seem happy with one another and their little family. Mrs. Wilder is one of my favorite professors. Everyone adores her. I can't imagine her having to stay at home just ironing Aaron's shirts while she waits for her kids to come home from school when she could be writing and teaching college students literature while the nanny does the ironing.

Mr. and Mrs. Wilder never yell, and they respect each other, even though they've been married for several years. They grind fresh coffee beans every single morning to make coffee, and they eat healthy salads with interesting vegetables, and Mrs. Wilder sometimes makes me a chocolate malt because she worries about how I'm "skin and bones."

They are rich and live in a big home that is beautiful and clean, but not perfect, so it feels comfortable and easy. They have a stack of music albums, including Amy Grant's newest one, *Lead Me On*, and they let me play it whenever I want. They do not believe in satanic beats. Maybe satanic beats aren't even a thing.

They also allow me to have my boyfriend, Chris, over to hang out. I got to know Chris last year when we were both on the homecoming court, and we ended up going to a missions conference called Urbana '87 with a bunch of students and hit it off. When we got back, we both volunteered at the Boys Club in St. Paul, and I could see myself with Chris for the rest of my life. We've even talked about getting married after I graduate next year.

I sleep in the Wilder's unfinished basement, and sometimes Chris stays late into the night, and we mess around after the Wilders go to bed. We both feel guilty about it, even though we never cross "the line." I wish Chris was more heavenly minded, like Peter was. But then again, I really don't. I could make out for hours and never get tired of it.

When the summer is over, the Wilders take me to a fancy restaurant for dinner and give me a gorgeous pearl necklace. I feel embarrassed, and I'm not sure I deserve it. I can't help but wonder if they were only pretending to like me because they are polite people. When I think about what I want some day, this is it. I want a peaceful, happy family.

Nanny

I love that you rubbed shoulders with the Wilder family. I love that you crossed paths with and learned from your relationship with Chris. The pearl necklace is a reminder of how precious you are to God and to others who have come into your life. One day you will be able to receive as fully as you give. We will get there together. I promise.

21

Saddle Up Your Horses!

I'm driving down 35W on my way to work with Steven Curtis Chapman's *The Great Adventure* blaring on my car radio. I have graduated from college, and now I teach English, Bible, and Typing to seventh through twelfth graders in a small Christian school. I love it. What I don't love is that I had to break up with Jerry.

Jerry was the love of my life. I'll never forget the first time I saw him at a regional singing competition through the Evangelical Free Church. We were in eleventh grade, and I was crazy in love with Danny, a boy I sang with in Freestyle. But when I saw Jerry standing in the middle of a cloud of adoring teenage girls, I fell instantly and hopelessly in love. It shocked me how quickly I transferred my affection for Danny to this cute new guy who made all the girls swoon.

All through college, I watched Jerry date girl after girl after girl, and I secretly wished that one day, he would look in my direction. I guess he ran out of interesting prospects because at the beginning of senior year, right when Chris was about to ask me to marry him, Jerry started flirting with me, and I liked it. I was a fickle mess. Chris would be happier in the long run without me, so I broke another good boy's heart and turned my attention to the bad boy I had always wanted.

Jerry had a reputation for being a womanizer, and I had just been voted "Miss Northwestern," supposedly representing all that was pure and right and holy on campus, but I didn't care about what others said. When my English professor and mentor, Dr. Brown, pulled me aside and asked me why I was dating Jerry, I had nothing profound to say. "I'm crazy about him. I always have been. He is my destiny." She gave me an exasperated look.

Jerry and I broke up and made up over and over. It was an exciting, emotional rollercoaster, and I was obsessively addicted to every minute of it. I learned how to dress better, kiss better, and look better all because of Jerry, but I struggled to keep up with everything he wanted me to be all the time, and I wasn't a submissive girlfriend, so we fought often. Finally, God told *me* to break up with *him* for good at the same time God told *him* to break up with *me* for good, so there was a bit of arguing over who broke up with whom. The long and the short of it is that I didn't stop bawling for days on end, and I cut off all my long, beautiful hair and permed it, making me look like a poodle with a new trim.

Along with my new poodle hair, I finally had an epiphany. I was never going to date again. I was going on a Great Adventure, and even now it gives me chills to think and sing about it with Steven Curtis Chapman, whose music, incidentally, has plenty of satanic beats. I have finally decided this music can't be wrong when it feels so right. I have already slipped too far down the slippery slope, but maybe, just maybe, if I only date Jesus, my renewed commitment will make up for the satanic music.

So here I am at the start of my new life. I've got my new job, and I've started going to a new church. I had been going to a large Baptist church in the Twin Cities after their pastor came to my college for a week's worth of chapel talks. But when I tried to get into their church choir in time to practice for the Christmas program, I was too late. They already had one practice, and I missed it. I tried to explain to the choir director (whom I found out later was sleeping with the church secretary, so looking back, I suppose he was distracted) that I had been singing in choirs my entire life and could read music and pick up anything I had missed in one session, but he scowled at me (maybe the secretary wasn't available that night) and said no. I drove home crying. Yup, I'm still the same old bawl baby I've always been. Why can't I just trust God and be happy?

Anyway, that old church doesn't matter to me anymore because my roommates and I receive an invitation to this new church from a mutual college friend who is getting married to a guy she met there. It's a little community church that used to be a Plymouth Brethren church where all the women wore head coverings. Two new pastors have moved into town to transform it into a seeker-sensitive church like Willow Creek in Illinois. So, no more head coverings. Thank God. Too weird for seekers. Head coverings are also too weird for me, and I graduated from "seeker" to "mature Christian" ages ago.

My new church is still small, but it's mostly singles or young married couples, so I feel right at home. Many of the young couples have shared their story of how they met and got married, and the story is oddly the same for almost all of them. A single man and a single woman decide to get a new small group started. They nurture that small group, pray together, work together, and grow together until God lights the fire of love in their hearts. One day, they wake up and realize they were always meant to be together. It's a God-thing, so they get married.

Many of these couples don't even like each other when they start working together, but God's ways are mysterious, and love comes softly with no dating required. Just lead a small group and watch your destiny unfold. That's how our college friend gets engaged, and her husband is going to be a pastor one day, so God has truly blessed her for not dating. It's like, if you date Jesus, He'll give you a husband on earth. Or something like that.

I love this idea because it removes the decision-making and angst of dating. I hate all the forks I've come to in my life so far. They require me to figure out which path is right and which path is wrong, and I'm always making the wrong choice. The right choice leads to blessings and love. The wrong choice leads to getting yelled at and kicked out of people's love circle. It's tricky.

This method of finding a mate takes care of all that. No more choices, really. It's like climbing to the top of a sledding hill, hopping on a sled, and sliding down. Actually, this reminds me of a slippery slope, but this is a *good* slippery slope. This slope leads to marriage and a family that glorifies God, which is always the right choice. I will never date another guy again. Saddle up your horses, folks! We are going on a Great Adventure!

We were always together, my bright little Natalie, and our adventure began at the dawn of time. No matter how you find a lifelong partner and no matter who it is, you and I will always be together. We will always be One. love thought of us before the beginning of the world, and you will see and experience more of love as you continue your great earth adventure.

22
Clicking

Pastor Luke is super popular, and he preaches amazing sermons about real stuff like sacrificing our lives and giving everything to God. He and his wife have sacrificed and left everything they knew in Iowa to come to Minnesota with a vision to start the biggest church in the Twin Cities. Pastor Luke has an inner circle of friends, like Jesus did, and I really want to be part of it. My roommates and I start babysitting his kids for free since he doesn't get much money as a pastor. After he and his wife come home from their date, she goes to bed, and he sits up until one or two in the morning talking about spiritual things with us. We listen intently and believe everything he says.

One day, he tells me I should go into full-time ministry. I could raise support through our church's parent organization and do missionary work with students at the University of Minnesota. He casts a vision for me, like a net, and I am enthusiastically caught in it. Being a missionary and serving God full time is exactly what I've always dreamed of, so when my year of teaching high school is over, I decide not to go back, and I spend the summer raising support. This means setting up appointments and meeting with hundreds of people, asking them to commit to a monthly pledge amount. While I'm fundraising, I also spend time at Pastor Luke's house, helping his wife homeschool their kids. She is the most godly, submissive woman I have ever met. Her voice is soft and high pitched, like a baby bird, and she always has a big warm smile on her face. I wish I could be like her, but my voice is low and loud, and I'm prideful and like to make my own decisions. I babysit for Luke and his wife sometimes without my roommates, and when his wife turns into bed, Luke and I have long talks into the night. Something inside me feels wrong about this, but I can't put my finger on what it is. He's a godly pastor, so if there was something wrong about it, wouldn't he recognize that and point it out? All I know is that I'm now part of Pastor Luke's inner circle, and I feel special. Since I've started only dating Jesus, I miss feeling special to a human.

Pastor Luke calls me on the phone every day to talk. If my roommate answers and I'm not home, he says he can't talk to her, but if I'm home, he'll talk to me for a long time. He goes out of his way to say hi to me at church. He invites me to be on the worship team and takes me shopping to buy pretty clothes to wear on stage. He takes me to his special praying place in the woods where we talk about God. But there is something underneath that nags at me, and I worry about what it might be. I can't trust my heart because the Bible says it is "deceitful above all else." I will need to trust Pastor Luke.

In the fall, I've raised enough money for a monthly check that will support me, and I begin planning student events, prayer meetings, Bible studies, and evangelistic outreaches for students at the U of M. Pastor Luke tells me to pick a few college women to work with more closely. These are the rules of discipleship. Pick a few people and keep them close. The rest are loved by God, but heaven knows we don't have time to build into everyone. There is some grumbling about this among the students once in a while because everyone wants to be chosen, but Pastor Luke is always there to encourage me to keep doing what is right even if people complain. Stay focused. Thank God for Pastor Luke. Like my mom, he teaches us that we each have a fragrance, and that fragrance will attract the right people that we are able to influence. We will "click" with them. This is why Pastor Luke has an

Clicking

inner circle. The people in his inner circle "click" with him. And this is why I must have an inner circle of my own girls who "click" with me. This reminds me a little of popular cliques in high school, and I have never thought of those cliques as being spiritual or healthy. But what do I know? I want to be teachable, and that means I know nothing.

Knowing nothing also means being confused, and the older I get the more conundrums I discover. For example, I've never been baptized because, according to my mom, baptism is no longer part of our current dispensation, and I have no reason not to believe her since she has studied this up and down and all around. She refused to be water-baptized as a result, and the little Evangelical Free church I grew up in made an exception in her case so she could be a member without getting baptized. Her infant baptism didn't count. Not to her, and not to our Evangelical Free church. This causes me to wonder what counts with God since the infant baptizers, the adult baptizers, and the non-baptizers all claim His stamp of approval. I secretly think God might not care either way.

I'm leaning toward getting baptized at Pine Tree Community Church, becoming a member, and being done with it. However, if I get baptized, my mom will be upset. If I don't get baptized, my church will be upset. I wish I could make everyone happy, but this is one of those uncomfortable situations where I'm forced to upset someone. Since Mom is used to being upset with me and most likely has a higher tolerance for it, I guess I'll upset her and get baptized. It's not like I'm going to hell for being baptized, right?

God loves all the children of the world, whether they follow this tradition or that tradition. Jesus didn't come to set up more traditions. Those are activities people set up to help them experience God. Their traditions help them make sense of their pain and ease their fear and shame. But love is right here inside of you, little Natalie, and you may experience God and love to the fullest of your capacity any time you wish, safely enjoying love's Presence within you. No traditions necessary. Just faith to believe this is all that is necessary.

23
Dating Jesus

I've been dating Jesus for a couple of years now while focusing on helping Pastor Luke and his family, evangelizing the University of Minnesota, and discipling the clicky students. I work with another guy on staff named John, who is lanky, unassuming, quiet, and behind-the-scenes. All the students love him.

Pastor Luke does not. Luke likes passionate people. He likes the movers and the shakers. He likes the leaders who rise up from the crowd of nameless faces. John is not passionate. John is not a mover or a shaker. John is not a leader. He's just . . . John. The first time I see John, he is introducing Pastor Luke at a student meeting on campus. John looks terrified and stumbles over his introduction. It's sort of adorable. When I meet John afterward, I notice he doesn't have a wedding ring, and I curse myself for looking. (I'm sorry, Jesus. I don't mean to be unfaithful.)

Here's the thing: I was never planning on marrying someone like John. I have always wanted to be with someone exciting, like Jerry, but when I remember how Jerry's huge personality eclipsed my own, I wonder if maybe a more passive man would be better for me. John isn't the kind of person who cares what my shoes look like or whether or not I'm wearing nail polish. John simply, faithfully shows up for everyone. He shows up for me.

I don't know how it happened, and sometimes I wonder if I made it happen because I was beginning to think I would be dating Jesus for the rest of my life. No offense to Jesus because I love Him with all my heart, but I want to have sex and babies before the rapture, and you can't do that with Jesus. I start to think that maybe I need to give John a nudge and initiate a conversation about a potential future together. I simply need the right opportunity.

That opportunity comes when John and I take the college students to a summer leadership training in Washington, DC, and we drive out early, which gives us time to talk. His sister and brother-in-law live in Philadelphia, so we stop by to see them for a couple of days. While we are there, I do the nudge. It's late one night, and we're in their basement when I suddenly feel the urge to give him a hug. He hugs me back and nervously tells me he wants to court me. Courting is like dating only you plan to get married at the end of it. I tell him I would like to be courted, and that's that. When John and I get engaged a few months later, Pastor Luke's wife takes me out to lunch and tells me how relieved she is that I found someone to marry. She tells me she was beginning to think God would kill her and give *me* to Pastor Luke as a wife! I stare out the restaurant window and can't think of what to say about that.

I used to say God put John and me together, but as I look back, I'm not so sure. I think maybe I put us together with my selfish desires. I think if I had been a good girl, a wise girl, a patient girl, I would have kept dating Jesus because when you make your bed, you know what comes next.

Love holds all the children in this story. Each one is reaching for love and meaning and relief from their own fear and shame, but they are reaching for solutions that will never satisfy them. They are reaching for acceptance, approval, and admiration. Love is not confused about any of this. Love is not wringing God's hands in despair. To the contrary, God already inhabits the time when every last child will finally discover that everything they were looking for was already within them. They are all whole and complete in love, seen, accepted, approved of, admired, and adored. And so are you, little Natalie.

24

Baby Girl

John and I have been married for six months when I take my first pregnancy test. It's positive. My legs buckle, and I drop to the floor of the living room with my face in the carpet while happy sobs rip through my body. There is a life inside of me! The problems my new husband and I are having melt away. God is showing me His favor!

The days that follow are a blur of sickness, exhaustion, and irritability as I count the minutes to the next hour, and the hours to the next day, and the days to the next week, longing for the first trimester to be over. I want to feel my baby, not the nausea. Finally, the nausea melts away, my belly rounds, and the flutters begin and grow stronger. I am in heaven.

Until one day, I wake up spotting. The doctor looks inside me and says matter-of-factly, "You're three centimeters dilated, and the bag of water is bulging into the birth canal. Your baby is going to be born and can't survive at this stage, so you need to go to the hospital, and they will direct you from there."

I cannot think. I cannot breathe. Everything hurts. John drives me to the hospital in the rain. *"I will trust in the Lord, even though He slay me."* I speak the words of the Bible verse inside my head, but they do not resonate. One minute ago, life made sense, and the next minute, it's utter chaos, and Bible verses are now empty words. I collapse beneath something impossibly heavy. I can't do this. I will never, ever be able to do this.

Baby Girl

Incompetent cervix. That's what I have. My baby is healthy, but my body is inhospitable, and it's kicking the baby out. The surgeons at the hospital put in an emergency cerclage that holds for two weeks, but in the end, when they cannot stop the labor from coming, they cut the cerclage out. I'm five months pregnant when Elizabeth Anne's little twelve-ounce, perfectly formed body slips out, and they take my hope away. I went into the hospital with a belly full of baby and a heart full of love, and I leave an empty shell. My baby is gone, and so is my soul.

My life is fuzzy—like I'm moving under water. I walk through Target and can't remember how I got my groceries. I look at people and think, "They do not know that Elizabeth is gone forever. Nobody knows she was even here." I do my job as an apartment caretaker and vacuum the halls of our complex. The residents ask, "How is your pregnancy coming along?" I tell them, and they say, "It's all for the best. You will have another one. There must have been something wrong with it. Next time it will be healthy," and other things that twist my heart.

I cannot bring myself to be happy. To smile. To laugh. All I do is stare or bawl. And John asks, "What's wrong with you?" Over and over and over. That's how I know I'm alone.

Why did God let this happen? Why would He give me a dream come true and then sadistically steal it away, like a bully holding a toy over the head of a child and never letting her have it? What kind of God would do that? Why does He intervene for some and not for others? What is the point of praying if He's just going to do what He wants to do anyway? Why is He distant when I'm suffering? Why does He get credit for anything good that happens, but if something bad happens, it's not His responsibility? Why do I always feel like He expects me to respond properly—like I'm in some big Universal Contest? I want to respond beautifully and neatly, with perseverance and endurance. But I can't.

I give up! I'm tired of having to be everyone's stupid example. I'm tired of trying to live up to God's expectations. I have given up my own dreams and desires to be obedient to Him. My every thought is constantly about how to please Him. Does He ever care about pleasing me? I feel like a horrible human to even have these selfish, demanding thoughts. I can't tell anyone how I feel. I've tried, but they tell me to trust God. I know the devil is ruling my thoughts, but if God is that much stronger than Satan, why isn't He speaking to me? I'm reading the Bible, but it's not saying anything to me anymore. Why is it that when I need God the most, He is a million miles away? There is a swirling pit of darkness growing bigger and deeper in the core of my being, and I am being sucked in and down. The only relief is when I sleep, but waking up is even worse. As soon as my brain comes online, this heavy weight rushes in and fills every cell of my body with screaming pain. I am utterly lost, and not even God knows where to find me. If only I had died with my baby.

Baby Girl

My heart breaks with yours, little Natalie. I know this left you grief-stricken and terrified that you and those you love are randomly spinning out of control. The world you are living in right now is like this. Life throws you curveballs and gives you whiplash when you least expect it. Nothing makes sense, and it isn't supposed to make sense. Not yet. But you will push through the pandemonium, and love will tuck priceless treasures into the folds of your faith for you to find when you need them most. Love will never leave you or forsake you. And love will never leave or forsake your children, either.

25

Bedrest

I walk into the clinic and say, "Hi! It's me again! Can I come back now? I'm pregnant again!"

I overhear the receptionist whisper to another patient, "It's that incompetent cervix case. I can't believe she's going to kill another one so soon."

I watch all the competent cervix cases with bulging bellies draped in pretty maternity tops confidently walking in and out. They belong here, and they know it.

"Please!" I cry out. "Can someone help me save my baby?"

I wake up in a cold sweat.

This second pregnancy gets off to a rocky start. By six weeks I'm spotting and cramping, and an ultrasound shows what appears to be an empty sac. "A blighted ovum," they say. I beg God to save my baby's life even though I don't think He will, and a second ultrasound a week later shows the beginnings of a healthy baby. I hope God will not count my doubts against me or this innocent baby. The baby can't help having a mother who's a faithless coward.

I'm on bedrest, and every day is the same. I awaken, slowly sit up in bed, watch the room go black for a moment, stand up when I can see again, and walk carefully to the bathroom. My legs feel like Jell-O, and the pressure of my growing belly on my weak cervix worries me. I check my pale, zit-covered face in the mirror for any new blemishes and then wobble back to bed to redistribute my body among the pillows. I mark time by meals, showers, the mail, my weekly doctor appointment, my favorite soap opera, two threads-worth of cross-stitching, and getting through one more week.

This morning I awaken to pain in my thigh. The doctor wonders if I have a blood clot. I've had contractions all day, plus cramping, nausea, and dizziness. It's hard to stay calm. I want to scream in frustration. My friend, Marlene, stops by with dinner looking radiant at eight months of pregnancy. She's getting a haircut tomorrow and looks forward to the arrival of their second child with no worries or fears. That lucky baby. That lucky mom. That lucky family. Happiness comes so easily to some.

I feel as ugly and as incompetent as my cervix. My poor, innocent, helpless baby is placed in the womb of a loser. I have this recurring dream where I'm holding my baby, but my arms are getting weaker and weaker, and I can't hang on. I'm aware my baby is going to fall, and I wake up with a sadness so deep I can hardly breathe. I'm probably on the verge of seeing another sweet baby die, and it will be all my fault.

Part of my cerclage knot comes loose at four months. I've bled off and on. I have to take medication to prevent preterm labor. And I'm lonely. John is rarely here. He works hard with the ministry, delivers papers at 3:00 a.m., and takes care of the apartment building, so we can live here rent-free. I'm just one more burden in his life, and I despise myself for that.

I'm selfishly hanging on too tightly to my baby. I am afraid I will lapse into temporary stages of madness and want to keep my baby close to me and away from God. If only I knew that God wanted my baby to be safely delivered into my arms for me to raise for His glory. I promise I would give him back to God if He would let me keep this one, like Hannah did with Samuel.

Little Natalie, both you and your baby will always and forever be safe within God's love. It is not selfish to seek safety and relationship and love. It is wise. I know you can't see this yet, but you get to keep every single treasure love ever gives you. Love never takes back its gifts because love is a fountain spring of never-ending gifts. The water comes up and over, offering refreshment, and then it falls down and in, only to spring back up again in a never-ending cycle of joyous grace. One day you will see. For now, drink in this miracle.

26
A Reason to Live

The week before Christmas I go to bed feeling slightly feverish and wake up around one in the morning, horrified to feel contractions coming at regular intervals. My baby isn't due until March, but an active strep B infection has reached my uterus, and the baby needs to come out. They tell me he is twenty-nine weeks gestation, and with a few weeks in the NICU, his chances of survival are very high. But I feel like the entire universe hates me and wants to spit me out. My body actively labors, but my heart is numb under a layer of ice so thick I can't move. If I do, the ice will crack, my baby will die, and then I will die with him. Better to stay frozen.

And then he comes. In spite of my frozenness, he comes all the same. They allow me to look at him briefly before they intubate him and rush him to the NICU. While they clean me up, I hardly know what to think or feel. My baby is alive. For now. Will he still be alive by the time they allow me to see him? I pray over and over, "Please, Dear God, I will do anything, anything, *anything* You ask if You will only save this baby. I will never ask You for anything again as long as I live if You will just save him. Please, I beg of You, don't take my baby away from me. Please don't take him." I keep the tears inside so nobody will think I am weak or stupid.

They eventually put me in a wheelchair and take me down a long, underground tunnel to the children's hospital, where my baby already has his own station in the NICU. And there he is. I look at him through a fish tank and can hardly believe my eyes. He is only three pounds of skin and bones, but he is a real, live baby. The tears come then, and I don't care what anyone thinks. My baby is alive, and he is really mine.

During the next seven weeks, I drive to the hospital every day and spend hours holding and rocking him. I pump breast milk around the clock, fight off painful and recurring breast infections, throw away all the milk with blood in it, and keep doggedly pumping so I can nurse him when he is ready. I deserve the pain. I have failed everyone in every way, and any pain I experience is only fair.

The hospital gift shop has adorable little handmade preemie clothes for sale, and I purchase several and dream of the day when he will not have all the wires and tubes in the way. The first time I'm allowed to dress him, I'm in raptures. He's so cute! The nurses teach me how to stimulate him if he stops breathing, how to feed him on a three-hour schedule, and how to turn him so his head will grow evenly on all sides. I bring him a cassette tape of my voice as well as a couple of lullaby tapes, and the nurses play those when I'm not there at night. I hope that my gratefulness and my hard work in pumping and rocking and praying will impress God enough to be convinced that letting me keep my baby is the best choice.

My son comes home on an apnea monitor, but otherwise, he is healthy, at least at first, and the next few months are heavenly. While friends complain about how tired they are with their newborns, I am relishing every minute with mine, no matter what hour of the day. I hardly notice my own constant illness, my bladder infections, my toe infection, and my continuing breast infections.

And as it turns out, our baby is not out of the woods entirely, either. He's getting ear infections and coughs. His head is also growing exponentially, and it's becoming obvious to everyone around us that something isn't right. Dr. Nagib, a pediatric neurosurgeon, is concerned he may have hydrocephalus. It becomes a waiting game as we keep an eye on his head growth and the fluid levels in his brain every month.

In the meantime, I grow sicker and sicker. Walking upstairs leaves me winded and dizzy. I'm losing weight, sweating constantly, and can hardly lift anything. Something is wrong, but I don't want to complain or be ungrateful. John served me while I was on bedrest, and now I need to step up and get back to serving him as a good wife should. I'm thrilled to be up and around, keeping house. I've even taken a babysitting job for a friend to earn money and help make ends meet. This is what I have wanted since I was a little girl. A husband, a home, and a baby. I keep telling myself that I have never been happier, and I'm not going to let my health stop me now.

But when I'm honest with myself in the middle of the night holding the one I love more than anything else in the universe, something has been getting to me, and I'm not happy. I'm deeply hurting in my marriage, and I'm struggling to forgive my husband for the mean things he says to me and the ways I feel so desperately alone. I beg God for the grace to endure and to overlook any wrongs, but I feel shredded inside. I worry that I'm not praying enough. I have talked to Mandy, who recently lost her four-year-old son to cancer, and she suggests I may be angry at God. I readily admit this is likely true. I have doubted His goodness and questioned His ways. I know I'm in sin, and I'm constantly scared that God will take my baby away from me to punish me.

My professor and mentor, Dr. Brown, has been trying to get me to come back to my alma mater to teach English. She tells me that if I pursue my master's degree, my alma mater will hire me as a part-time English professor until I'm finished with school and can teach full-time. I want to teach so badly that I have to push the thought straight out of my head because I know if I leave my child now and put him in daycare while I work, God will think I don't love my son enough. God will think I don't take my job as a mother seriously enough. He will wish He had not given me this treasure. I cannot, *will not* take that risk. I tell Dr. Brown no and then press onward. I've gotten used to pushing pain away. I hope God will see me making every effort to obey Him in spite of my selfish heart.

One day I get out of bed and fall on the floor. My heart is racing, and I wonder in a fog if I might be dying. John takes me to the ER where we learn I have Graves Disease and require radioactive iodine treatment. This means I can no longer nurse my baby or even be near him for several days until the treatment has left my body. I'm crushed but also relieved that it's a treatable issue, and it won't kill me. I finally have an incredibly precious reason to live.

A Reason to Live

You have many incredibly precious reasons to live, little Natalie. Not only to love and protect and shape this new person you've willed into existence but to love and protect and shape your own person as well. Love gives you spaciousness in which to live and move and have your being, and I want you not to step precariously through your life but to dance in freedom in these wide-open spaces offered for your joy. You can freely take up space because love is spacious, and you are in love, and love is in You.

27
Enough Faith

Our baby has hydrocephalus and needs surgery. The week before his surgery, Mandy encourages us to ask the pastors if they will lay hands on him and pray for healing. Our church is not that kind of church, but we are desperate, and the pastors humor us. Mandy says in order for the prayers to be effective, the pastors must have faith God can do it. I'm relieved about this because my own faith is not at its peak, and if it were up to me, I'm more likely to hold out my baby to God and scream, "FINE! TAKE HIM! HAVE IT YOUR WAY SINCE YOU OBVIOUSLY DON'T HAVE ENOUGH BABIES WITH YOU AND NEED ANOTHER ONE SO BADLY!" I know. Rude.

But like I said, it's not up to my faith; it's up to Pastor Barry's faith, and apparently, he has enough of it to make the miracle work. Dr. Nagib orders one last MRI to check fluid levels, and this time, the scan shows an ever-so-slight decrease. Not enough to put my son out of the woods, but enough to cancel the surgery and see if it will continue to resolve on its own. A few months later, our baby is diagnosed with "benign macrocephaly," which means "not a big deal, just a big head."

But my baby is still sick with ear infections, puking, and coughing. And then there's me. I'm having a laparoscopy and hysteroscopy the day before we leave for our ministry's Leadership Training, and John's family is coming to stay the next week while John is gone camping. The cupboards are being stripped, and my friend Jessica is moving in, and there are thank you cards to write. I'm supposed to be calling people on bedrest, supervising in the nursery, helping another friend with her garage sale, grocery shopping, cooking, cleaning a dirty home, and weeding flower gardens. I've got infected gums and Jessica's birthday to worry about. People are slowly leaving our financial support team, and we're worried about bills.

John and I plug away on staff with Great Commission Ministries, but everything is shifting, and they want us to move to Columbus, Ohio. We've fasted. We've prayed. We even drove there for a visit to see if we could catch a longing or a calling or a . . . a *something* to go there and do ministry. We could not catch a thing in a drab, gray city that left me depressed. I would rather poke my eyeballs out with knitting needles than move away from everything I know with a man I'm not even sure loves me. I want to prove my love for Jesus by doing my duty, sacrificing whatever I need to sacrifice, and laying down my life if necessary. But I will not do all of those things in Columbus, Ohio. Call me rude and a flagrant rebel, but if I'm going to die to my own dreams for the next fifty years, I will do it in my own home state.

I invite my mom to go to the Mary Hill Retreat center with me for a time of prayer and Bible study. When we get back, she comes over to see the sponging technique I'm using to paint my living room, which gives the walls a rustic, textured look, like a Spanish restaurant. She doesn't like it. She warns me that I'll get sick of it, too. The walls would be better in a plain, neutral color. I would be happier in the long run. Maybe she's right, but I want to try my brightly colored Spanish restaurant walls. I keep painting my way, but not without nagging doubt, fear, and even guilt. Is it rebellious to try something colorful? Something normal people might not do? Maybe when people come over to visit, they will be uncomfortable now? Maybe it's too much. Maybe I'm too much.

I have this powerful desire for safety and security on *this* side of heaven, and I want it *now*. My dreams at night are full of terror, anger, sensuality, and sorrow, and I'm afraid if people truly knew me, they wouldn't want to be around me. Larry Crabb writes, "*When relief from the inevitable pain of living in a fallen world becomes our priority, at that moment we leave the path toward pursuing God.*" I definitely long for relief. Maybe I have left the path to God, and all is lost.

John has been applying for secular jobs, and he keeps getting turned down. His most recent ministry performance review from Pastor Barry was not good. There is no vision, direction, or hope for the future. I am utterly at a loss as to what to do or how to help. I don't know if God is trying to help us, and John isn't listening, or if I'm supposed to be helping more. How can I support my husband's leadership when he will not lead? We are in a boat out in the middle of the ocean going nowhere, and my job is to support and respect his choice to do—*nothing*? Every fiber of my being objects to this apathy.

I don't deserve my beautiful son. I am forever doing anything I can to avoid pain to the point of becoming defensive when John hurts me. The things he does to me stir up so much indignation that I've fantasized about him getting sick or dying in a car accident. My fantasies scare me. How could I be that angry at someone, let alone my own husband? In the Bible there is a story about a woman who keeps banging on the judge's door. Banging, banging, banging until she gets an answer. That is what I will do. I will keep banging on God's door until He fixes me. I need more faith.

Enough Faith

I see your endless toiling and your relentless thrashing for relief from the questions, the fear, and the shame. And in the center of your being, there is God. The Great Beginning and End. Quietly loving you. Quietly holding you. Quietly knowing you, your history, your present, and your future. Also, your eternity. You are blindly banging on an open door. Love is not a judge who refuses to help. Love is your life and your hope. One day you will stop desperately banging long enough to look into Love and enter into Peace. In the meantime, I am with you, little Natalie.

28
Sex at the Beach

I've never had an orgasm. I have always thought I was an oddball, but apparently most women don't have them, and I discover this fact at Myrtle Beach. John and I spend three days traveling there with our son for six weeks of Leadership Training at the beginning of the summer. I have exploratory surgery on my uterus the day before we leave, and there is a bunch of gas in my system from the anesthesia. The pain is almost unbearable, but I think about how hard life is for women in third-world countries, and I tell myself to "buck up, buttercup." On top of that, our car breaks down several times along the way, and once we finally arrive, I find out I'm allergic to the mold that seems to proliferate in coastal South Carolina and have to constantly pop Benadryl. I keep nodding off like an elderly woman everywhere we go. John and I fight nonstop, and I'm a hypocrite around the other staff wives, pretending life is awesome when it's actually a hot mess.

One day all the staff wives get together to talk about sex and how to enjoy it and give it to our husbands as a way of supporting them in their ministry work. I'm shocked when they bring up the subject of orgasms, and several of the wives openly admit to never having one. John can be mean in the kitchen, but in the bedroom he's kind and patient, so even though I can't have an orgasm (I'm not even sure what that is for a girl—it's not like I have a penis or anything), I feel loved when we have sex. The only problem is that it hurts. And if I were a swearing person, which typically I'm not, I'd say it hurts like hell. I squeeze my eyes shut and hold my breath and pray for it to be over.

That's a lot of pressure on John, which only makes the sex drag out, and by the time he's done, my body is screaming in agony. I try to pretend I'm fine. I don't want to embarrass him or make him feel bad when he's trying so hard to make it good for me, but I dread sex with every fiber of my being.

So, no. I don't want to discuss my sex life with a bunch of women I don't know, but they keep chit-chatting about it like we're talking about going to the mall to buy a new dress. I pay attention because I want to be a good wife, and I want to please my husband and make him happy. After our wives' sex talk, I go home and try out some of the suggestions that night: Think about how grateful you are for your husband and how he takes care of you. Concentrate on his kisses and how it feels. Move your body. Get into it. Let yourself go. Make noises. It's all good. Anything is game. I think, "*Okay, I can do this.*" I'm nervous, but I give it my everything. I'm a go-big-or-go-home kind of gal.

John notices. Right in the middle of my enthusiastic efforts, he suddenly stops everything and says, "What are you doing? Why are you acting like you're some kind of movie star or something?"

He found me out.

Something is seriously wrong with me, and it's not only that I can't have an orgasm. I feel bad for John. He's married a self-centered fraud. If anyone is in pain, it's him. I will go back to holding my breath, closing my eyes, and disappearing.

Feeling loved is worth it.

Sex and marriage were never meant to be this way, and it is a curious thing to see so many precious souls suffering under layers of broken ideas and mistaken beliefs, everyone looking to fill the gaping holes inside by hiding, pretending, and demanding—all in misguided efforts to feel safe and worthy of existence. There is a Great Healing coming. For now, know that you are seen and loved, little Natalie. Not from a distance, but from inside of your very being.

29
Even If It Kills Me

I may have made a huge mistake. I have told my pastor about what is going on in my marriage. I feel terrible, like I have betrayed my husband, but what if my pastor can help us? I want to have a healthy marriage that honors God more than anything else, and now there is a child involved. I feel naked and exposed sitting in Pastor Barry's home, trying to explain things. Pastor Barry and Conner, my husband's best friend, who is also an elder, sit back comfortably on easy chairs at one side of the living room looking peaceful, engaged, and in control. John sits next to me on the couch with a blank mask on his face. He's covering it up, but I can feel his embarrassment and anger, and I also imagine those men empathizing with John. *How humiliating to have your wife expose your sins. I'm glad my wife would never do that to me.*

My body flushes and closes in on itself with shame. What if I'm one of *those* wives? The kind who can't love and submit well because her selfishness and unsubmissiveness get the better of her. And now here I am turning the story all around and upside down and telling the pastor and John's best friend that *John is the problem*. I feel terrible for John and guilty for putting him in this position. I don't want to humiliate him. Is it possible he's only a problem *because of me*? Am I the stumbling block to John's being a good husband? If I were a better wife, would it be easier for him to be a better man? Does John wish he married Conner's wife, Betsy? John and Betsy dated and slept together before John met me, and I didn't find out about it until after John and I were engaged. That was when I discovered John slept with other women as well, which made me feel cheated since I had saved myself for my husband so I could have a great marriage. But one of our pastors told me *he* had slept around before *he* got married, and his marriage was great because of this thing called *forgiveness*. I should try it. Just forgive John and move on. If I had sex with one of the boys I dated, I'd have been put on the Used Goods table, and that would have meant giving up my hope for a good marriage unless I had a spouse who was willing to forgive *me*. Thank God I was a virgin when I got married.

So many couples at church have great marriages even though they started out on the Used Goods table, but I have obviously failed somewhere along the way. Now I'm stuck with a man who treats me like dirt, and John is stuck with a wife who tattles on him for it. No matter how I beg God for forgiveness and deliverance from my selfish wish to be loved, I still struggle with this sin. Once I even threw a treasured teacup from my collection against the wall in a crazed effort to get him to stop making me feel invisible and worthless. I thought he would take me seriously if he saw that I was willing to destroy one of my collector pieces. I had resorted to physical violence by throwing something, and I had become one of those drama queens you see in the soap operas.

And now, here I am in this quiet living room, fiercely hoping maybe there's a chance that a different man will hear me and help my husband understand that I'm not asking for happiness. I can easily make myself happy every time I think about how lucky I am to be a mother, to have a home, to be alive. What I'm missing is the *love part*. I wish to be *loved*.

I stumble through some examples of the ways I feel neglected and hurt. They make sense in my head when I'm at home alone with John, but now, as I hear my shaky voice push them out of my strangled throat, they sound as whiny and dumb as I feel. When we leave, John gives me the silent treatment for several days, broken only by subtle, sideways remarks reminding me of how disrespectful I am. To make up for humiliating him by going to Pastor Barry, I try extra hard to be good, make him his favorite meals, and keep the house clean.

Pastor Barry pulls me aside in church a few days later and tells me that he understands and believes me and that he's going to talk to John about everything. He reminds me that my circumstances are not a mistake but perfectly engineered by God to develop godly character in my life. He also tells me that I need to be prepared for John *not to respond at all*, and that this response will probably be the worst one I might be called to bear up under, but that I must be faithful and know that I'm not alone in my sufferings. Jesus also suffered, and He will carry me through.

One Sunday morning, Pastor Barry talks to John in the hallway during the church service. I'm on pins and needles with my entire future hanging in the balance. On one side is healing and hope and deepening love and intimacy with my husband and the father of my children. Everything I've ever longed for. On the other side is a cold, dark maze of dead ends I will wander around until I die.

We get home from church that day, and John is silent. I nervously make a casserole for lunch, but he doesn't want anything to eat and goes to the bedroom to take a nap. I eat a quiet lunch with our little boy and then numbly set about my household chores. John never brings up his conversation with Pastor Barry, and neither do I.

A few days later, Pastor Barry's wife takes me for a long walk and gives me one of her favorite books on how to be a good Christian wife. I eagerly read it, desperately searching within its pages for the key to fixing our marriage. I take notes, determined to put into practice any ideas I haven't already tried. And then I add it to my growing bookshelf of Godly Christian Wife books. I have learned one thing through this experience. I must not be a good Christian wife for John anymore. I know now that he doesn't love me and may not even be capable of loving me. I must be a good Christian wife and mother *for the glory of God*. Even if it kills me.

If only you could see in this moment how your existence in the universe already points to your Creator! What you do or don't do is not a reflection of God. <u>Who you are</u> reflects God because you and God are One. Here's a little secret. You are going to discover who that woman is one day, and it won't kill you. <u>It will save you.</u> One day you will push past the tide of voices programming you with the lies that you are unimportant, insignificant, and even wicked. When you get to know the woman Creator love made you to be, that is when you will begin to catch a glimpse of how near love is. That's the way love works. Love comes in unexpected ways. Hidden ways. Unpretentious ways. Can you see it? One day, little Natalie, you will.

Part Two

Oh, do hear me, oh, do hear me,
Else I think my heart will break.
In the longing be thou near me
And my burning thirst—oh slake.
Oh Lord Jesus, hear my crying
For a consecrated life,
For I bite the dust in trying
For release from this dark strife.

THESE WORDS FROM AN UNKNOWN WRITER PERFECTLY CAPTURED the state of my soul in my early years of motherhood, and I copied them carefully in my journal. I was desperately biting the dust in an effort to please God by living a "consecrated life," and this was fueled by filling journals with Bible verses and quotes from "godly womanhood" books, books written by Puritan authors, books by John Piper, Elizabeth Prentiss, Watchman Nee, Fenelon, Ian Thomas, Oswald Chambers, Amy Carmichael, and dozens of others. These books were like little demigods to me, instructing me on how to appease the God I both longed for and feared. I soaked up their teachings and fervently set out to apply their insights to every area of my life. These insights all seemed clear on paper, but in the reality of my life, everything dissolved into confusion. I often felt like I was living in the upside-down world of *Alice in Wonderland,* where nothing was as it seemed, and I couldn't figure out the patterns or find the key I needed to unlock the truth and be free.

In recent years, I've learned about and applied Internal Family Systems theory (IFS), a way of looking at ourselves that recognizes we each have different parts inside of us, and those parts have their own beliefs or programming based on our life experiences. Some parts of us, called "manager parts," try to *prevent pain* by working hard to manage the circumstances and people in our lives. They might do this by trying to please people, control people, manage other people's emotions, judge people, and so on. These manager parts of us might think, for example, that if only we could make people like us or do what we want them to do, we would be happy and avoid pain.

Other parts of us, called "firefighter parts," spring into action if our manager parts are unsuccessful at preventing the pain. These firefighter parts attempt to "put out the fire" of the pain to make it go away. They may do this by overeating, overdrinking, overspending, self-harming, or using drugs. These parts of us believe immediate relief is the answer, and we must do whatever it takes to make the pain go away. They don't understand that some of the methods we use to get immediate relief often lead to long-term damage.

When trying to explain this to my children, I gave them this analogy: Imagine your life is a bus. In the front of the bus is our Self, and we drive the bus through life wherever we want to go. The Self is interconnected with God and is whole, complete, and resourced. God didn't put our Self in charge of anyone else's bus—only our own. We are the driver, connected and at one with our Creator God. But there are other parts of us on the bus, too. Sitting on one side of the bus are our manager parts with all of their ideas and thoughts about how to manage our lives in order to prevent pain. On the other side of the bus are our firefighter parts ready to fly into action as soon as we feel negative emotions.

Way in the back seats of the bus are our exiled parts. I think of them as younger versions of us, hiding and curled up in the fetal position. These parts of us carry all our pain, past trauma, and confusion. We might acquire exiles from being bullied in school, getting lost in a shopping mall, losing a friend in an accident, going through a natural disaster, having a hard time finding friends, growing up poor, growing up in an overly strict home, having a parent with a mental health issue or substance abuse problem, or anything else that caused us harm or emotional pain.

The parts on my bus sometimes disagree with one another about the best course of action. They judge each other. They fight. I used to think there was something wrong with me because I had all these opposing thoughts dictating orders, and I couldn't figure out which ones to obey. I saw them as more scary little gods in my life shouting orders and threatening me if I didn't do everything "right." But now when I feel particularly chaotic in my brain and body, I'm aware of what's going on inside of me. I'm no longer afraid of these little parts, and I can think, "*Oh! My parts are having a food fight on the bus right now!*" That's when I try to slow down, tune in, and listen to what each individual part is trying to communicate to me. I'm not listening to something outside of myself. I'm listening to my *own beliefs and inner thoughts*. If I don't stop to listen, I will never know what is going on inside of me. I will never have the self-awareness I need to address the issues I'm struggling with. Because guess what? These parts *also* need an empathetic witness to heal and to find peace and calm in our body, and *we* are that empathetic witness for ourselves. It is miraculous and comforting to know that God within us *partners with us* in our core Self to be an empathetic witness.

Richard Schwartz, the therapist and former professor who developed the IFS theory, teaches that when we are attuned to our core self, we will experience the Eight C's: compassion, curiosity, calmness, clarity, courage, connectedness, confidence, and creativity.[1] In her book, *Altogether You*, licensed therapist Jenna Riemersma makes the connection between these Eight C's and the fruits of the Holy Spirit found in Galatians 5:22–23: love, joy, peace, patience, goodness, gentleness, kindness, and self-control.[2] When we are aligned with the Holy Spirit within us, we will experience these qualities. How might we react to having someone in our lives who is kind, compassionate, curious, calm, clear, courageous, connected, confident, and creative? How could someone like that help us when we are scared, angry, frustrated, overwhelmed, sorrowful, or worried? What if we *do* have Someone like that within us? What if the only thing keeping us from actually experiencing that Someone is our own lack of belief that this Empathetic Witness is already there? Riemersma says experiencing this Someone is like knowing the sun exists, but we can't experience its warmth when the clouds are in the way.

I also use the cognitive behavioral therapy (CBT) triangle tool, which shows how thoughts, feelings, and behaviors are all interconnected. This tool helps me examine my thoughts and beliefs to discover how they make me feel in my body and how those feelings cause me to show up in my life and in my relationships. Combining the ideas of IFS together with this CBT triangle tool might look like allowing one of those exiled parts to come up to the front of our bus and tell us what they are thinking. "There is something wrong with me!" they might say. When this part believes that thought, we might feel shame in our body. When we feel shame, we might hide, cover up, pretend, shut down, play small, be indecisive, or refuse to take risks. And when we do these things, they end up confirming in our minds that, yes, there truly is something wrong with us. This creates a never-ending loop we can't escape from unless we examine and interrupt that belief within us.

What happens when we share something important, scary, or confusing with someone, and they listen, empathize, and care? We feel heard. We heal a little bit. They are an empathetic witness, and being heard and seen helps us process our emotions and integrate our experience into our life story. Well, guess what? We can offer to listen, hear, and understand our frightened, confused, and panicked parts inside of ourselves, too! We can turn to ourselves and say, "I can understand why you would think that way, precious part of me. You were told there was something wrong with you over and over by different people in your life. No wonder you are worried it is true. I'm so sorry people told you those things. The truth is that there is nothing wrong with you. You are a human being with totally normal reactions and responses to the kinds of things you have experienced. I am here to listen and love and support you from now on. I promise to always have your back. Together, we will find hope and peace and love and healing."

This is a simple example, and working through the quagmire of all our programmed thoughts and beliefs is not an overnight fix. I've been doing this work for many years now, and I anticipate doing it until I die. It is the ongoing work of being a human—not a perfect human, but an honest, authentic human. It means accepting that some of the parts on our bus have dark impulses, behaving like little gods who try to control us from within. But it also means recognizing that those parts are only trying to protect and help us, even though their ideas of how to do that may be misguided and destructive. If we want to neutralize some of the negative effects their beliefs have on our lives, we will need to acknowledge these darker parts of us and befriend them. We will need to listen to them. We will need to love and witness *all of our parts* in order to heal them and absorb them into the God of Love. Incredibly, when we do this work, we can then offer this kind of love to others around us. Whenever I am triggered by someone's behavior or words, that is my signal that a part inside of me is activated and needs to be heard and cared for. I won't be able to effectively listen and understand another person until I can listen to and understand myself.

So, what does all of this have to do with Part Two of my story? Well, I'm going to do something a little different and let some of my own inner parts come to the front of the bus to tell the next part of our story. You'll meet Rude, Freaked, Melancholy, Wonder, Spiritualizer (a name coined by Riemersma in her book), and sweet little Rosie with her rose-tinted lenses. But before we get started, I want to say one more thing. As a child, I had no control over my programming. Neither did you. We were programmed by our environment, parents, siblings, teachers, peers, churches, and experiences. We had no choice about what was planted in our minds. But as we move into adulthood, we do have choices about what we will allow or not allow into our lives; however, most of us will make those choices based on the programming of our past. In Part Two, I made choices that I look back on now and regret because at the time, I chose to continue in much of my early programming. On the one hand, I understand why I made those choices, and I have compassion for the young adult version of me. She did the best she could with the resources she had. On the other hand, if I want to heal and grow into the next version of myself, I need to take personal responsibility for my adult choices and the programming I reinforced through my choices of friends, books, music, churches, and intentional experiences. If I don't take responsibility, I will always blame my lack of growth and stuckness on outside forces, and that leaves me in a powerless position. I've chosen to take my power back by being an adult who takes responsibility for my *own self*. I can't blame my family, my ex, my kids, my church, my pastors, or anyone else for my own choices. But I also don't blame myself. Taking responsibility is not blaming. It's owning. And owning is something only adults can do.

But I'm getting ahead of myself. For now, let's find out what some of my parts have to say about what happened next.

30
Trust God

Rude: My son is sick again. This time with hand, foot, and mouth disease, a gift from the church nursery, thanks to all the inconsiderate parents who don't care about anyone else except their own kids. His immune system is crap, probably due to being born so early.

Freaked: Then he develops croup and another ear infection within three weeks! His whole body goes into convulsions, and I call 911 in a panic. At the hospital, it takes *four* nurses trying *five* times to get an IV in his vein!

Melancholy: He cries and repeats, "Okay! All done! Owie! All done!" My heart breaks in a million pieces. His convulsions turn out to be a febrile seizure, probably due to my not giving him any baby Tylenol. I'm a horrible mother.

Freaked: I'm only trying to do what is best for him! He is constantly sick, and a couple of *way* more experienced moms from church tell me a fever will fight the infection. I mean, it makes sense, right?! When you take a fever-reducer, you prolong the illness. Right?!

Rosie: Those moms are only trying to help. God bless their souls.

Rude: The "perfect" mothers never have to watch their children have febrile seizures. From now on, I'm giving my baby Tylenol.

Melancholy: The seizure is terrifying enough, but what happens next is even worse, and once again, it's all my fault, even though I try so hard to prevent danger.

Rosie: I'm having a quiet day filled with doing laundry, reading to my son, praying for our family, and cleaning up. When it's time to make dinner, I want to put my son in a safe place where I won't have to have my eyes on him while I work in the kitchen.

Freaked: To my horror, I notice the basement door is slightly open. Just a tiny little crack. But I never leave it open like that! Our son could fall down the long, narrow stairs and break his neck!

Rude: John must have forgotten to shut it again. He doesn't have to think about everything that could go wrong. He floats down the river of life on his inner tube, and whatever happens, happens.

Freaked: Which usually leaves me holding all the responsibility for making sure our son stays safe!

Rosie: Once we went to a friend's cabin, and the husbands were going to watch the two toddlers outside while the wives were in the cabin getting food ready.

Freaked: I was nervous to leave our son alone with John!

Rosie: But since there were two men and two toddlers, I comforted myself with the thought that even if John got distracted, the other father might be more like my own dad, who was overly paranoid about bad things happening. John's friend would surely make sure the boys were safe.

Rude: But when I checked on the boys to be sure, the two men were in their lawn chairs yucking it up like nothing bad ever happens in the universe, and the toddlers were nowhere to be seen.

Freaked: After some frantic yelling and running on my part and much calmer searching on the part of everyone else (*Why weren't they panicking?*), we found one child had crawled from the dock and into a boat on the water, and my child was happily dangling his feet in the water from the edge of the dock! The water there was four feet deep! Had either child fallen in, they would have drowned!

Rude: *Not okay.* And I made sure they all knew it.

Rosie: The other couple calmly suggested that everyone makes mistakes, and I should trust God more. They weren't wrong.

Freaked: I was the ***only one*** of the four of us who went to bed that night riddled with anxiety, despair, and increased pressure to be on top of every single thing! If I should let up for one second, death could, and probably would, claim my child! I already killed one, and if another one died on my watch, I would *never* survive it!

Rude: I don't have the luxury of assuming life is just a bowl of cherries. So, back to the kitchen with the basement door carelessly left open by John. I march to the door and shut it all the way—loudly, so John will get the message.

Freaked: But to my utter horror, I notice a slight resistance on the other side of the door, and then I distinctly hear the sound of a soft thud! I instantly fling the door open, only to watch my child's limp, helpless body as it finishes flipping down the long stairs, landing in a crumpled heap at the bottom! I stand there, frozen for a split second, wondering if I am having a night terror, and then I run down the stairs, yelling for John to call 911. I am certain our son's neck is broken, and he is dead!

Rosie: The medics arrive a few minutes later and look him over. He is fine. He doesn't even cry.

Melancholy: I am a hot mess. I ask myself, "Is God in control, or am I a victim of life's chaos? Did I make some colossal mistake somewhere along the way, rendering me completely out of God's will and, therefore, out of His loving Hand?"

Spiritualizer: "*He is like a tree planted by the waters that sends out its roots toward the stream. It does not fear when the heat comes, and its leaves are always green. It does not worry in a year of drought, nor does it cease to produce fruit*" (Jeremiah 17:8).

I'm resolved to sink into His love and stay green through whatever drought comes my way.

Rude: What choice do I have? I'm also pregnant again and sick around the clock with nausea.

Rosie: But this means I'm having another *baby*! So even though I'm facing a high-risk pregnancy that will require surgery and medication and bedrest, I am so happy! Drought? I can do drought.

Spiritualizer: Hannah Whitall Smith writes, "*Will you follow Me into suffering and loneliness, and endure hardship for My sake and ask for no reward but My smile of approval and My word of praise?*"

Melancholy: (*sniffing*) I will try.

Freaked: John regularly calls me a ditz head, stupid, and ridiculous, and he recently told me that I think I'm superior to everyone else and that my church friends also think I'm stuck up!

Rude: None of my friends in high school or college ever said things like this to me, and my church friends have never said this to my face. John's a liar.

Melancholy: But what if he's telling the truth? Are they talking to John about me behind my back? Are they afraid to tell me? I'm mortified. I have always been conscientious and intentional about trying to be supportive. I am devastated at the thought of being "*dreaded by my friends . . . I am like a broken vessel. For I hear the slander of many . . . O Lord, let me not be ashamed, for I have called on You*" (Psalm 31).

Rosie: I can make sense of things when I read the Psalms. Even David was confused, so I'm probably not crazy.

Spiritualizer: I now see the key to my future. It is death. I must die so Christ can live in me and have full reign. If I lay down my rights, I will have joy, and if I have joy, I will be able to be a good wife and mother and daughter and sister and friend. I will set my face like flint to accept and do His will.

31
A Crucified Life

Rosie: I'm having another boy! I love being a mother despite all the illness it has brought, and I can hardly believe I get to do it again! I'm on bedrest, and one of the things I miss the most is doing laundry. I love seeing big daddy socks, big mommy socks, and itty-bitty little boy socks all in the same basket. Now I lie in bed and shake. I'm taking medication through a continuous infusion pump in my leg to keep me from going into preterm labor. I wear a belt around my belly, and it sends data to a nurse at the hospital. She reads the data and lets me know if I'm having more contractions than usual, and if I am, I need to increase my dose. Most of the time, my days are pretty quiet. I would do anything for this baby. For my miracle family. And I am so incredibly grateful.

Melancholy: I'm also lonely. This time around, I also have my little boy, and he plays nicely, for the most part, on the living room floor while I lie on the couch. John is frequently gone, but when he is here, he takes out his frustrations on me in a variety of ways. Sometimes at night I dream about some other faceless person here with me, loving me, wanting to be with me, and I feel pretty and lovable. When I wake up, a heavy feeling washes over me. I pray every day for strength to return good for evil, but I'm not very successful at it. In my pride, I defend myself and disrespect my husband. My mom was right. I'm rude. It's my fatal flaw. I speak my mind. I loudly protest when others hurt me, and I beg for them to stop. Oh, why can't a quiet, gentle, and long-suffering spirit come easily to me? I have to work hard to pretend I'm godly enough to deserve blessings.

Rude: How can I respect and trust my husband when, if I met the same kind of man out in the world, I would never, in a million years, bring myself to respect or trust him?

Melancholy: But he is my husband, and that changes everything, although I rebelliously have a hard time accepting how. I worry about our son and how our marriage impacts him. I'm trying hard to respond correctly, and by God's grace, I've made some progress. But I hurt so much inside at times, and today I am weary of the ache. I wish my life could change faster. I wish John would show me love in front of our son instead of anger. I wish I knew what to do right away, and I wish I could maintain a bright, cheerful attitude when I'm hurt. But it seems I'm only capable of bawling and hiding. I once dreamed of having some influence and making a difference in this world, so I am disappointed when I realize the only way I can change the world now is to either 1) be a man or 2) be the wife of a man who is changing the world.

Rude: I would have liked to do a million things to help people and make this world a better place if only I had been allowed to do them, but because I'm a wife, I must sit back, watch, wait, and hope my husband will do them instead, but my husband shows little interest in any of it. The whole situation feels wrong.

Spiritualizer: Most likely, my rebellious heart is whining instead of submitting to God's quiet and hidden plan for me.

Melancholy: My body is growing weaker by the day. My muscles are like jelly, and my back is weak. Bedrest has taken a toll on me.

Rosie: I'm beginning to see that perhaps the way I will change the world is through Motherhood. If that is the case, then I will be the best mother I can be.

Spiritualizer: I will raise children for the glory of God. I will invest my days in educating and training them to grow up and change the world.

Melancholy: I could be content with this role if I knew my children would go and do everything I dreamed of doing.

Spiritualizer: If I invest my time in prayer for this next generation, they will be my mission. Their lives will be why my life mattered in the end. Their future work will be what gave me the right to have lived at all.

Freaked: But what if they do not want to follow God?! What if, after all that hidden effort, they walk away from the faith?! I'm worried for our two-year-old son's heart even now! There is an undercurrent of resentment there! I can see it—a tiny thread of rebellion that I've never seen before! He says "no" all the time now for no reason! He doesn't understand why I am lying down all the time. He shows me little affection but seems to have transferred his attention to his dad, and they hang out together when John is around. I have this nagging fear we have already embarked on a path toward the destruction of the souls of our children because of our sinful pride!

Rosie: There is one bright spot in my bedrest darkness, and that's Gretel, a godly pastor's wife who has been my mom's mentor since my mom was born again. This veteran soldier of the Christian faith has agreed to come to my home once a week and mentor me in trusting God and loving my husband. She sits by my couch and listens to me pour out my heart, and then she offers me encouragement in her quiet, strong, and motherly voice. She teaches me how to be thankful for my husband and reminds me that John cannot be kind to me unless he feels safe, and I am bound by duty to create safety for him. By the time Gretel leaves, she has smoothed and calmed my ruffled insides, and I hope one day to be just like her.

Spiritualizer: "*Be of good cheer, for I have overcome the world.*" I can believe it and live it and trust God to save my marriage and my children. If God can change *me*, that is all that will be needed. I must stay focused on that. Jesus, set me free from my prison of Self.

32

I Am a Sheep

Rosie: After months of being on bedrest and monitoring contractions, the doctor takes out the cerclage at thirty-seven weeks and then . . .

Melancholy: Nothing. My cervix holds tight all on its own for three weeks. John's mother comes down from Duluth so she can be here for the birth, and then after a few days of nothing, she goes back home. I thought we'd be going to my dad's company picnic at Cedar Lake Farm with our new baby, but I walk all over the farm with an oversized belly instead. My atrophied muscles and back scream in pain the entire time.

Rosie: But my heart is full of happiness! John is always kind when my parents are around, and they all dote on my son and me. Our little boy rides the ponies, I eat all the prune kolaches I want, and that night my water breaks. After several hours of bringing glory to God with the worst pain of my life, I give birth to a giant baby boy. When we bring him home, he lies in his crib and breathes all by himself without an apnea monitor. What a miracle! I fill pages and pages of my daily journal with Psalms and beautiful, encouraging quotes from books.

Melancholy: I also write my confessions of sin—how I am impatient in hardship and rebel against my sufferings.

Rosie: Help me respond in humble and loving tones. Help me to encourage and build up John and support him unconditionally. Where I am weak, be my strength!

I Am a Sheep

Freaked: My "prohibitive conscience" is getting a workout again. I've been feeling guilty about everything and fearful that God will take my little ones away! My nightmares have increased a thousand-fold since the baby's birth. During the day, intrusive thoughts and horrifying images plague me out of nowhere! Is this to be my own "thorn in the flesh" for the rest of my life? Set me free, Jesus! I don't want to be afraid of You!

Melancholy: My friend Jessica tells me she is pregnant. I'm so happy for her, but part of me is jealous. I envy her happy-go-lucky outlook on life. She's so giving, so unselfish, so peaceable. Her vices are unnoticeable and rare. I long for her friendship again, but she and Dale are moving to Plymouth to be near Don and Monica. The other perfect couple. Not even one of these beautiful souls suffer from a "prohibitive conscience." They don't wake up in cold sweats crying in the middle of the night. They aren't afraid of God. God makes perfect sense to them. They do this, and then, predictably, God does that. But my depravity runs deeper than I can fathom. It is a bottomless pit.

The Empathetic Witness Within: [*I see you. I love you.*]

Melancholy: If only those words could penetrate and illuminate my dark heart. But Augustine said, "*All those in the church today who only know how to ask God for temporal happiness belong to Ishmael. Their worship is carnal worship. Earthly blessings are all they seek . . . victory over enemies, numerous sons, abundant fruit. One who has this Ishmael kind of faith will always be in darkness.*"[3]

That's exactly me. The "Ishmael Faith" person.

I write in my journal after reflecting on the words of St. Francis of Assisi: "*How quickly are you offended, scandalized, and stirred to anger by a single word, all because you count it as a personal injury? How quickly are you offended when something you feel is yours is wrongfully denied you? If you find this is true, then it simply means you are not yet poor in spirit, counting nothing as your own."*

It is hard to be poor. Poor financially. Poor in spirit. God is teaching me to be both. To crucify my flesh and joyfully accept God's plan for my life.

Spiritualizer: We learn about sheep in church, and it is fascinating! Sheep can't find water or food for themselves. They follow their shepherd without asking questions and trust that he will provide what they need. Sheep are susceptible to wolves, dogs, and foxes. They don't have anything to fight with. They don't have camouflage to hide them. They rely on the shepherd to protect them. Sheep are dirty and unable to clean themselves. Their wool is full of lanolin and dirt and dung and blood. **We are sheep.** We have a Great Shepherd, Jesus Christ. And then we have other shepherds who lead and guide us. They are our pastors and leaders, appointed by God to be our authority.

Melancholy: As a sheep, I feel helpless. I feel dirty and ugly and dependent on someone who will take care of me despite my disgusting nature.

Freaked: As a sheep, I'm afraid! To ensure I get the help and protection I need, I will bow down while I serve and uplift those in authority over me! *I will be careful!*

Rude: People, this story is *so* off base. Good grief.

Melancholy: I tend to be a rebellious soul, so I do not dare trust anything that comes from deep within. I am a sheep. I will lift up my desires to the Lord, but even as I ask Him to bless us in material ways, I am discouraged to see such a greedy, depraved heart in me. I think of the Christians in other countries who are poor, sick, and alone. I think of the tragedies of others and the pain they endure. I cry tears of repentance, and I experience God's forgiveness.

Rosie: How much God's mercy covers. I may be a fallen creature, but how amazing is God's grace!

33

Forks

Freaked: Is life just one big fork in the road?! Sometimes it feels that way, and it's overwhelming and scary when I don't know which way is the right way and which way is the wrong way!

Spiritualizer: I know God set it all up so I wouldn't have to carry that burden of decision on my own shoulders. My husband is the head of our home, and I can bring all of my decisions to him to pray over and decide for me.

Rude: The only problem is that John is more paralyzed than I am with forks in roads. So sometimes I decide instead. For example, I decide to stop doing music ministry at church and focus on parenting and homeschooling. I make a unilateral decision, and I am pretty confident this is God's right choice for me, so I don't run it by John.

Freaked: But I have a nagging fear I'm not being submissive! Then, I find out John hasn't been paying our tithe! He tells me he hasn't paid it because we are struggling financially, but I believe we are struggling financially because he hasn't paid it!

Spiritualizer: I encourage him to think about ways we can pay bills *and* still pay the tithe, and he comes up with a plan to sell our computer. The sale brings in exactly the amount we need to pay off the tithe money we owe.

Freaked: I am relieved to have that debt paid off, but again, am I wearing the pants in our family by controlling that situation? Yes,

God wants us to tithe. Should I have let John's decision go to see what would happen without my input? I'm pretty sure the tithe would never have been paid, but how will I know if I don't trust God to speak to my husband?

And then there's Y2K. John has been reading about this event, which is now less than *two years away*! He tells me what he is reading and learning, and I wonder if we are on the brink of the Tribulation! I'm afraid for my children! I don't want to watch them starve to death! I don't want to watch our son die of an asthma attack because we have no electricity! What if the mid-Tribulation or post-Tribulation folks are right, and we have to go through it? I don't know what certain verses mean because people have different interpretations of them! If only I knew the truth instead of having to sift through everyone's various debatable opinions! In the meantime, I make my plans for homeschooling and raising children, and I wonder, *are my plans in vain?*

And what about having more children? Biblically, is there precedent for avoiding pregnancy? I don't think there is, but now I'm *scared!* If we have another baby before Y2K, how will we get diapers or food or medicine? What if we have no heat? What if another Great Depression hits? How will we provide for them?

Spiritualizer: I need to buckle up and trust that whatever God lays on John's heart—whatever John has peace about—*that* is God's plan for us. I will trust His perfect plan to lead our family through my husband. I need to think eternally and trust God completely.

Freaked: Except that John originally told me he didn't want us to have any more children until Y2K is over, and I am not so sure that is a decision based on God's Word!

Spiritualizer: I want to make decisions based on God's Word, not my fears. But then, according to God's Word, I'm supposed to submit to

John's leadership. If he says, "No more kids," then I need to submit willingly and trust that God will work out all the details.

Rude: Why are we put in these impossible situations where if we do one thing, we are disobeying in one area, but if we do the other thing, we are disobeying in a different area? That makes zero sense.

Freaked: I really don't know what is right and wrong at the end of the day! I'm not sure what scares me more: starving or freezing to death after Y2K or getting to heaven, discovering I had it all wrong, and God is disgusted with me! I guess the second one? But I really, *really* don't want to experience the first one either! No matter which way you slice it, it's all a LIVING NIGHTMARE!

Rosie: And then, out of the blue, John says we can have another baby. I am not sure I heard right, but he insists God is leading us to try.

Rude: But a few days later, he changes his mind. Again. Which message from God does John misunderstand? Whichever one it is, I get pregnant from one night of unprotected sex at a marriage conference. John must have been right the first time when God told him we should try. (*Eye roll*)

Rosie: It's a miracle!

Freaked: Until I miscarry the baby!

Rude: I guess John was right the second time when God told him we shouldn't try. (*Another eye roll*)

Spiritualizer: Never fear! We need to have faith that God will give us more kids at the right time.

Freaked: I really want more children!

Rude: So, I take matters into my own hands again and convince John that adoption would be a good idea.

Rosie: These babies already exist, so they would face the atrocities of Y2K regardless. This makes sense. And, in fact, we find out about twin boys who need a family.

Freaked: But we need to *act quickly* to complete the adoption paperwork!

Rude: John drags his feet, as usual, and another family gets the babies.

Rosie: I notice the more I submit to John and do what pleases him and do not give him any feedback or disagree with him in any way, the more peace we have in our home. I've been actively practicing this for seven months now, and it does seem to work.

Melancholy: But while I feel a sense of relief that he isn't mistreating me, I also feel like something has died inside of me. Deep inside me is a volcano of energy building up and begging to be let free. I know it is there, and God knows it is there. The older I get, the more I see the scum inside this volcano. It's disheartening, and I feel like my very soul is underneath the surface, boiling in the fires below. I like to think those fires are purifying me, burning off the dross so I can come forth as pure gold. I also wonder if I am a zombie pretending to be alive and making random decisions at forks in the road.

34

Y2K

Rosie: Y2K is right around the corner, and we've installed a wood-burning stove in our living room and stocked our small basement storage room with canned goods and whole wheat berries. I now grind my own whole wheat and make homemade bread every Saturday for my family. We'll be prepared. It's all under control.

Freaked: I'm nervous about what's going to happen when Y2K hits, and I'm really hoping Jesus comes back this year before it happens; but then again, I don't *want* Jesus to come back this year because I can't tell if our children are really trusting Him for the forgiveness of their sins! Our oldest son is now five, and I'm pretty sure he is a Christian, but the second one is only three, and it's hard to tell with him! It terrifies me to think of either one of them *burning forever in hell*. How could I have dared to bring a child into this world with the understanding that this might be their *eternal fate*? All because I wanted so badly to be a mother.

Melancholy: The depth of my selfishness astounds me sometimes, but then I'm not sure which part of my selfishness is the worst: the selfishness of not being willing to take chances and allow God to create another soul who may or may not spend eternity with Him, or the selfishness of saying, "No! I will not take any chances, and I will not allow God to create another soul because it may not spend eternity with God."

Rosie: Whether right or wrong, we take a chance, and our baby is due in March of the year 2000.

Melancholy: I'm not sure what we are thinking.

Spiritualizer: But I am determined to trust God.

Freaked: While I trust God and wait for Y2K to *destroy the world as we know it*, I've given up all ministry at church to focus on my children and make sure they get saved!

Rude: But I get bored and can't help myself . . .

Rosie: I organize a monthly newsletter to encourage young mothers and give me an opportunity to write.

Melancholy: (*sniffing*) I get in trouble for it. One of the pastors' wives scolds me for thinking that I could "teach" young moms through a newsletter when I am only a young mom myself. It's the *older women* who are commanded to teach the younger ones. And at thirty-three, I don't qualify yet. She's probably right, and I'm mortified at my gall. Yet I have such a desire to communicate in some way. I don't care how. I would sing, speak, teach, write, but I must communicate. Despite my presumptuous and prideful youth, a bunch of women have signed up for my newsletter and have even told me they look forward to receiving it each month. I'm torn. If I stop writing it, I will be a humble, normal mom who doesn't presume to know anything, who has time to play Chutes and Ladders with her children, and who is quiet, teachable, and lovable. This would please the pastor's wife and probably my husband, who says I'm a terrible communicator anyway.

Rosie: But on the other hand, if I keep writing the newsletter, I will have something interesting to do, and I might encourage a bunch of young moms like me.

Melancholy: I decide to keep going even though I feel sheepish about it, and I'm bad at communicating.

Rude: Eh, the women who get my newsletter don't know that yet, so I'll keep going until they figure it out.

Rosie: I may not be able to do meaningful ministry work at church anymore, but I am able to give away a red sweater I love to a woman who is visiting our church from Guatemala. One of the pastors' wives suggests that giving this sweater away is the kind of ministry I could do. I don't have many nice things, but this visitor has a much worse situation than I do, so I'm happy to share my sweater with her.

Rude: If this is going to be my ministry, I'm going to need more sweaters.

Melancholy: At home, John still finds fault and blames me for everything that goes wrong. No matter what I say or do to try to fix it, it backfires, and I am lonelier than ever. Every day I teach my boys and wash clothes and cook meals and clean up after the meals and clean up after the boys and wish there was something more. Sometimes the sadness is unbearable, and I think about how nice it will be when Y2K hits. The Russians will bomb us, and we will die and be done with the whole thing. But then, maybe hanging around here on earth might be worth it one day?

Spiritualizer: So, I will meditate on God's words to me: *"I waited patiently for the LORD; He inclined to me and heard my cry. He lifted me up from the pit of despair, out of the miry clay; He set my feet upon a rock,* *and made my footsteps firm. He put a new song in my mouth, a hymn of praise to our God. Many will see and fear and put their trust in the LORD"* (Psalm 40:1–3).

    Use me, Lord Jesus . . .

Melancholy: . . . despite my weakness and deep-seated propensity to look to others for love and approval.

Spiritualizer: Help me to carry on with hope and love, trusting You to make my life worthy of You.

35

Red Heifer

Rude: We are still here with heat and running water. Russia did not bomb us off the planet. Our wood-burning stove sits empty and cold in the corner of our living room. We wake up on January 1 to a day like every other day.

Rosie: And then on March 25, 2000, exactly seven years to the day when I lost my precious Elizabeth Anne, I give birth to another daughter. I once again give glory to God through the suffering of natural labor, even though I hemorrhage from the stress of it. I've read natural childbirth books and gotten advice from friends who do it the natural way, and they say hemorrhaging mostly happens if you don't have a natural childbirth. My friend Bess, who always gets an epidural, plays cards and doesn't feel one ounce of guilt during her labors, which are smooth and happy. If I could hemorrhage while giving glory to God, then what if I could give glory to God while also having an epidural?

Rude: A rebellious seed of an idea is planted, and I'll mull it over because I don't want to go through natural childbirth again. If I'm going to have a million babies, I'd like it to be a little easier.

Rosie: Regardless of the hemorrhaging, I don't die, and my daughter is healthy and strong. For some reason, I'm not afraid for her life like I was for the boys. This baby feels like a merciful gift from God to make up for the first baby He took. It's like He said, "Here you go,

Natalie. The first one was Mine. This one is yours." So, I don't worry she will die. I can safely enjoy her.

Melancholy: The only problem is that I am unable to sleep, even when she is sleeping. After I finish feeding and changing her, I try to sleep for an hour while she does, and all I can do is lie in a state of panic over my desperation to sleep. I beg God to give me rest, but it continues to elude me. I'm not able to keep up with life due to my exhaustion. John seems annoyed with my inability to function at full capacity. I try to give up my right to sleep, to be healthy, to have support, to experience love, and to be respected, but my life feels so heavy I can hardly bear up under it. My sins, weaknesses, and failures are ever before me. I cry out to God for help every day and feel depressed that my children have been given a mother who cannot find her footing because she is so selfish. Once again, I am longing for this life to be over, but just then, there is hope on the horizon.

Rude: Jesus is supposed to come back on a Sunday morning in September during the Jewish holiday of Rosh Hashanah. At least that's what this teacher named Joe Good says. He studies Jewish holidays and Bible codes about the rapture, and my husband and I meet with a few couples every week to go over his latest teachings. We are told to look for the sign of a rare red heifer sacrifice seven days before Rosh Hashanah. It has to be a *very* red heifer. If it's a *sort of* red heifer, then this is not the year of Christ's return.

Melancholy: "*Please let the red heifer be sacrificed seven days before Rosh Hashanah. Please come and get me out of here.*"

Rosie: And sure enough, we hear that a rare red heifer has been sacrificed! This is it! Christ is coming! The morning of Rosh Hashanah I am scheduled to work in the church nursery, and I wait in more anticipation than I waited for my wedding day for that blink of an eye when we will find ourselves with the Lord!

Rude: But apparently the red heifer isn't red enough, so instead of flying up through the clouds to heaven, we drive our van through the rain back to our house. Someone royally screwed up and got something wrong again. I swear to God, this is getting old.

Melancholy: I feel betrayed. Jeez.

Spiritualizer: Watch your slang and let us move on to a more productive subject. Pastor Barry and Pastor Jim are preaching on anger right now. The cure to anger is to let go of your rights and to believe the best about others instead of hanging on to a belief that life should be fair. When you allow your emotions to adversely impact you, your anger turns to bitterness. Expect to be wronged by your spouse. Fix your thoughts on what is good about your spouse. Forgive them. Listen to their criticism. Quit looking at what your spouse is doing to you and focus on your own sin. Never bring up past hurts. Instantly apologize when your spouse is offended by your feedback or your thoughts that are different from his.

Rude: I have tried to follow all these instructions, but it continues to rankle me that John doesn't see the need to do the same. I must let go of my rights, but why can John keep his? I must believe the best about him, but why can he call me names? I must forgive him and never bring up any past hurts. I must listen to his criticism, but why am I in sin if I tell him to watch our child more closely by lakes, cliffs, and busy roads? Is this because he has a penis, and I do not?

Spiritualizer: I'm going to ignore that last vulgar comment and take copious notes every Sunday morning and every Wednesday night as I set my face like flint to obey.

Freaked: But I can feel a dragon of anger quietly growing inside of me, and I must carefully keep it down, down, down, so it doesn't come out and *hurt my beloved family!*

Rude: Because now I'm pretty sure Christ isn't coming any time soon.

36
Crying Out

Spiritualizer: I haven't been to a Bill Gothard seminar since high school, but now, here I am attending the Institute in Basic Life Principles with my husband. I forget how simple the Christian life can be by following biblical principles. College and freedom and rock music might have distracted me from the truth I once knew in high school, but now I have repented and committed my life to God to do as He pleases. My heart is teachable now, so God has given me the insights and truths I so desperately need to conquer the rage inside my heart.

Freaked: I'm still worried that the only way God may be able to get through to John is by taking a child! *One of my kids is going to die!*

Spiritualizer: But I've committed them to God, and I'm determined to trust His plan. My one heart's desire is that all my children will know and love Jesus and serve Him with all their hearts. This means I will need to have His steady flow of power pouring out from me to my children all day long. To get this, I have committed the first part of my day to the Lord to read the Scriptures and pray. I have a prayer notebook, and I pace my kitchen floor for thirty to sixty minutes every morning before the kids wake up, begging God out loud to pour out His Spirit on my children and make them strong and mighty in spirit.

Melancholy: The only thing standing in the way of my vision for my kids is my parenting. I'm not sure if praying can override all my mistakes and failures. My adorable, dimpled son was diagnosed with

Tourette's syndrome. My mom says tics come from watching too much TV and playing video games. My cousin's child has Tourette's syndrome, too, and he plays a lot of video games.

Rude: Seriously? My son is only six, and the extent of his screen time is playing Reader Rabbit for thirty minutes a day, which is fun and educational.

Freaked: But maybe this diagnosis is a punishment for allowing our children to learn the lazy way with a computer!

Melancholy: My heart is breaking into a million pieces watching him struggle with his facial twitches. Right now, he is licking his upper lip so much he has a red mustache. I want to hold him and bawl, but that might scare him, so I pretend everything is okay and tics are just part of life. I feel devastated that he has to suffer the consequences for my laziness as a mother.

Rosie: But then again, having Tourette's doesn't have to stand in the way of becoming a world changer, right? When I was a little girl, I always thought I might grow up and be a world changer like Corrie Ten Boom. I remember reading the Psalms, especially Psalm 71, and feeling such a powerful stirring in my heart. I knew somehow that it was my *life Psalm*. But now I see that it is not *my* mouth that will tell of God's righteous deeds and saving acts, but the mouths of my children. I will be like Susanna Wesley, John and Charles Wesley's mother, quietly raising mighty warriors for the glory of God, and my offspring will be the ones who declare God's power to the next generation!

Melancholy: Even though I've committed to praying every morning, I've been sorely tested. I've been sick almost nonstop since I started, and I'm still struggling with insomnia. The kids have been sick as well and often wake up as early as I do, with wet beds, unable to go back to sleep, thus interrupting my prayer and reading. I must admit, I am tempted to give it up. Sometimes my rebellious heart rears its ugly head and whispers, *"If God wanted to spend time with you, wouldn't He make it a little easier?"*

Spiritualizer: But I know this is only the voice of the devil who does not want me to do this, and God is only testing me to see if I meant what I said. Will I fight to spend this time with Him? Will I guard it with my very life? How important is God to me? I am resolved to show that I love Him, and He is worthy of my time and effort.

Rosie: One of the things we learn about in the Institute for Basic Life Principles is the power of crying out to God when we need Him most. Bill Gothard shares several stories of people who cried out to God for various miracles and answers, and God honored their crying out and answered accordingly. So, I'm determined to try this out for myself. I'm big on prayer, but crying out? I have never tried that. One morning, John mails over $200 worth of rebate forms he carefully collects during the holiday season. John is careful with money, and every dollar counts in our house. I look out the window about an hour later and see a beat-up car drive up to our mailbox. A man takes out all our rebates and drives away.

Freaked: I run out the door, *screaming* at them to stop before returning to the house bawling like a baby!

Rosie: Then it hits me. This is the perfect time to cry out!

Rude: But first I call the police.

Melancholy: I don't know, maybe that's a mistake. Maybe that's why the crying out part doesn't ultimately work.

Rosie: But what if God wants to use the police to catch them? The police come over and take down a description of the car and then leave to go drive around and look for it. While they are doing that, I cry out.

Freaked: And by crying out, I mean, I literally yell, "DEAR GOD ALMIGHTY, HAVE MERCY ON OUR FAMILY! WE REALLY NEED THAT MONEY! CATCH THOSE THIEVES! MAKE THEM CHANGE THEIR MINDS AND COME BACK AND PUT THE REBATE FORMS BACK IN OUR MAILBOX! MAKE THEM MAIL THE FORMS IN THEMSELVES! MAKE THEM DROP THEM ON THE GROUND FOR THE POLICE TO FIND! GIVE US BACK OUR $200 DOLLARS FOR I ASK THIS IN THE POWERFUL NAME OF THE BLESSED LORD JESUS CHRIST, AMEN!"

Rosie: And then I'm quiet, half expecting the doorbell to ring and the thieves to hand me the forms and apologize. I mean, God can do anything right? I truly believe. I have the faith. But we never see hide nor hair of the thieves, the forms, or the money again. God can do anything, but maybe He doesn't always want to. And that's why we need to have faith.

Freaked: I can't help this nagging fear that if God doesn't pay attention to my crying out for the money the thieves stole, maybe He won't pay attention to the hours of prayer I'm putting in every week for my children! I mean, money is one thing, but what if one day someone *steals a child*? How can I bear up under that?! Where will my faith stand in that case? I'm afraid I might *fling my faith and my body out the window* and be done with it!

Rude: Why should I cry out again if it makes no difference? It's better to say, "God's will be done," since no matter what happens, I can always say, "God's will was done."

Melancholy: I want to be a more faith-filled follower. I'll never get this right.

Rosie: I am comforted by this verse from Isaiah 49:23, 25, *"Those who hope in me will not be disappointed. I will contend with those who contend with you, and your children I will save" (NIV).*

Spiritualizer: God does not bring our money back, but He does seem to be leading our lives through the Institute in Basic Life Principles, and we've dodged a bullet as far as bringing evil toys into our home. Our kids want some Star Wars Legos, but why would we bring anything questionable into our home when there are thousands of other options? Other families may play with Pokémon cards, but *we may not*. God sets certain people apart to be holy. That's our family. Set apart to be holy.

Melancholy: The only thing standing in the way is my petulant heart, especially regarding my marriage.

Rosie: So, while I pace the floor to pray for my children, I am also . . .

Melancholy: . . . desperately . . .

Spiritualizer: . . . praying God will make me a wife who guards and heeds her husband. That God will help me cover John's offenses with love when he sins against me or the children. That I will be a channel of forgiveness and teach my children forgiveness and overlooking faults.

Melancholy: How many times do I do the opposite and interfere with shock and indignation? I bring attention to my husband's sin and give my children a reason to do the same. I tear down my own home, and I feel remorse and sorrow over my own sin of pride and self-righteousness.

Spiritualizer: I want to walk in God's agape love and let it flow through me like a meek, humble, quiet stream of healing to my children and my husband.

37

Epidurals

Rosie: I plan to birth my fourth living child God's way, without any medication, giving glory to God throughout the suffering of childbirth. My cerclage is removed a few weeks before my due date, giving my "weak cervix" almost a month to let go of its grasp on this baby. Yet, it holds on tight, and I'm overdue when my body finally goes into labor in the early hours of January 9, 2002. I check into the hospital with painful contractions only to learn I am dilated to one.

Rude: This isn't my first rodeo, and I expect to be at least a four for the pain I'm in. The doctor on call says it's obvious I'm in active labor, and we'll have to hope I start progressing soon.

Freaked: A couple hours later, I am still at a one. And LORD GOD ALMIGHTY, the contractions are becoming increasingly unbearable! I panic in the same way now as my last labor and delivery, but at least then I was making progress every time they checked!

Rosie: Different doctors come in to check, but nobody can figure out what's going on. One finally recommends I get an epidural since it looks like a long road ahead for me.

Freaked: I am concerned about not laboring to God's glory, but I am also concerned I might MURDER everyone in the room!

Rosie: So, I ask the doctor on call to kindly explain the risks of epidurals again. He tells me that labors with epidurals are statistically smoother and safer for both baby and mother. He also tells me that because I have been in active labor for so long and have not dilated any further, there's a chance I may need a C-section, and having a block anesthetic would be necessary anyway.

Melancholy: I am worried he might be lying to me, but I decide to take the risk of not bringing glory to God, and I compromise my values and convictions by accepting the epidural.

Rosie: Blessed relief!

Rude: Unfortunately, I have an old, bossy nurse who believes epidurals are a copout, and she says as much with a scowl on her face every time she bustles in to see if I've progressed.

Melancholy: She lectures me about how epidurals cause labor to slow down and sometimes stop, and that is why my cervix is still at a one, even after nine hours of hard labor. I meekly ask if it's possible that my cerclage hasn't been removed completely and perhaps it is holding my cervix shut. But she dismisses that as ridiculous.

Rude: When she goes off duty, I consider cheering out loud.

Rosie: She is replaced with a younger, sunny nurse who fills me with hope that good things are around the corner and that having an epidural was a wise choice. All I can feel is gratefulness and joy, but I'm still at a one. I offer the new nurse the same suggestion. What if the cerclage is still lodged in my cervix? Is that possible? Would that be enough to keep me from dilating? She thinks this is a very real possibility and goes to find out. In the meantime, Dr. Cho, the doctor who removed my cerclage four weeks ago, unexpectedly comes into the hospital in her street clothes on her day off to pick something up, and my nurse grabs her and pulls her into my room.

After examining me, Dr. Cho announces that yes, indeed, there is a part of the cerclage embedded so deep into my cervix, she will need to cut my cervix to get it out. Once again, the epidural is necessary, and I'm beginning to suspect that God planned this all along, and maybe it isn't a sinful compromise after all!

After she removes the remainder of the cerclage, my cervix dilates from one to ten in five minutes, and my son's healthy, strong body emerges in a couple of painless, easy pushes.

Rude: My only regret is not being able to say "I told you so" to the crabby nurse.

Rosie: I deliver my next five babies easily and successfully using epidurals every single time with great exultation and not one ounce of guilt. Maybe God doesn't have one set way to bring Him glory through childbirth. Maybe He lets me decide some things for myself, and He just cheers me on.

Rude: Finally, some common sense.

38
Dodgeball

Spiritualizer: I've been reading a book called *Me? Obey Him?* It teaches that wives should submit with a happy attitude even if their husbands ask them to sin. It explains that this is God's plan, and we bring glory to Him when we obey our husband without questions.

Rosie: Thankfully my husband doesn't ask me to sin.

Melancholy: I feel terrible that sometimes I submit on the outside while chafing on the inside.

Spiritualizer: I've also been listening to a teaching by Pastor Denny Kenaston called *The Hidden Woman*. He talks about how the role of a wife is to be hidden, submissive, and prayerful. I take careful notes in my journal, as I usually do. It's my heart's desire to be a hidden woman and please God and my husband. Toward the end of the sermon, Pastor Denny addresses what we should do if our husband is not who he should be.

Rude: I perk up at this. My husband is most definitely not who he could or should be.

Melancholy: And I've been searching for years for the solution. Could this be it? Kenaston quotes Jeremiah 9:17–18: "*Summon the wailing women; send for the most skillful among them. Let them come quickly and take up a lament over us [the men of Israel], that our eyes may overflow with tears, and our eyelids may gush with water [in repentance].*" We are not supposed to give our husbands feedback or try to manipulate them to repent. We are supposed to **pray** that our husbands' eyes might gush out with tears of sorrow and repentance. I'm disappointed in this solution because I *have* prayed fervently and consistently for my husband to see how he hurts the kids and me and for him to repent, yet I have never experienced him repenting of anything. He doesn't think he does anything wrong, so why would he see the need to repent? Everything is my fault, not his.

Spiritualizer: I need to trust God and be more patient.

Rude: John must have read my journal notes on this sermon because later I find these words in my journal in his small, slanted handwriting: "*Yes—and especially your wife's eyes so she would focus on her carnal self and humble herself.*" It looks like he tore out some pages of my journal, too. I used to love playing dodgeball when I was a child in school, but now that my life is one big dodgeball game, I'm over it. The balls of insults and accusations keep getting thrown at me, and I am sick to death from dodging them.

Melancholy: When can I get out of this game and rest? I remember a little book I had growing up with a picture of a tiny bird hidden in the crag of a great mountain while a terrible storm raged all around. I want to be that bird, but I'm still desperately flapping my feathers out in the storm, looking for a safe landing place to hide. Psalm 3 says, "*O LORD, how my foes have increased! How many rise up against me [fears, guilt, burdens, sin]! Many [my husband] say of me, 'God will not deliver him.' But You, O LORD, are a shield around me, my glory, and the One who lifts my head. To the LORD I cry aloud, and He answers me from His holy mountain. I lie down and sleep; I wake again, for the LORD sustains me.*"

Rosie: Oswald Chambers writes, "*I will spend myself to the last ebb for you. You may give me praise or give me blame, it will make no difference.*"[4] That is the true heart-attitude I wish to have toward my family. It is easy to serve to the "last ebb" when I get praise or appreciation.

Melancholy: Serving is hard when I am condemned and mistreated. I wish God could get me to the point where "it makes no difference." Maybe if I had more time to rest, read the Bible, and pray, I could be a godlier woman, but with the new baby, all the plates are spinning constantly. I could really use even a short break of an hour or two, but John is gone all the time, even on nights and weekends, "running errands." Maybe he wants to get away from the kids and me.

Rosie: God knows my frustrations and desires. If He thinks I need something, I know He will provide it at the right time. For example, John tells me I can take two days off and attend the Minnesota Association of Christian Home Educators (MACHE) Conference. I can hardly believe my good fortune!

Melancholy: But a few hours later, he asks me where all the money in our education budget has gone, and I tell him that I used it for homeschooling curriculum and supplies last fall. He gets upset and tells me that if I want to go to MACHE, I will have to come up with the fifty-dollar ticket fee on my own. I'm devastated. I think if I could find a way to make some money on my own, then I would not have to worry so much about it. Maybe John would appreciate and love me if I made money and contributed financially to our household, but I don't know how I could ever find the time with running the home, teaching the kids, and nursing babies around the clock.

John is also upset with me because I threw out one of his old, torn lunch bags. He had two of them, so I used some grocery money to buy him a brand-new one for Valentine's Day and threw out the one with holes. He hollers at me to return the new one and to never, ever, under any circumstances, throw out anything without first asking his permission. He regularly goes through our garbage to make sure I am obedient in this area, and I'm sorry to say that sometimes I do try to throw away old toys or things I don't use anymore to try to declutter this house, which is getting crazier every year. I sit bawling on the couch, which is rare for me as I usually try not to act like a baby in front of him because it annoys him. I tell him I am sorry, and I won't do it again, but that I long for him to notice and appreciate all the work I do for our family. He scowls and says, "At least you said you're sorry."

Rude: And then I lose it. I say a swear word in a rude tone and run to my bedroom, slamming the door shut.

Melancholy: I bawl like a stupid, out-of-control, rebellious little girl. I am ashamed of myself at how angry I get. I can't help but think of the mother of a high-profile ATI family who raised eight kids and loved her husband and was a doormat for his selfishness for almost two decades until he left her and married his younger, prettier secretary. I wonder if she is looking out her window at the dead, barren day right now, the way I am looking out mine, knowing in her heart that she is unloved and that her family loves her only for what she can give to them. They need her, but they do not see her.

Rosie: God must look down at this cold earth knowing that His children love Him for what He can give them. They need Him, but they don't really see Him. Has His bride left and married the world? Does He give up? No. His love never fails. And this is the love He wants to give to me so I can then turn around and offer it to others.

Melancholy: I'm not only having trouble with my husband. I'm having trouble with my mom, too. Sometimes she says or does hurtful things, and I keep forgetting to keep my mouth shut. I always regret when I let her know how her words hurt me. Why, oh **why** can't I keep my feelings to myself? Now I'm in a real knot with her again. I want to unravel that knot, but that will mean I have to say I'm sorry, pretend nothing hurt me, cover it all up, and forget about it. That's what I do to keep the peace, and then I hurt inside while nothing gets resolved. I'm so tired with the new baby I can hardly think. Everything is a blur.

I feel blind. My days are only little pieces of a whole I cannot figure out. The path often looks rough and treacherous and sometimes dull and monotonous. I'm in uncharted territories as a mother, dealing with sins in my own life I had no idea were so deeply rooted in me, as well as dealing with the sins of those around me. I feel responsible for all of it, and it is a burdensome weight. I feel like a hypocrite most of the time, trying to correct and guide the children along the paths of righteousness that I often stray from myself. I argue with John about issues that seem to me to be so crucial in the moment, so good and right, and then I go off on a rampage, fearful that our children will not get the truth unless I loudly make it known. I'm not only getting hit with dodgeballs. I'm lobbing them myself. The fruit is that my children see a fearful, angry, self-righteous windbag in action, rebelling against the authority God has placed over me.

39
Standards and Convictions

Rosie: I love homeschooling, but the more we've learned about the Advanced Training Institute (ATI), a homeschooling program through the Institute in Basic Life Principles, the more I believe this program will give our children the Very Best Christian Education. Academics are not as important as character, and I want my children to grow up mighty for the Lord.

Every month we go through booklets and study a different Christian character like virtue, endurance, and obedience. We memorize a different principle each month, like "Small compromises produce great consequences;" "Godliness brings verbal attacks;" "Ineffectiveness brings harsh consequences;" "Humility comes by understanding depravity;" and "Meekness requires dying to self."

We also study the forty commands of Christ and seek to follow them. When we are tempted to disobey or compromise because His commands feel like a prison, we can ask ourselves, "Do I view His commands as expressions of His love or restrictions on my happiness?" So even though my boys adore *Lord of the Rings*, we sold all our Lord of the Rings movies, posters, and toys to avoid the murky waters of compromise and Christian carnality.

Spiritualizer: These are high standards, but I have never wanted to be a casual Christian, and I don't want my family to be a casual Christian family. I want us to strive our hardest to be set apart for God and to bring Him glory. We've learned in the kingdom of God the rule is "Thy will be done, and my will be undone." My calling is to lose myself to save what matters far more. My goals are helping others find happiness and fulfillment, giving generously, and glorifying God. My object is eternal gain. My right is to lay down my life. My concern is obedience. The price I am called to pay is death *now* so that I can experience life *forever*. Here is how I will know God is at work in my own life: self-effacement, self-suppression, and abandonment to something or someone other than myself.

With all these new convictions, I am growing more and more discontent with our church. They are compromising by tickling the ears of the people with things they want to hear so the church will get bigger. My kids are watching *Veggie Tales* in Sunday school and singing meaningless songs.

Melancholy: But there is another reason I feel discontent there. Mentoring leaders is a big deal at this church, and the church leaders are overlooking John.

Rude: In fact, they put a younger man in charge of mentoring John, which, on the one hand, bothers me; but if I'm honest, I understand why. I'm ashamed that I married this man. He mistreats me. He's a bully at home, but nobody at church knows because when he's there, he is passive and quiet. At church, he does nothing more than what he is told to do. Because he is not a leader at church, the church pastors sideline him, yet he bullies me at home, and I am supposed to follow him.

If John doesn't make a decision that needs to be made, I'm left with three choices: 1) beg for my husband to decide and be accused of being a dripping faucet and a nag; 2) make the decision and be accused of wearing the pants; or 3) say nothing and don't make any decision, and then we miss out on an event or opportunity. When that happens, I often get accused of not reminding him or saying anything. I've tried it all three ways, and I'm damned every time.

Melancholy: It shames me to admit that once in a great while, when I'm feeling particularly desperate . . .

Rude: . . . *deciding to wear the pants and make the decision is worth it.* I have a hard time respecting my husband, and I have a hard time respecting the pastors, too. They lack spiritual sense and talk like spiritual children. One of them told me that I probably wasn't even saved until I started going to their church. What in the world? They could fool me about some of my beliefs, but not that.

Spiritualizer: I'm embarrassed to tell people what church I go to because outside of our little bubble, we are viewed as a church for baby Christians. I like to think I'm a little more mature than a baby, what with reading Puritan authors and being part of ATI and all.

Rosie: But then I remind myself that God also loves His little babies, and why should I be ashamed to be one or to mingle with them? God wants me to get under every single leader, including my husband, regardless of their level of maturity and humble myself. In fact, I heard one elderly woman explain it this way: "If your husband won't lead and is just lying on the ground like a dead man, your job is to get under his dead weight and stay there. That's what obedience will look like for you."

Rude: Well, I can say from firsthand experience that obedience like that is insufferable.

Spiritualizer: I know God's ministry for me is to be a help and support to John and to lovingly train, educate, and raise our children. My ministry to John is forgiving him, overlooking his insults, and dying to my own rights and desires for care and love.

Rude: Should I take the blame for his sin, too? Can I accept that?

Melancholy: This is what I am resisting within the core of my being. I don't want to suffer for John's sin.

Rude: *John* should bear the consequences of his own sin.

Spiritualizer: God has called me to a life of sacrificial death.

Rude: But sometimes I sit up on that altar and scream!

40
Death and Life

Melancholy: 2003 starts off horribly with everyone being sick almost nonstop, and then I get pregnant, and I am overcome with morning sickness on top of everything else. The kids and I are studying the concept of dying in our wisdom booklets, and I realize that this pregnancy is a time of death. I am dying to my right to feel good and be healthy. Dying to my right to be seen, heard, and understood. Dying to my right to sleep.

Spiritualizer: But isn't this the Grand Opus of the Christian life? May God give me the attitude of Christ, who did not seek to be served but to serve and to spill His life out.

Melancholy: I have another opportunity to die to myself when my sisters take my mom out for her birthday without me. I know I should not continue to be surprised when this happens, but it hurts, and I spend too much time bawling and losing sleep about it. If I tell them not being invited hurts my feelings, they tell me, "Self-pity is of the devil." If I ask them why they did not invite me, they tell me, "We just assumed you were busy." When I tell them I feel like they are intentionally excluding me, they say, "You're just making that up in your head." I decide not to say any of those things this time around. There is no point when I already know all their easy answers that somehow make my pain my own fault. ***And maybe it is.***

Rosie: Instead, I shop for my mom's gift by myself and give it to her the next time she comes to play with the kids.

Melancholy: I don't fit in with my family of origin. I dread our yearly trip to the cabin with them. Every year I come home from that trip exhausted, hurting, and angry. I keep hoping for connection, conversation, and love, and all I get is left behind. I hole up in my cabin with whatever toddler and baby I have at the time and count the days until the trip is over.

Rosie: I don't expect anyone to help me or cater to me in any way. I can take care of my own family no matter what challenges come my way. My sisters have children the same ages as mine, so they are also busy and full of responsibility. I long to be friends with my sisters and my mom. They tell interesting stories about all the people they know and make me laugh. I admire their sense of fashion and their sense of humor.

Melancholy: They seem annoyed with me, and maybe they wish I would disappear. I try to do that as much as possible, but boy is it boring, lonely, and sad.

Rosie: But that's only the first half of the year. The second half of the year is nothing short of miraculous. We move!

Rude: I guess John *can* make decisions.

Rosie: We move from our little three-bedroom rambler on 130th street to a big, two-story home with four bedrooms, a gargantuan basement, and an expansive flat yard with a swing set. John picks out some used furniture on Craigslist, including a beautiful cherry wood dining table and china hutch. Did I die and go to heaven?

Despite my pregnancy, I spend the last few weeks in our old home running on adrenaline as I pack and clean, and one week after we move in, I give birth to our fifth blessing. She is the smallest full-term baby I've had, coming in at just over six pounds, but she is also the strongest. I know she's a fighter.

I take her into JCPenney's for newborn pictures, something I've never done with any of my other babies. Some of my friends have had newborn pictures taken with their babies all curled up like they are still in the womb. Those pictures are so cute, I have to try it with my new little one. But my baby will not stop stretching and pushing her body out. We curl her back up, and she instantly uncurls herself with a stubborn energy that surprises both the photographer and me. In the end, we get pictures of her tiny toes and one picture of her hand gripping my finger. I guess this child will do things her way.

So far, I have had the easiest postpartum experience. Despite not wanting to pose properly for pictures, this new one is an easy baby. John is also in a great mood fixing up our new home and yard, and I wonder if all along, we simply needed more room to grow and be a family. I love our new neighborhood.

Melancholy: But I will miss the two large Christian homeschooling families from our old neighborhood. Here in the new neighborhood, we are the only homeschooling family, and we are also the only big family with five kids. Our next-door neighbors, an older couple who live with their dog, seem annoyed with us. The woman hollers at me for putting our new rescue dog on a line in our backyard. She says it's inhumane. I try to explain that our rescue dog is always trying to attack our kids, and we want the kids to be able to play outside without getting hurt, but the neighbor isn't convinced and says we need to figure out another way because putting dogs on lines, rescue or not, is wrong.

Rosie: In the end, we rehome the naughty dog, and I make our neighbor and her husband some homemade bread to help smooth things over. I pray God will help me show them love.

Melancholy: Deep down inside, I want them to like me, but I suspect they don't because we have too many kids, and I feel ashamed.

Rosie: I also understand. Before I had my own convictions about allowing God to give us as many kids as He wanted, I would drive by the home of the other big family in our old neighborhood, and every spring I'd see the wife in the garden with either a big belly or a baby in a sling. *Every spring without fail.* This seemed weird and irresponsible at the time, but now I know they are trusting God with the size of their family.

Melancholy: Still, I'm sure others view me with disgust, and maybe they think poorly of my children, too.

Rosie: So, I need to double down and be sweet as honey in return! Things have been going so well that I take on another responsibility outside of the home. I have been asked to go on the board of Amnion Crisis Pregnancy Center, which involves meeting once a month on Tuesday nights, and John has given me permission to accept this role! Had I been asked any other year he probably would have said no, but he has been in such a good mood lately. Thank You, Jesus! John also buys me a CD teaching series by Michael Pearl called *Sin No More*. I love the book Mr. Pearl wrote with his wife called *Created to be His Helpmeet*, and usually I must save my allowance to buy books or teaching CDs, but John has been generous lately. This is the happiest I've ever been in my marriage.

41
Tongues and Quilts

Rude: Nobody told me how boring being a mother could get.

Freaked: I've engaged in dark blasphemy against all of God and motherhood for even thinking that, let alone saying it out loud!

Rude: And when I say bored, I don't mean "nothing to do." I have plenty of brainless work, but my brain is aching for a challenge.

Spiritualizer: I need to find something *godly*. It can't be teaching, making money, or writing a book. I need *women's* brain work, like sewing or quilting or something.

Rosie: And that's how I get obsessed with sewing and quilting! I can always justify the hours of picking out coordinating fabrics, cutting out pieces, and sewing them together to create blankets, children's clothing, and gifts by saying I'm being a good Christian woman by making blankets for others and clothing for my family. Exactly like the Proverbs Thirty-One Woman. Who can argue with Proverbs Thirty-One?

I love how the patches for the quilts come together in beautiful patterns. You'd think all the different shapes cut from different colors and patterns couldn't possibly transform into a picture or cohesive design. But they do. They all work together like pieces of a puzzle to create a work of art. I make practice quilts for my kids, and after I gain more skill, I make extravagant quilts for my mom and sisters as well as baby quilts for friends.

Melancholy: I make beautiful things to keep my mind off my troubles and give me something to distract me from the tsunami of rage building up inside. This rage sometimes leaks out through my tongue. I'm forever biting it to keep the rage tucked safely away.

Rude: My mom models a clever tongue with well-placed, potent words that could drive a stake in the heart of a vampire. She thinks on her feet and puts anyone nasty or stupid in their place, and she has the ability to make an argument that wins every time. I guess that's why God made her a prophet, but she could have been a lawyer.

Dad and my sister Marcy are quick learners. They always keep a low profile, safely under Mom's radar. But Alice is Mom's sun, moon, and stars, so she's unaware Mom even has a radar. As for me, I have spent my life *triggering* Mom's radar, and I lose every single time. Now in my late thirties, I'm finally figuring out a way to deal with my mom. I've been watching Dad's strategy, and while I have little respect for it, I can see how I would have had more peace in my life if I had hung my head in shame or smiled and nodded more.

Maybe that's the humble Christian way, but now, as a mom myself, I can't smile and nod when the kids don't want to do chores or math. I'm now living with six humans who all, baby excluded, use their tongues like little cowboys, expertly lassoing everyone around them. I'm unsure of how to help them overcome their sinful little lassoes when I have a hard time bridling my own in the face of injustice, deception, and cruelty. How are we supposed to expose evil yet bridle our tongue? This balance I have not yet discovered.

If I use my tongue in the way my mother uses hers, I should get the same results. She's even told me, "*If I had a husband like yours, I'd tell him this, that, and the other thing, and he'd NEVER speak to me like that again.*" Or, "*If one of my daughters ever talked like that, I'd spank it out of you, and you'd never do it again.*" And her methods effectively produced three nice, obedient daughters, which inspired my childhood church to invite Mom and Dad to teach a parenting Sunday school class so others could learn how to get the same results.

Melancholy: For some reason, I haven't been able to make it all work the way she did. When I talk back to John, I dig my own grave. The only way out of that pit is to say, "*I was wrong. You told the truth. You really did have 3,496 reasons for calling us names. You truly are an awesome husband. Please forgive me for being an asshole again.*" Only I would never say "asshole" out loud. I hate the silent treatment, the passive-aggressive rage, and the feeling of walking on eggshells.

Rosie: I must do *something* to get out of this pit as soon as I can, and groveling usually works!

Melancholy: Why, oh **why** have I been unsuccessful at being an agent of peace and change? I've sacrificed my entire life for this. I've devoted my prayers and my efforts to this end. And yet, there is never anything to show for it but utter confusion, frustration, and dissonance. My husband regularly asks, "*Who is the common denominator in your issues with your mother and your husband? Hmmmm?*" And he's not wrong.

Spiritualizer: If I want to be a good wife, I need to use as few words as possible, especially in the morning. Don't correct him or give him feedback. Pray for God to give him insight into family needs. Hug and kiss him often. Be inviting. Use soft words. Praise him. Show him gratitude every day. Never argue. Bite my tongue.

Melancholy: But how can I? I'm a mother, for crying out loud! I'm constantly being forced to give orders, directions, corrections, and rebukes, and *I don't want to!*

Rosie: I want to spend my days with my kids laughing and romping in fields of wildflowers or at least being able to say, "*Wow, Honey! Look* *at you getting your math done and playing so nicely with your baby sister!"* And *"Thank you, Sweetums, for putting the dishes away!"* And *"Bless your heart, Darling, for sharing the truck with your brother."*

Melancholy: Some children make efforts to please while others make efforts to complain and be lazy. I want to do my part to help them be happy and positive, but I struggle to find the Fruits of the Spirit in their lives or in mine. Instead, I find my own attitude matching theirs, and I'm responsible to turn it around. I'm the parent after all. What kind of example am I setting for my kids? One of them recently told me, "We're not a very good family."

Rude: Stick a dagger in my heart, child.

Melancholy: This is my greatest fear coming true—that we are not a very good family, and it's all my fault. If I could find and fit only beautiful shapes perfectly together—good girl, good daughter, good wife, good mother, good sister, good friend, good Christian—then this family could be a treasured heirloom of lasting value.

Rosie: I buy three books with money Mom gives me: *Classic Sermons on Family and the Home* by Warren Wiersbe, *Affliction* by Edith Schaeffer, and *The Sovereignty of God* by John Piper, and I can't wait to dig in. I will keep searching for that elusive answer I can feel is out there—a patchwork piece of the puzzle that, once in place, will finally make the quilt of my life make sense.

42

Marriage Conferences

Spiritualizer: We finally leave behind the casual Christianity of our former seeker-sensitive, numbers-obsessed church so we can get back to real, expository preaching again instead of listening to men who have never been to seminary teach us their quiet time thoughts. I can hardly believe my husband agrees to make a solid, Bible-preaching church our new church home. It helps that some of his friends have started coming here as well.

I love conferences of all kinds, and our new church emphasizes conferences. In our old church, the conference speakers were the same pastors who spoke every week anyway, and the women's conferences always featured their wives. But our new church brings in big-name Christian authors and speakers, and there are hundreds of attendees.

Rosie: One of the music leaders for the women's conferences is someone I knew in college, so I get to help lead worship occasionally, which is a thrill. Being a mom means giving up many of my dreams, so having a little taste of singing occasionally has been a drink in a desert.

Melancholy: John and I rarely get time alone together unless I plan for us to go out on our birthdays or our anniversary, and overnight trips are extremely rare.

Rosie: But our new church has an annual marriage conference, and with some planning on my part of arranging childcare and persuading John this would be good for our marriage, I convince him to go with me. His friends and their wives are faithful attendees, so that helps.

Melancholy: Last year I had to bring our newborn, and I had a sinus infection and fever, so I hardly remember any of it.

Rosie: But this year, I am sure everything will be amazing. It's at a beautiful conference center, and we are staying in a nice hotel room, having fancy dinners, and wearing our wedding clothes! I can hardly wait. Once we get to the conference, we settle in to hear the speaker talk about communication problems. He shares how Adam took a passive position when Eve sinned, how the purpose of marriage is to help our spouses become their future glory-self through sacrificial service, and how our spouses aren't here to make us happy but to make us holy.

Rude: All the things I've heard a million times before.

Rosie: But then he says something I have not heard a million times before. He says to have intimacy in a marriage, each partner needs to feel safe and understood. He says both safety and being understood need to be present to have deep conversations. A spouse cannot anticipate bringing something up only to be criticized and blamed by the other. When this happens, the spouse who doesn't feel safe will withdraw, and the marriage becomes a coexistence.

Melancholy: *That's it.* I do not feel safe or understood. Every time I bring up a concern to John, he criticizes and blames me, and I have to withdraw to keep the peace.

Rosie: Someone finally put my marriage into words, and maybe John will be willing to talk with me about this. When the session is over, we go back to our hotel room to get ready for the fancy dinner where the women dress up like brides again. John has been talking to some of his friends, and he's in a good mood. While we start changing into our wedding clothes, I lightly bring up my notes from the earlier session and say, "This is how I feel much of the time. Can we talk about this?"

Melancholy: Suddenly, John is driving us home. I stare out the car window, my face hard and still as a brick, but I can feel tears running down my icy cheeks. I have perfected the art of the silent bawl. I sit all night in my rocking chair in our bedroom, and John goes to the basement to sleep. The kids are at my mom's house, so I numbly rock and rock and rock. I cannot put a coherent thought together. Trying seems pointless. Nothing makes sense. I start slipping into something very dark, and I feel hopeless. I can usually figure something out—a way to cope or a plan of action, but I cannot think straight about anything anymore.

Spiritualizer: Instead of wishing to be known, loved, and understood, I need to wish to know, love, and understand God. I hope, I pray, and I long to be at the end of myself. ***I am sick to death of myself.***

Rude: This is what comes of my taking initiative and pushing my husband to attend a conference. I will never do that again.

Melancholy: And as it turns out, I never do. That is the last conference we ever attend together.

43
Visionary Woman

Melancholy: What kind of woman am I? How do I want to define myself? I dislike myself, yet I have an insatiable, selfish desire to be loved, and I feel self-pity because I am not loved. I am forever looking for the approval of others.

Freaked: I'm terrified I will suffer because of the choices and behaviors of others!

Spiritualizer: I am impatient toward others and discouraged when I see laziness, apathy, unloving attitudes, lack of purpose, wasting time, and selfishness.

Freaked: I fear all of these things destroy our potential for God's glory—that my own life will have been for nothing!

Melancholy: I have given up any influence in the world I might have had as a professor, writer, or ministry-focused leader in order to raise children and be someone's wife. I'm not doing anything of significance if my own kids grow up and throw their own lives away. My pain and sacrifice will have been for nothing. I have hope that one day I can stand before God and say, "Here I am, and here are the ones you gave to me. All of them! All Yours!"

Spiritualizer: Our pastor shares that the judgment seat of Christ for the believer will be like this: He will have a file for all our days, and most of those days will have Fs, Ds, and Cs on them. A few will have

Bs, and a very few might have an A. God will take the big stack of Fs, Ds, and Cs and burn them. Then, He will pick up the As and Bs, hold them up, and cry out, "Evidence of My grace! Evidence of My grace!" Oh, how I need to hear that.

Rude: So, wait, no grace for the Cs, Ds and Fs? Am I the only one who thinks this doesn't fit with what Jesus showed us?

Rosie: My marriage is hopeless, and nothing is going to change. So, I've started a blog called Visionary Womanhood to encourage Christian women. I figure if my life as a Christian woman is confusing, painful, and tottering on the brink of being utterly meaningless, then maybe other women are feeling the same way, and I want to help. We need each other.

Spiritualizer: After receiving permission from my church elders and having a specific elder put in charge, I start a small gathering of homeschooling moms, also called Visionary Womanhood. We meet once a month to watch a video sermon from Vision Forum, an organization for building up Christian families and helping parents raise the next generation of world leaders. One day, Christianity will rule the world with God's perfect law, and I want to do my part. I love to inspire vision in the other women, and we spend a good deal of time praying for our husbands and children during the second half of the meeting.

I tell the women our meetings are about a battle between God and Satan. Our posterity will either rise up and bless the name of the Lord—a people set apart as holy unto God our Creator—or our posterity will melt into the world and be lost. This is not a game. This is war. And here in this Visionary Womanhood gathering, we are doing battle. Our work will *not* be in vain! I post an article on my blog encouraging women to go to the Word of God for direction concerning the election, but I don't think very many women did that.

They say they have "no time," and yet I wonder if they have time to watch TV or read magazines or go shopping.

Freaked: I don't know, and I feel bad for judging, but everything feels like an uphill battle, and God's side is losing! Will His Church prevail? Is it doomed to slink toward Gomorrah until Christ returns? Will the Church be triumphant? Or will she crash and burn and then be rescued at the last minute? I wish I could clearly know what God is doing!

Spiritualizer: Our nation has ignored and rejected God by electing Obama to be our new president.

Freaked: Dear God, grant me faith to trust You when I don't understand.

Spiritualizer: I decide to repost a review by Kevin Swanson about the *Soul Surfer* movie. Christians love that movie because the main character is a Christian, but the setting takes place at the beach, so there are half-naked women in this movie. Do we really want our sons and husbands to be looking at half-naked women?

Melancholy: I receive pushback for sharing that review, and I am embarrassed.

Spiritualizer: Someone must be willing to speak the truth! The lives of our children are at stake! At church I see a young woman wearing fishnet pantyhose and stiletto heels. Her fingernails are long, and her skirt is short, and I feel a mixture of pity and animosity toward her. Doesn't she know we don't dress like this in church? Will my boys or husband get turned on by her? How can I protect them? What does it feel like to look pretty like that? *My* nails are short, and *my* skirt is long.

At our family reunion, my cousin's wife, who is the picture of sophisticated fashion, looks at me with amusement and says I look like Ma Ingalls straight out of a scene from *Little House on the Prairie*. I don't even care. I laugh lightly and walk around our family reunion picnic feeling blessed with a baby in a sling on my back. Relatives are looking at me with curiosity, and I notice someone looking at me with open disgust, but I don't let their stares take away my joy.

Rosie: I love my hilarious, clever, fun aunts, uncles, and cousins. I can hardly contain the joy I feel when I am with them, even when they question my clothing decisions.

Melancholy: But this woman with the fishnet hose and stilettos sitting in front of my family and me at church? Do I love her? This feeling in my body is not love but judgment, an uncomfortable feeling I don't know how to process. We haven't learned anything about handling judgmental feelings in our character booklets. I don't want to feel this way toward people.

Spiritualizer: I'm reading *A Time of Departing*, which is about how the New Age, Mysticism, contemplative prayer movement is sweeping the Christian church. Very scary. Anyway, the author compares this mystic and contemplative kind of worship or practice (which has the appearance of being God-centered and beautiful and good) to Cain's sacrifice. Cain thought he could please God by thinking up a "better" sacrifice—less bloody, gross, and stinky. But God rejected his "man-wisdom" offering. God is who God is, and He is the one who makes the rules—not the maggots He created.[5]

Someone at church asks me if John and I will encourage our daughters to go to college. I say "probably not" since I want them to focus on raising the next generation, and college will only distract them from their true calling. Then another person listening in says special needs children should be educated in the public schools where they can get the help they need. I walk away from this conversation dumbfounded. How quickly, how easily, we turn to cultural wisdom to solve our deepest problems instead of the Word of God. Imagine all that God could do if we would cry out to Him, seek Him, love Him, and ask Him for wisdom. But we don't. Why go to God when the government has a ready, easy, available option? Sometimes I get into arguments trying to convince people of the rightness or wrongness of things. I'm scared of confrontation, but am I being a responsible Christian if I allow people to believe lies?

Melancholy: Sadly, I don't trust God to do inner spiritual work in others, and I take the burden for their spiritual health upon myself. I know I need to do my part, but I would be more joy-filled and hope-filled if I could truly know and believe God would fulfill all His plans for my children and our family. I'm afraid I will end up hindering God by not doing my part or by neglecting something.

Spiritualizer: We had a conversation with a couple last night concerning our decision to throw away our *Lord of the Rings* paraphernalia. They did not approve of our choice, but I am not my own. I belong to Christ. If He asks me to stop eating bread, I will. If He asks me to stop growing roses, I will. I don't need to rationalize His directives in my life. And I'd rather hang out with brothers and sisters who radically follow God and obey His Word than lukewarm, argumentative, compromising, pill-popping brothers and sisters who live joyless, apathetic lives of devotion to the flesh. And I don't want to be that kind of casual Christian, either.

Dear God, light a fire in my life. Change me. Transform me into a visionary woman. Pour out your supernatural, powerful grace in my spirit and life so I can live a life empowered by You, Your presence, and Your Word. I'm getting sick again, but I will obey You today in loving and patiently serving and training my seven children despite my physical infirmities. Your grace is sufficient for me!

Onward!

44
The Letter

Melancholy: Since I turned forty, I've had two painful miscarriages, including one I thought would never end. The thought has crossed my mind that if I am to be obedient to God and allow Him to give me as many children as He wants, then I may have a lot of miscarriages in my forties. Can I endure that physically and emotionally?

Rosie: My friend Lori, who teaches the parenting class at church, recently wrote me a letter encouraging me to persevere no matter what. This is a high calling, and it is always our privilege to suffer for the glory of God. So, I am pregnant for the third time since turning forty, and this one sticks. Not only does it stick, but I am not even sick for this pregnancy!

Freaked: Right before my miracle baby is born, my sister Alice sends me a letter that *knocks the breath out of me!* After reading this letter, I don't sleep for several nights in a row, and I even end up getting physically sick for a while! Alice explains her disgust about my lack of control over my five-year-old daughter, who hit Alice's twelve-year-old son and hurt his feelings. She wants me to spank my daughter more, but she doesn't realize how much we do spank her already! Our daughter is stubborn and physical, and honestly, she is starting to terrify me with her uncontrollable tantrums! She hits her younger sister as well, and nothing we do changes her behavior. But that isn't the worst of the letter. Alice also accuses me of thinking I'm better than everyone else because I wear skirts and talk about Vision Forum and Bill Gothard stuff!

Melancholy: I'm so ashamed.

Rosie: I have noticed during holiday gatherings that my mom and sisters are animated and full of laughter and fun when we're talking about movies or TV shows or shopping. I usually listen to them and laugh. They're all hysterically funny, and I love their stories.

Melancholy: When I bring up something meaningful to me, like a book I'm reading, something I am learning at church, or a new curriculum I'm trying for homeschool, they get quiet and look down at the table. I feel awkward and stupid, like I don't belong.

Rude: Some of the things in Alice's letter are not even true. I don't know how or where she got the ideas to create the stories she made up. The letter describes someone I don't even know. Some of her complaints are exaggerations and misunderstandings that she has never talked to me about, so I had no idea she was interpreting anything incorrectly. I sort of understand where she may have formed those ideas because I am more conservative than she is. I dress differently, and I'm having a million babies, which *is* kind of weird. But Alice takes our differences and puts a spin on them so far from what I have actually said, done, thought, or felt.

Melancholy: At any rate, Alice is at the end of her rope with me, and I need to shape up, but I'm not sure how. She ignores and avoids me during family holidays.

Rosie: I smile, reach out, and try to intentionally show kindness at the beginning of every holiday to get her to warm up to me. She usually does eventually!

Melancholy: But I guess, according to the letter, she has harbored deep anger and resentment toward me, and I don't understand why. We almost always do what Alice wants to do so that she is comfortable and in a good mood. As far back as I can remember, *this is the goal.* I'm the one who is expected to sacrifice my own wishes and needs to keep the peace, and I try hard to do that. But now I wonder if I had it all wrong. I know I'm selfish. Maybe what I think I've experienced is inaccurate? It's so confusing, and my entire body hurts.

Rosie: I constantly remind myself that she is five years younger than I am, and I need to set a good example by letting go of my own rights. On our most recent family cabin trip, I intentionally practice two things, and it makes the trip better than any other year. First, I keep my big ugly mouth shut. I say very little. And second, I never make any requests or get in anyone's way, and I don't annoy anyone. Instead of offering any of my own ideas, I *cheerfully* agree with *everything* Alice wants to do, and the cabin trip goes great! I stay in my cabin as much as possible to avoid bothering anyone, which works out well, and I get a bunch of things done. I finish a quilt, plan our fall schedule, work on my recipe book, take an online photography course, and organize our pictures on my computer. I need to remember to keep my head down and stay out of trouble at all family functions. I don't want to cause others to be uncomfortable or to feel upset because of my selfishness. And I don't like sitting around feeling sorry for myself and giving the devil a foothold when I could be productive and focused.

After several sleepless nights and thinking and praying about Alice's letter, I see clearly what I need to do. I write her a letter apologizing for my sin of pride, and I thank her for helping me to see my disgusting and self-serving attitude.

Spiritualizer: I promise from now on to check my thoughts when they stray toward the negative; check my tongue when I'm tempted to open my big mouth; remove myself from environments where gossip is taking place; and encourage right thinking and speaking in the lives of our children.

Rosie: I decide to name my miracle baby after my mom and my grandmother. Alice's middle name is also my grandma's name, and I'm going to ask Alice if she will be my daughter's godmother. I hope with all my heart this will help to patch things up, and Alice will see how much I love her. I hope she will want to be around me again.

Melancholy: I feel miserable and full of shame when I think someone is angry with me. I will try harder to be a more loving, thoughtful, and sensitive sister. I hope she will one day be able to forgive me.

Today is my daughter's due date, but she arrives a little early and is already sleeping next to me on my bed. There are many strange emotions after birth. I am relieved the baby is safely here, but I am sad the pregnancy is over. The old routine is done. Life changes overnight and begins a new routine. I have to say goodbye to what was and embrace what is to come. I notice the fragility of life in a more acute way, so I'm gripped by fears of losing those I love. I feel sorrow over how quickly my children's babyhoods came and went. How wonderful and sad to watch them grow, change, and eventually, one day, leave.

I pick up my toddler out of her crib this morning, shocked at how big she is. Before the new baby's birth, my toddler was a tiny little two-year-old, yet overnight, she has grown into a Very Large Person. She stares up at me with her big eyes, and I cry because she isn't my baby anymore. That baby is gone forever, and soon, this new one will be gone, too. What is it all for? All this birthing life and then losing it? All this joy and this pain wrapped up in a single package? It all has a divine purpose I can't see. I will never fully know this purpose in my lifetime. The Bible says we are like the flowers and the grass, here one day and gone the next, and oh, do I feel that today.

Spiritualizer: Motherhood is another kind of death. A beautiful, sacrificial death. A mother is invisible and does invisible work. She has no identity of her own so that she can be the soil where her children are planted, fed, and raised to reach their full potential.

45

Soap

Rosie: I'm not sure how it happens, but I start a successful business making and selling cold process soap! It starts out as another homemaking hobby I can justify as being semi-godly. (Cleanliness is next to godliness, right?) After watching dozens of YouTube videos and reading articles and books on the subject, I begin to formulate different recipes and come up with over fifty different bars, including a couple dozen shampoo bars.

Every time I have a problem, I look up the solution online and solve it. Every time I have a new idea, I try it out. Some ideas work, and others don't. I focus on creating an excellent customer experience that includes lightning-fast shipping, free samples, and pretty packaging. And, of course, the bars are beautiful, practical, and smell amazing. When I first start, I ask my husband if he will loan me $1000 to buy initial supplies. To my surprise, he agrees, but not without tossing me a John-style blessing, "I know I'll never see that money again."

Rude: I'm not sure why he gives the money to me if he knows he'll never see it again, but I am determined to prove him wrong. In less than a year, I give him back his money plus a few thousand more.

Rosie: Each year I contribute more and more to our family bank account. I pay for all the homeschooling materials, swimming lessons, camps, violin lessons, piano lessons, field trips, birthday and Christmas presents, and I even buy my husband a used car and pay off some of the principal on our home.

Melancholy: I am hoping John will be proud of me and love me and appreciate me. Maybe he will stop criticizing me for how I "spend all his money." Instead, he finds other things to criticize, including the way I run my business. Apparently, I don't run it the way he would, and if I did it his way, the business would be much more successful. I can't win with him.

I can't win at parenting, either. My children are getting older and making their own decisions. They don't always agree with me or respect my thoughts. All those adorable little babies who once needed me and loved me and wanted me? They grow up and have minds of their own. I'm not sure what I expected, but somehow this is a sad surprise.

Rosie: But I'm successful in the soap business! I do A and predictably get B. I'm in control, and people love my soap. They love the funny descriptions of my soap. They love my customer service. I get so many kudos from everyone else that I no longer look for anything from my husband. I keep my head down around him and find all my joy in creating and selling soap and learning how to run a business. I'm finally good at something.

Melancholy: But, oh no! *Big Problem.* The soap business is no longer a godly, homemaking hobby but rather a money-making enterprise, which makes me *a work-at-home mom.* And that's bad. That means my kids aren't as important as money. That means I'm being selfish with my time.

Rude: It's true. I'd rather be making soap and packing orders than playing Duplos.

Melancholy: I'm riddled with guilt over this. I didn't intend for the business to grow to become a Thing. But here we are. One of my church friends makes little comments every chance she can to drive this point home, and I'm feeling more and more uncomfortable being around her. I have a sneaking suspicion that she thinks our daughter's problems might stem from my making and selling soap even though I keep up with homeschooling, make three meals a day, keep the house clean, and regularly practice hospitality.

Rude: I've also stopped trying to make life work in a skirt. I'm regressing to my rebellious, carefree college days. I now wear jeans every day, and I must say, it's a relief.

Rosie: I provide a job to the mother of another family from church who is struggling financially. I teach her how to make soap, and now she makes a few loaves a week. I teach her how to set up her own business, so she can "sell" me her soap wholesale and make more money for her time than she would if I paid her by the hour.

Melancholy: In this way, I assuage my guilt over being a work-at-home mom. I tell myself I'm helping another Christian family. I give my kids paid jobs, so they can learn the importance of working and earning money. I am doing the best I can, but I know I could do better. I could work harder. I could be a better person if I weren't so selfish. After all my efforts in life, I've discovered that making babies and soap are my only successes. I've failed at everything else, and God has given up on me. So, I work, work, work to keep my mind off how my actual life is unraveling around the edges. I can sense a tsunami on the horizon even if I can't quite see it, but maybe if I ignore it, it will go away.

Rosie: Ooh! I have an idea for a new soap line: Literary Soap. I'll start with a Charlotte Brontë bar that smells like roses and lavender.

46
The Fool

Melancholy: John is unhappy with the boys' progress in math. Our oldest son scored in the ninety-ninth percentile, and our second son in the ninety-seventh on the Iowa Test of Basic Skills last year, but that is not good enough. John tells me he's disappointed in me for this and other failures. According to John, I am stupid, and I never listen. And here I thought we were doing so well. Our oldest son is two years ahead of his actual grade level, and our second son is at grade level. Math is my least favorite subject to teach and has taken far more of my time and emotional energy than any other subject, and now to hear that my efforts are disappointing? I have no words.

Rude: Except I do have words because the words are like a fountain I cannot stop, and I have to solve this problem. I wonder if John might be willing to teach the boys math himself since I am unable to figure out what his expectations are and never seem to meet them. But he is not willing to teach them math and threatens to put them in public school if I do not do a better job of it. I will keep plugging away because while I have given up wearing skirts and baking bread from scratch every Saturday morning, I draw the line at homeschooling. I will die before I give that up. But I have to say, I'm angry. I'm so angry I could tear out my hair and scream like a crazy witch and not even care.

Wonder: In my Bible reading, I come to the book of Proverbs, which I have read dozens of times in my life. But this time I connect some dots I have never connected before. I start noticing *only* the verses about fools, and I write those particular verses out in my journal.

Melancholy: When I read them back to myself, it hits me like a stomach punch. Those verses are describing my husband.

Wonder: *Is John a biblical fool?*

Freaked: I don't write this thought in my journal because I am *unkind* to even think this thought! I'm betraying his trust! Aren't wives supposed to overlook their husband's sin? How is seeing his sin in Proverbs overlooking it? Instead, I am zeroing in on it! How can this be good? Both the relief I feel in seeing this and having language for how I see John also feels wrong somehow! What kind of person would feel relief because her husband is a proverbial fool?!

Wonder: *And yet, if I'm honest, I do. I feel deeply relieved.*

Melancholy: All these years I have felt like I might be crazy, like there is something fundamentally wrong with me not even God can fix.

Wonder: Now I see a glimmer of hope that I'm not crazy—that maybe what my husband does to me is as bad as it makes me feel. Maybe John is the problem.

"Do not speak to a fool, for he will despise the wisdom of your words" (Proverbs 23:9).

"Fools despise wisdom and discipline" (Proverbs 1:7).

"The complacency of fools will destroy them" (Proverbs 1:32).

"He who hates correction is stupid" (Proverbs 12:1).

"The way of a fool is right in his own eyes" (Proverbs 12:15).

"A rebuke cuts into a man of discernment deeper than a hundred lashes cut into a fool" (Proverbs 17:10).

"A fool does not delight in understanding, but only in airing his opinions" (Proverbs 18:2).

"Drive out the mocker, and conflict will depart; even quarreling and insults will cease" (Proverbs 22:10).

"Like a madman shooting firebrands and deadly arrows, so is the man who deceives his neighbor and says, 'I was only joking!'" (Proverbs 26:18–19).

"A stone is heavy and sand is a burden, but aggravation from a fool outweighs them both" (Proverbs 27:3).

Melancholy: I know the weight of living with the man these verses describe, and now I know *God knows it too*. I feel relief, yes, but also deep sorrow shredding my heart to pieces. What am I supposed to do with this? The older kids and I sit down with John and try to share the ways he causes pain in our lives. They tell him, with tears, about their hurt when John lectures them for long periods when he is displeased. Sometimes he heaves them into things when he is angry. He grabs their faces and yells into them. He interrupts them and won't let them talk. He tells them they are dumb, ridiculous, rebellious, and selfish. He yells at them when they are only laughing and having fun. But talking to him doesn't work. He makes fun of our tears in the days that follow and accuses us of disrespectfully "ganging up on him."

"Whoever corrects a scoffer gets himself abuse" (Proverbs 9:7).

"Do not reprove a scoffer or he will hate you" (Proverbs 9:8).

Once I dreamed of a family full of love, but what we have here is a family where hate, sorrow, fear, and shame thrive.

Rude: And I don't know what the hell to do about it.

47
Road Trip

Rude: For many years, John's parents come home to Duluth in the summers from where they winter in Arizona, and I am obligated to plan for three weekend trips to Duluth with all the kids since his parents do not enjoy making the two-hour drive down to the cities to see us. I plan a trip in the spring when they arrive, another one mid-summer, and a final one in the fall before they leave for Arizona again. I arrange for and plan these trips because that's what a good wife does, but nobody seems to appreciate the time and emotional energy required to clear everyone's schedule, plan for all the packing, include all the paraphernalia for babies and toddlers, and then actually *get it all packed*. I suppose I am fishing for some empathy and encouragement when I mention the work involved, but John tells me I am making a big deal out of nothing. *How hard could it be to pack a suitcase?* I am being ridiculous.

After I load the bags by the door, his job is to somehow fit them into our car. He does this at the last minute and gets annoyed by how much stuff we bring for our big family. After we get up to his parents' house, our visits are enjoyable, but several of us have allergies, and we sleep poorly with all eight of us packed like sardines in two hot rooms. Once we reach six kids going on seven, I tell John if he wants to visit his parents, he will need to set up the trips. I am happy to go along with whatever he arranges, but I will no longer make any arrangements myself. I have a hopeful hunch he will not take the initiative to plan any trips at all, and my hunch proves correct. His family

Road Trip

probably blames me for being a bad girl because we don't travel up there anymore, but I am too busy trying to raise a million kids. I don't have the bandwidth to wring my hands over being judged. I put in my time for many years, and I am done. Another adult can step up if getting together is important enough to the family.

Melancholy: But I make a huge error in judgment when I agree to take a road trip across America in our Sprinter van with our camper trailing behind. I knew from the very beginning of our planning that *this* was going to be a Bad Memory. At least for me.

Rude: John has idealized childhood memories of camping, and he wants to recreate them using our kids. In his memory, there are no late-night campground arrivals and set-ups. There are no mosquitoes. No injuries. No one-year-olds with fevers of 103 and rashes all over. No storms in the middle of the night. No driving with eight children for days at a time. No sick wives pregnant with number nine.

Rosie: There are moments of fun that peek through the clouds for us.

Melancholy: The desperate exhaustion, nausea, demanding children, a stubborn man, and anxiety over my baby who is extremely ill all taint any of the moments of fun for me. I spend entire days and nights with nine other people, yet I am completely alone. When we arrive at John's sister's home in Idaho, I am beside myself with sleep deprivation. Feeling like I have the flu, I fall into a real bed and sleep hard for several hours.

Rosie: John is in a good mood the next day, and our time is peaceful and fun.

Rude: But as soon as we pile back into our van to continue the journey to visit more of John's relatives, he is crabbier than ever. By the time we arrive at his parents' apartment in northern California, he is in such a bad mood he bites his mom's head off, and she looks at me and whispers, "He gets like his dad sometimes." I already knew that, but I didn't know she knew that.

Melancholy: A strange wave of relief washes over me even though I know she doesn't have any answers or help for me. Men are this way. There isn't anything to do but accept it. We visit more of his relatives for a couple of days, and then we begin the week-long trip back home. I am getting sicker with the pregnancy, and trying to manage all the kids in a strange environment is taxing on my body. Normally, I would push through like a martyr, knowing I won't die in the process; I'd just feel like dying, which is okay.

Rude: This time, I decide to listen to my body. I am forty-four years old and pregnant with my ninth baby, and I am tired of nobody in the universe caring about my life, my body, and my well-being. Heck, I am getting tired of how I don't seem to care about these things, either. So, I decide to look out for me for once. In front of his relatives to make sure he says yes, I ask John if I can fly home, even though I know he hates to spend money and will think plane tickets are a waste.

Freaked: I am being intentionally manipulative and using his desire to look good in front of his family against him! I felt terrible about that!

Rude: But it works. He says yes.

Melancholy: The next day, my eleven-year-old daughter helps me take my one-year-old and three-year-old home on a plane. I remember getting the kids into bed after we arrive home that night and crawling into my own, shaking with fever. What is all this about? This family? This marriage? I can't talk about it. I can't tell anyone. There is no help on the face of the earth.

Spiritualizer: *So, I will lift my eyes to the hills, from where does my help come? My help comes from the Lord, the maker of heaven and earth.* I know there is coming a day—a glorious day of liberation, when the burden will roll off, and I will be free. I will be able to finally, at long last, fly away.

Melancholy: But in the meantime, I wonder what my life's destiny is. I know it's somehow wrapped up in motherhood, but I don't have a clue what the harvest will look like, and I don't want my life to be wasted.

Wonder: I have this nagging thought deep inside there might be something else I'm supposed to be doing, but I don't know what that would be.

Freaked: I am afraid this question is meant to sidetrack me and lure me off the present road with lofty ideas of "really making a difference doing something of tangible importance."

Wonder: Why is the destiny of all women to simply bear children so those children can make a difference in the world? And why is it that those children, in turn, are supposed to grow up to be adults who bear children who can make a difference? What if I want to be one of the people who makes a difference myself and not only through my offspring? And what if my offspring want to do the same? Why can't we all, as individuals, make a difference in the ways that inspire and move us?

Melancholy: But then I come back to my Christian duty. Nobody cares about what I'm doing or how it brings glory to God. I am an obscure, selfish, sin-wracked suburban woman making food, cleaning it up, teaching children, changing diapers, doing laundry, and trying to get along with nine other people under the same roof, all of whom try me to the limits of my patience. I fail every hour. I go backward more than forward. Every day, like an ant, I build my hill and wait for it to be wiped out with the next rainfall or stomp of a toddler in a grown man's body.

I want to do great things for God and make Him proud, but I fail miserably.

48
The Hotel Room

She didn't remember what they were fighting about or how she arrived in that hotel room in the middle of the night. She never remembered their fights even ten minutes after they had run their circular course, and she was left choking, not only in her throat, but in her whole body. It felt like a rope, or maybe a living thing, encircling her flesh, round and round, tighter and tighter until she thought she might suffocate.

Last night, that's all she wanted—to suffocate and die.
She didn't sleep.
She writhed.
All night.
Without a break.
The minutes ticked by
while every cell of her skin, muscles, organs, and bones hurt.
Yet she was relieved to be alone in the belly of a hotel
where nobody could interrupt her with their needs.
Nobody could judge her.
Nobody could find her.
And that meant she could cry.
But also,
if she wanted to
slip away forever,
nobody could stop her.
A white bathtub silently waited in the dark
for her to step inside its welcome warmth and go to sleep.

*She thought about that white tub all night.
She would fit perfectly in its embrace.
But she wasn't alone in that hotel room.
The white tub would have to hold someone else, too.
Her baby boy was a month away from being born,
and he, like the rest of her family, was oblivious to her pain.
He rolled and pushed and kicked her,
calling her back to life.
And yet . . .
But still . . .
That's how the night went.
Over
and over
like a fever dream of never-ending circles spinning
down,
down,
and deeper down
into hell.
A million little pins, a few insignificant, imperceptible,
no-big-deal pricks poked each day,
every day,
for years
and years
and relentless
pricking
years.
Until the dam of her Self could no longer sustain the pressure
with all the millions of tiny holes.
And her life blood squirted through them inelegantly until the sun rose,
and she lay empty
and quiet.*

The Hotel Room

With shades pulled up in the early morning light,
the room looked like a normal hotel room.
The bathtub, another cold white object with no meaning.
But something changed.
The woman who stumbled into that room the night before was gone.
And in her place was someone she hadn't seen for a long time.
God, I missed her.

Part Three

"The best way to keep a prisoner from escaping is to make sure he never knows he's in prison."

—Dostoevsky

Several people harmed me in this next part, and while they should be held accountable for what they did to me and other women, my book is not the vehicle for that; therefore, I have chosen to change their names. Rather than exposing the darkness specific abusers have brought to their relationships and communities, the purpose of this book is to light a way for victims to see what is possible. There will always be people, ideas, communities, and even our own inner parts that will lay claim to us and desire to control us for their own agendas. I want survivors to know that it is possible to break the chains of all these scary little gods we have historically fawned after and placated. Why? So, we can fly free into the light of the powerful God of Love, who requires nothing from us other than to be exactly who we were created to be. Exactly who we are.

The only trouble is those scary little gods do not easily let go.

49
Shifting

The morning after I spent that night in the hotel in February 2012, I packed my bag and took my laptop to the local Barnes & Noble to do some research. I Googled terms like "passive aggressive man," "painful Christian marriage," "my Christian husband never says he's sorry," and "when you've tried everything, and your Christian marriage is still falling apart."

I didn't find much that day other than more of what I had already heard: "You can make a difference if you just do A, B, and C, suck it up, and be a martyr." I mean, not in those words, but you get my drift. I had already done A, B, and C, plus every letter all the way to Z. I *had* sucked it up, and I was *sick* of being a martyr. I was looking for something different. I was looking for the truth.

In the months that followed, I continued my search and went down some Internet rabbit holes that eventually led me to a book by Henry Cloud and John Townsend called *Who's Pushing Your Buttons*. That book described emotional abuse without actually using the word "abuse," and at that time it was the only resource I could find in the Christian world that addressed exactly what I was experiencing. A year later I would discover *Foolproofing Your Life* by Jan Silvious, and then Leslie Vernick's book, *The Emotionally Destructive Marriage*.

Although I didn't find any answers at the Barnes & Noble Café table that morning, I knew something had shifted within me. I had come to the bottom of a dark pit, and like Katy Perry sings in her song, "By the Grace of God," I had decided not to die. I knew I was in for a fight to get up and out; but what I didn't know was how many people—how many *Christian* people—were invested in making sure I stayed in that pit to die.

I eventually went back home that day. Eight children were wondering where I was, and the relentless merry-go-round of life kept going even if I wanted to get off for a while. John and I celebrated our twentieth anniversary a couple of weeks later, and I bought him a platinum band to commemorate this milestone. John unemotionally accepted and then returned the ring to the jewelers. Shortly after that, my ninth baby was born.

The doctor asked if I would like to "catch" my last child as he came out of the womb, and I did. It was an empowering moment, and I took that baby home and relished every second I had with his tiny self. I loved the newborn stage and had a routine that worked well for both me and my baby. In the past I would try to get back into full-time mothering and homemaking within three days of giving birth. John seemed agitated and unhappy when I was out of commission for any reason, and I believed it was my wifely duty to make sure he was emotionally comfortable.

Not this time. This time I announced I would be coming home with the baby and locking myself in the room for two weeks. Whatever happened outside of that room, happened; but for two weeks, I was going to rest and heal and get to know my baby. To this day, I have no idea what went on outside of my room during those two weeks. I only know I felt my power returning, and it felt right.

Those two weeks flew by, and then I emerged to pick up where I left off. My nine-year-old daughter was screaming and running around like a bat out of hell, destroying everything in her path simply because she was asked to clean her room or do her schoolwork or get in the car so we could run an errand. I was scared to make simple requests from her. If I implemented a boundary or a consequence, I might get kicked in the back or screamed at until 2:00 in the morning. My life felt like one long "pouring out" to nine children who needed me, plus one adult who relentlessly criticized everything I did or said. I couldn't remember the last time anyone said thank you. My days blurred together in a series of demands, insults, whines, and accusations. Anything that went wrong (and in a family of eleven, things were forever going wrong) somehow traced back to my failure to come through for someone in one way or another. I tried to take responsibility for my own behavior; however, if I dared to point out how someone else could potentially be responsible for a thing or two, even just partially, I received loud howls of protest. I was so desperate for peace that I slipped into the familiar scapegoat role by default.

Even though much of my life was out of control, I found order, beauty, and peace in my writing and my soap business. In these activities, things made sense, and my decisions created positive results for myself and others. I was in control. But in every other area, I was set up to fail. My husband would mutter things like, "You're retarded, and you never listen!" His words and behavior provoked me, and I disrespected myself at times with sarcastic responses to his abusive behavior. In one particularly volatile verbal exchange between John and me, I threatened to start cutting notches in my thighs every time John did or said something mean. I had been considering this for a while. Nobody could visually see what was going on, and when I told them, they didn't think it was a big deal, so what if I could make a visual for them? For myself? For John? I imagined walking into a domestic violence center and saying, "Help! My husband never hits me, so I can't prove anything, but I did keep a record of his abuse on my thigh. See?" And they would look at my leg and see hundreds of little scar lines, each one a visible validation of how much pain I was feeling inside, where nobody could see. Maybe they would believe and help me then? Those scars would also remind me of what I had been through. I would not allow myself to keep forgetting anymore.

I mentioned this idea to my sister, but she warned me that John could use it against me, perhaps making a case that I was mentally unstable. I decided not to do it, but I definitely *felt* mentally unstable and had to fight the temptation to cut on several occasions. A couple of years later I shared this with a pastoral counselor who, in turn, talked to my husband and the elders at my church about it, bringing up the idea that I might have borderline personality disorder. She was not trained, qualified, or licensed to make diagnoses, nor was she acting in good faith to spread that kind of rumor among people who were already biased against me. I would later be diagnosed with complex-post-traumatic-stress-disorder (C-PTSD) by a (licensed) clinical psychologist who would tell me that the symptoms of BPD and C-PTSD overlap in some areas.

So many cognitive shifts were happening during this time. For example, I no longer believed I was responsible for John's bad behavior, and this revelation alone lightened my emotional load. I realized that I wasn't fighting the devil or John. I was fighting a twisted version of Christianity as it lived and breathed in the religious culture around me. John was as much a product of the toxicity as I was; he just played a different role. The answer didn't lie in changing him or in changing my controlling religious environment. That was a fool's errand. The solution was always going to be about my own transformation, but before I could rise like a phoenix out of the flames, I had to get burned at the stake by the worshippers of a scary little god I wasn't sure I believed in anymore.

50
First Domino

She screamed for hours at a time, almost daily, for years. She also hit, kicked, bit, and scratched. Nobody was exempt from her wrath. Not even the house. She punched holes in walls and broke chairs, doors, and toys. Until I saw it play out with my own two eyes, I was completely unaware that children could be this dysregulated.

The rest of our children were your garden-variety kids with an assortment of personality styles and varying degrees of cooperation, and it wasn't like I was a new mom with no experience or intuition. But despite my sensitivity to behavioral patterns and my dogged ability to manage everyone's emotions, I couldn't crack the code on this one.

Her babyhood was uneventful. I nursed her the longest of any of my other babies—until she was about fifteen months old. She was a content baby who ate and slept well, and she was surrounded by music, talking, reading, and playing due to growing up in an active homeschooling family. When she was one year of age, she contracted scarlet fever and had a lengthy febrile seizure. She was blue and lifeless, and I thought she had died in my arms, but by the time the ambulance arrived, she was pinking up and moving slightly. I always wondered if something shifted in her tiny body at that point in time.

She entered her toddler years and gave new meaning to "The Terrible Twos." I had been through this four times before and told myself that everything would work itself out, and it would all be okay. Potty training was a nightmare, and we were still in the full swing of it when she was old enough to start kindergarten. Since the Bible never mentioned psychology (at least in modern terms), I avoided any dangerous exposure to the modern, new-fangled ideas about child development and instead insisted on *Growing Kids God's Way* with the Ezzos, who had figured out God's exact formula for turning out godly children. Spanking was involved. All of this felt normal to me because I had been raised the same way, and it "worked" for my four oldest kids in that they (mostly) followed the family rules and cooperated when we asked them to do or not do something. And wasn't that the sign of good parenting?

Another unfortunate belief that had been downloaded into my brain was the idea that the government was out to steal our kids and our freedoms. Because I ferociously clung to these beliefs and my fears, I failed to get my daughter the help she needed when she was younger. I could *do this on my own with the Bible and by the grace of God*! But as she grew up, her symptoms worsened, and when you put her issues together with my issues and John's issues, you had a perfect storm. The day before Easter of 2013, that storm hit.

Our daughter had been raging all day, and because I was her target of choice most of the time, I had spent much of that Saturday locked in my room or bathroom. John came home from only God knows where and settled in at his computer in the formal dining room that had been turned into his office, and so I came out to make dinner knowing that John and this child would keep one another occupied with their collective drama. Am I proud of this? No. But at the time, I didn't have any better solutions. I wasn't strong enough to take her body anywhere other than where she chose to put it, but John was. He could pick her up and bring her downstairs and then come up and lock the door—which is exactly what he often did.

Lest you imagine our basement was a dark dungeon, it was not. It was well equipped with toys, a comfy couch, bright lights, and a TV.

She could do whatever she wanted down there until she calmed down and no longer presented a danger to the rest of us. But she would rage and scream and try to break down the door, and sometimes she succeeded. We had to put multiple locks on it so in case she broke one, the others might still do the job.

The problem was that John wasn't content to only bring her downstairs. He was a man who liked to control things, most often passive aggressively, but when it came to this incessantly screaming child, he would shove his fingers down her throat to stop the screaming even though it never worked. Not even once. We could hear her choking and gagging down there, but none of us knew what to do. He would spank her over and over again, telling her that as soon as she stopped screaming, he would stop spanking. Again, it didn't work, but that didn't stop John from trying.

To be fair, I tried this once, too, when John was gone. We had been listening to the raging and screaming for a couple of hours, and I asked my two oldest sons to hold her down so I could spank her. I focused on outwardly appearing calm and repeating, "Please stop screaming, and then we can stop spanking," and I swatted her butt every few minutes, giving her time in between to consider whether or not she wanted to continue. She screamed louder. That fiasco ended about thirty minutes later with me crying and the other kids glassy-eyed and emotionless. I didn't know what trauma was back then, but we were all traumatized. That was it for me. I knew at that moment that something was deeply wrong with spanking, and I was done with it.

On the night before Easter, she was arguing with John, and there was an altercation in his dining room/office. I didn't go in to check on anything because what was the point? What would happen would happen, and I had no control over any of it. I could tell it wasn't good but hopelessly made dinner with my heart pounding out of my chest.

John eventually brought her to the basement, and the rest of the kids and I could hear screaming and banging, but we knew there was nothing we could do about it, so we tuned it out, like little emotionless robots. I learned to dissociate when things became this chaotic, and I spiritualized it by saying I was "forgiving and forgetting" until it became second nature to me. The next morning, we all got up to go to the Easter service, and when this child came out of her room, both sides of her face were black and blue. I could hardly comprehend what I was seeing. Trembling with anger and fear, I brought her to John and demanded to know what he had done to her. He looked at her nervously, but stubbornly mumbled, "She did that to herself."

"HOW?" I yelled, my mind reeling with panic and rage.

"I just put my hands on both sides of her face, and she batted her head back and forth between my hands and must have bruised herself."

An irrational argument ensued with me trying to convince him that this could not possibly be true from a physics standpoint, but he told me I was stupid and what did I know about physics? And what kind of person did I think he was? And it was my fault anyway because I couldn't control her.

I kept her home from church that day. My old friend Rude screamed at me through my upset stomach, headache, and pounding heart, "*Your husband physically assaulted your daughter, you freaking idiot. Wake up! Call the cops!*"

And my other friend Freaked screamed back, "*What if John is right?! Maybe she did it to herself?! How am I supposed to betray my own husband to the police?! What if the police take all my kids away?!*"

And then Rosie tried to calm me down with, "*He's never done anything this bad before. I'm sure it will never happen again.*"

I told John he had to leave, or I would tell the men in our small group at church what he did, so John left for a few days. Then I called

First Domino

one of the pastors' wives and asked her what I should do. I remember noticing something about this. It was a whisper of a thought, but I noticed I was still living like a child, relying on other adults to make my choices for me. "Mommy, should I call the police? Mommy, what if they took our children away?" The older woman—the Adult—said no, it wasn't necessary to involve the police. Maybe one of the pastors could talk to John about it. Obviously, our family was hurting, and maybe John needed some support and encouragement as the head of our home.

I should have just called the damn police or at least taken pictures. But I wasn't quite there yet, and this woman seemed so sure of herself. I conceded to believe what I had always been told that I tend to do: make a mountain out of a molehill. I was being overly dramatic. I must be looking for attention, failing to overlook a wrong, and wallowing in bitterness. I didn't want to be the kind of person who did those terrible things. I wanted to be a good Christian woman; I wanted to be loved; and I didn't want to lose my children. That terrified me more than anything else.

Ironically, while I felt like a child, I also still took responsibility to fix everything for everyone, so when a friend of mine told me about a local counselor who did two-day marriage intensives for $7,500, I thought God answered a prayer. I had just finished a writing project that brought in about that amount of money, and I believed it was a sign from God. I would tell John that he could come back only if he agreed to go to this marriage intensive with me. He agreed to do it if I was paying for it, so I scheduled the intensive, and the bruises faded. But the first domino had already fallen.

51
Marriage Intensive

I had heard about marriage intensives. They were luxurious getaways in the mountains or by the beach where couples would have group sessions, individual sessions, and time alone with their partners to talk about their relationships and enjoy one another in a beautiful setting. Those couples would then go home with healed marriages. They were expensive, but you couldn't put a price on an amazing marriage, right? So, when a friend of mine recommended a local counselor who was "known for his successful marriage intensives," I knew this was what I needed. This was Custer's Last Stand. It would be my greatest, most expensive, and last-ditch initiative to fix our marriage. Rosie was convinced this was our Miracle Moment. The Turning Point.

I was secretly hoping it would be in the mountains.

When I called to make the appointment, I found out this marriage intensive would be two days in the counselor's local office a few miles away in cold, slushy Minneapolis. We would have to bring two other couples along with us to observe and offer support. Also, the counselor wanted $7,500 up front in a money order before he would put us on his schedule. Also, his schedule was full, but he could take us in two weeks if he didn't take a vacation he was planning. Also, I needed to decide immediately.

Something was off, and I felt disappointed and somehow betrayed, but I quickly set my heart aside knowing it was deceitful above all else, and who could know it? It didn't matter if the intensive was in an ugly setting, expensive, and not private. I was just short of being willing to sign my soul over to the devil if only my marriage could be fixed. And this couldn't possibly be a devil if he would actually cancel his vacation just to help us. Plus, miracles can hide in dark places, right? *Believe the best, Natalie!*

One of the support couples we found had been in a church small group with us for several years, and the husband, George, was serving as a church deacon. He would eventually work with John to help him be "the husband Natalie needed." George would also give me a book called *Fierce Woman* to drive home John's narrative that I was the problem because I had a brain, a voice, and words, and sometimes I had the audacity to use all three of them despite not having a penis. I thanked him, read the book, took notes, and then told George I could not relate to the woman in the story, but it was an interesting read. And that was true. The woman in the story was a bitchy pastor's wife who tried to control her quiet, hardworking pastor husband, and eventually she repented and got nicer and wrote a book that played right into the hands of controlling, misogynistic Christian men who had wives who sometimes made a peep about it.

Anyway, I got the intensive set up, and John reluctantly drove us there on the first day. He would have been relieved to turn around and go back home to research used cars on his computer in peace—and for $7,500, he could even buy one. But this horse was out of the gate and galloping down the racetrack, and there was no stopping it now.

For the first couple of hours in the office, the counselor told us all about himself, his practice, his trips, his wild success in saving marriages, and his lovely daughters who looked hot in their stilettos. Would we like to see a picture? Eventually we got down to business, only interrupted here and there with related anecdotes, as well as some speaking in tongues, which made John and me uncomfortable, but what did we know? Maybe it was the secret sauce? By recording the time of his stories in the margins of my notebook, I calculated that about $2,500 of my investment was spent on learning all about our amazing counselor and his amazing life.

When he did finally focus on our issues, I learned that 25 percent of my pain was because of how John had betrayed me, 25 percent was because of how I betrayed him, 25 percent was because of how I betrayed myself, and 25 percent was because of how I betrayed God. So basically, I was responsible for 75 percent of my pain, and that was supposed to make me feel empowered. The key to solving our marriage issues was intimate friendship, amazing grace, and extravagant love. And all three of these would, in turn, give us the added bonus of hot, erotic, orgasmic sex. I was all in, but that wasn't the problem. I tried to tell the counselor again what I perceived the problem to be: my husband was hurting me, and he didn't care, and he wouldn't stop.

At that point the counselor told both of us to stand up and face one another. Then he told me to put my hands around John's neck and look at him like I wanted to kill him. I was following all of the instructions perfectly because I still believed that's how you make things work—*and I really needed this to work*—but even as I obeyed these strange instructions, I felt my brain exploding with the insanity of this request. What was he trying to prove?

The counselor took a picture of me strangling my husband like a deranged killer, and then he showed the picture to us. John gave a sad, knowing nod. I burst into body-wracking sobs. The only thing I could think was, "*This is what John has been telling me for twenty-one years. Every time I point out something hurtful he has done, he tells me I am a horrible person. I'm stupid. I'm mean. I bring nothing to the table but trouble. I'm a terrible daughter, wife, mother, and friend. Yes, I wished he was dead a time or 3,495, but I'd never kill him. I was only hoping he'd die of natural causes so I could find some relief. I really am a selfish wretch, and how can anyone stand to be within three feet of me?*"

I don't remember what anyone said or did while I sat there crying and shaking. But when I had calmed down enough, I asked timidly through my snot, "Is there any chance you could take a picture of John doing that to me? Because that's why I set up and paid for this intensive. I was hoping John might see how he is hurting me for a change, and maybe even want to stop. But instead, this is getting all turned around again, and we are examining how *my* very existence is somehow victimizing *John*. I don't think I can keep doing this if you are going to enable John to continue to deny, minimize, and justify how he hurts me."

I was scared to cross this professional counselor, but if there was any time to speak up, this was it. The Miracle would require me to speak about my experience no matter what. The counselor agreed, and we set the scene up again, with John putting his hands around my neck. The counselor snapped the picture, everyone looked at it briefly without any comment, and then we moved on to the next exercise.

I got the message loud and clear. What John did to me was irrelevant; in fact, it would always be twisted to become my responsibility somehow. If I chose to react, that reaction would be the new focus and the reason why John mistreated me in the first place. It would always and forever come back to me because, in this religious culture, it was always the woman's fault. All the way back to Eve.

I shut down and don't remember much of anything after that. I do remember going into a workout room where the counselor told me to pretend a punching bag was first John and then my mother, and I should say whatever I wanted to it while punching it. I said I didn't want to punch it, and I had nothing to say to a punching bag. I didn't want to pretend it was my mother, my husband, or anyone other than what it was. He insisted I had to do this. It was part of the transformation process. I still wanted the Miracle, although I was pretty sure by now this was another dead end. But just in case, I cooperated by pretending to be angry at the punching bag so the counselor would think I had obeyed him and would make the exercise stop. Then we went back for more prayer and speaking in tongues. I pretended I was okay with all of it, but every cell in my body was aching to get away. "*This is going to change your marriage! You can do it! This is the Miracle you've been waiting for! It will be worth it! Just wait and see!*" Those are the thoughts that made me stay.

Thanks a lot, Rosie.

There was one incredibly healing thing that happened there, though. I shared a haunting dream I had a few years prior to this, and I told the counselor how I could not seem to shake the feeling of foreboding and terror it still evoked in me whenever the memory of it skirted across my mind. In the dream, my own family had lured me to an empty football stadium with the promise of a birthday surprise. But when I got there, everyone I had ever known had gathered together to stone me to death. I had always suspected that I was unworthy of life, and the dream confirmed that I deserved to die.

The counselor had me close my eyes and retell the dream in as much detail as possible, only this time he told me to look for Jesus in the dream. To my surprise, it was not hard for me to find Jesus. When I got to the part where everyone started laughing and throwing rocks at me, the entire stadium melted away and quieted. I stood in a wide-open field, and Jesus was there, smiling at me with kindness, compassion, and total love. He wasn't loving me because He had to. He was loving me because somehow, in that moment, I was lovable.

I was never again haunted by that dream. I could recall it without any emotion other than gratefulness that Jesus had me no matter what. In this world, I could be hated and killed, but in the Real World, I was loved and held. Always. I'm not super woo-woo. My mom inoculated me with her scorn for anything emotional, and I'm not sure if that's a plus or not, but I do know beyond a shadow of a doubt that God gave that dream to me and even used a narcissistic counselor to prepare me for what was around the corner.

The week after the intensive was over, the counselor requested that we write a review about the outcome of our marriage intensive. John had been in a good mood and on his best behavior that week, and I was invested in believing the Miracle had occurred because the alternative was unthinkable. I wrote a glowing review and pressed the *send* button.

I should have waited three more weeks.

52

Detach

I had checked off all the boxes, some of them numerous times. The Marriage Intensive Miracle had failed, and I felt betrayed by John, the counselor, and God. I was beginning to expect betrayal from people—*but God?* I had trusted that He provided that money to do the intensive for a reason, and that reason was to *do a Miracle, dammit.* But just a few weeks later, John was worse than ever, and I finally admitted to believing several destructive lies.

I believed I needed to choose my husband's taste over mine. I believed things were bad between us when I wasn't being submissive enough, and being submissive meant not holding a different opinion or thought from John's. I believed I was responsible to keep the peace at all costs. I believed giving my husband feedback for any reason was disrespectful. I believed I needed to protect my husband's reputation. I believed he would be kind to me if I were a better wife and mother. I believed those in authority over me were always right, and when I thought they might be wrong, I was wrong about that. I believed if my relationship with John or my mother or anyone else was bad, then my relationship with God was also bad. Because I had believed these lies my entire life, I felt confused, unable to make decisions, and fundamentally flawed. I pretended, placated, tried harder, blamed myself, and asked for help repeatedly to no avail.

Just recognizing the *lies* began to unhook me from them, and interestingly enough, my older kids woke me up and gave me insight to see that this was not about me. They were experiencing the same dynamic with their dad, and while their relationship with John was different in that they weren't married to him, the same patterns were all there. After talking to them, I experienced a desperate hope that maybe I wasn't crazy. Maybe I was just living in a crazy, abnormal relationship dynamic. Okay, what next? I tried everything, and John remained unchanged. I could see this finally, but what was I supposed to do about it?

Around this time, I read *Who's Pushing Your Buttons*. For the first time, I read something that perfectly described my twenty-one-year experience with John. I could hardly believe what I had been experiencing was actually a real thing—real enough that two men, John Cloud and Henry Townsend, actually wrote an entire book all about it. Because this book gave me words to describe my life, I decided to write a letter using those words to explain our marriage dynamic to the men in John's accountability group from church. I hopefully thought, "*What is an accountability group for if not to hold one another accountable?*"

Using several quotes from the book to describe the situation, I explained the repetitive cycle of behavior, which I would later find out had a name: the Abuse Cycle. I wrote about how the older kids had come to me with their own pain over the same issues they were having with their dad, and how we had tried to talk to John only to be ridiculed and accused of ganging up on him. I shamefully admitted to blowing up in anger as well as resorting to other ineffective strategies for dealing with this problem, and I admitted I was at the end of my rope. My kids and I needed help and support. I was quite literally begging them. If I could have thrown dirt on my face and hair and groveled in the mud at their feet, I would have.

Glorifying God was constantly at the forefront of my mind, and I was still trying to figure out how I could glorify God with a marriage that sucked. Looking back, I was terrified that if I didn't glorify God, He would abandon me, like everyone else had. If I got it wrong with all the people in my life, I could survive. **But I could not get it wrong with God.** God was Everything.

One of the men who received this letter was Conner, John's best friend. He told me he didn't plan to read the letter, and that while he was all for people confessing their own sins, he found it "very disrespectful" for me to talk about John's sins. His wife, Betsy (the same Betsy whom John used to date), wrote to me that I needed to obey Ephesians 5:33, "*And let the wife see that she respects her husband.*" I was devastated and filled with shame.

Once I could see his accountability group was not interested in our reality, I decided to make things feel more real to John. I told him that unless he changed his behavior, I would not sexually service him. He rarely slept in our bed anyway, so nothing really changed except that he garnered some sympathy for himself by telling the elders at church his wife was no longer giving him sex. Since the marriage intensive, he had been regularly meeting with George and Pastor Don. I had tried to get a meeting myself with Pastor Don, but he wouldn't return my calls or emails to set up an appointment with me. John, on the other hand, got all the appointments with Pastor Don that he wanted, and George and Don seemed pleased as punch with John's self-reported progress. I found out the next year Pastor Don even referred John to an attorney so John could protect himself from "his wife's abuse allegations."

One night after a busy day homeschooling a bunch of kids and running a business, I had already fallen asleep when John came into the room and *woke me up* to apologize for something. I suspected George or Pastor Don had instructed him to practice saying he was sorry, but I wasn't sure if he was sincere or not, since he picked such an inappropriate time to decide to be sorry and was also unable to articulate exactly what he had done in the first place. I sleepily asked him a couple of questions to see if he knew what he did, but he loudly interrupted me and began listing my faults. I was bone-tired and just wanted to go back to sleep, so I asked him to please leave. He ranted for a while longer while I quietly waited for him to be done, and then he finally left muttering under his breath about how hopelessly ridiculous and impossible I was.

After being in a sour mood for a couple of days, he went to talk with George and came home almost jubilant. I remember thinking that George must have stroked his ego that morning. He was in a fantastic mood all day, and then again, late at night after I was asleep, he came into my room and crawled into bed with me. I woke up, startled, and I said, "You can't sleep in here. You haven't acknowledged anything or made anything right."

"But you said you forgave me," he scowled.

"Yes," I replied nervously, "I do forgive you. But that doesn't mean you've repented."

He got out of the bed yelling, "You're just judging me as usual! Nothing I do is good enough for you. Wives should not be kicking their husbands out of the marriage bed. You have no right. This isn't over. You will explain this to me another time."

I said, "I will try to explain things again, as I have numerous times in the past, but if you continue to refuse to hear what I'm saying, then nothing will be solved."

"How long is this going to go on?" he barked.

"That's entirely up to you," I said. I was shaking, but I felt in control of my thoughts and my responses for a change, and it felt good.

Historically, I was the one who initiated spending time with him on our birthdays and anniversaries—the only times he would agree to going out with me alone. I initiated conversations about important things for our kids and our relationship. I initiated attempts to solve any problems we were having. But I decided I wasn't going to initiate anything anymore. I had a sneaking suspicion that if I didn't push this dead jalopy of a marriage forward, it would just sit by the side of the road and rot.

And that's exactly what happened.

53

The Table

In 2013, Leslie Vernick's *The Emotionally Destructive Marriage* was published, and I eagerly devoured it like a starving dog, not once, but multiple times. This was the second book that described my situation with accurate precision. The big difference was that this book called my experience by its real name: *emotional abuse*. I hired Leslie to coach me for six months, and she introduced me to boundaries, growing up and making my own adult choices, not taking responsibility for the emotions of other adults, and learning how to tolerate the disapproval of other human beings.

Right around this time our family needed a new dining table. I had been dreaming of a large Amish-built table to accommodate our large family, but John found a giant, ugly floor model on clearance at Home Depot that he thought would do the trick, and I let go of my Amish table dream. I was good at letting go of dreams.

Then, that fall, our daughter's piano teacher purchased a new table, and I had never seen anything like it. It was an artisan-created piece built with repurposed, distressed wood, and it came with a beautiful long bench that looked like a church pew. This was the mother table of all the world's tables, and I could picture my family around it for the next forty years. I wanted it. I wanted it *bad*.

My soap business made enough profit throughout the year to pay for all the things our children needed related to home education, clothing, music lessons, swimming lessons, camp, Christmas and birthday gifts, and so on. At the end of the year, I put whatever profit was left into a joint account. Once the money was in that joint account, I was not allowed to use it without permission, other than paying for groceries. I felt good about contributing to our family economy and being able to enrich the life experiences of our children. I never purchased anything nice for myself. I went without a chiropractor for my bad back. I went without nice clothes. I went without quality makeup or hair products or new bras or nice underwear. I didn't think I deserved those things, and I was still longing for John to approve of my thrifty spending behaviors.

But then, I really wanted something, and this table wasn't just for me. It was for our family and our future. This table represented something important to me. I wanted to ask John if I could buy it, but I was scared he would say no. I talked to Leslie about my fears, and she asked me, "Are you an adult?" Yes. "Do you have the money?" Yes. We talked about how it was respectful to talk over large purchases with my spouse, but I also didn't need to ask his permission as if he was my daddy and I was a child. So, I finally got up the courage to ask John *as an equal*. I wrote it out in a letter so I wouldn't stutter over my words, which I often did when I had to approach him about something. Predictably, he did not respond, and I bought the table. He made negative comments about it whenever he could. I tolerated his disapproval and did not pressure myself to manage his emotions.

To this day, that table has brought my family tremendous joy. Everyone who sees it remarks on its beauty and functionality, but more importantly, it represents a mile-marker in my own liberation. It's another wink from God. This experience stretched me beyond my comfort zone and ultimately was a pivotal turning point in my life. For the first time, I could see that I was in a cage, yes.

But the door was always wide open.

54
A Little Note from Rosie

I know things were hard for me, and the story is about to get even more crazy, but before we get there, I want to make sure people know about the good stuff, too. Because there was so much to love about my life, even during the darkest moments. On September 24, 2013, I started a Spotify playlist that would encourage me when I was feeling sad. I included songs like "Hurricane" by Natalie Grant, "Need You Now" by Plumb, "Healing Begins" by Tenth Avenue North, and "Oceans" by Hillsong United. I kept adding to my playlist, and over the years I started listening to music other than Christian contemporary music. I added songs like "Stronger" by Kelly Clarkson, "Human" by Christina Perri, "Rise" by Katy Perry, and "Brave" by Sara Bareilles. Music kept me going. Music kept me sane. Once again, I made the delightful discovery that God can be found everywhere, even in secular music.

I also kept a gratitude journal, and I'd like to share a few entries.

- *Watching my teenage son holding his baby brother and thinking about how pudgy baby legs grow up to be hairy teenage boy legs.*

- *Tiny white baby teeth peeking through pink gums, six little buds, all in a row.*

- *Driving on rolling country roads with wide open spaces that make me want to fly.*

- *My son's dimpled smile and eyebrow tricks as he sits across from me at Panda Express.*

- *My toddler's cute growl.*

- *Middle of the night feedings with my last precious infant.*

- *Four big kids driving to Target ALONE with their oldest brother who just got his license!*

- *Nachos with my daughter.*

- *The sound of baby hiccups in the monitor.*

- *Little girls in ballet outfits and braids.*

- *Reading to kids in jammies.*

- *Four boys ages two to nineteen sitting on the couch in a row together watching a movie. Does the two-year-old know how lucky he is to have those big brothers around him? Do those big boys know how lucky they are to have an adorable two-year-old next to them?*

- *Watching my four-year-old daughter eat an entire Costco hotdog in five minutes.*

- *Birds singing in my kitchen.*

- *Begging God for mercy on the bathroom floor, and then opening my Bible to Psalm 116.*

I loved being a mother. Yes, each child had their own personality quirks and challenges, but when I thought about my family in general, all I felt was love and gratefulness for every single one of them. I could hardly believe God gave them all to me, and I often thought I did not deserve such a generous outpouring.

I didn't just birth children, though. One of the projects I worked on during that time, on top of homeschooling and running a soap business, was a book called *Three Decades of Fertility*, the story of ten women who gave their fertility to God and had children in their twenties, thirties, and forties. Several of these women were contributing writers for my blog, Visionary Womanhood, and their stories were, I believed, powerful testimonies of what God could do if women would trust Him with their bodies and choices. Many of those women would later divorce their emotionally and spiritually abusive husbands. But we couldn't see in our desperate bids for God's love and approval how we were indoctrinated to believe we were selfish and had no common sense of our own unless we followed and obeyed our foolish husbands. This was the pond we swam in, and we didn't know what we didn't know.

But just as our children grew up to shed their toxic bonds and beliefs, so their mothers woke up as well, in some cases, traveling together with our children away from all the right answers *about* God and toward the mysteries of what it meant to deeply *know* God, personally. And in other cases, the children traveled to darker places where we could not follow, and our hearts shattered in a million pieces. In all cases, regardless of how we were treated, our love for our families was a powerful force. That force continues today to bring not only the deepest agonies but also the highest joys. And this is what I choose to think about.

Because love feels good.

xoxo,

Rosie

55
Flying Free

In April 2014, I started meeting with some other women from church who were also experiencing chronic pain and confusion in their marriages. These were all women I had known for many years, three of them for over two decades. We had been together through the births of our babies, and then we watched those babies grow up. At this time, we met to go through a study called *The Ultimate Journey*, and as part of this study, we completed some powerful journaling exercises.

In one exercise we wrote letters to our younger selves to discover how we felt toward them.

> *Dear Little Natalie,*
>
> *I want to figure out who you were inside because all I can see is what you appear to be on the outside. You are like an ugly duckling, sort of gawky with weird hair and ugly glasses. The kids don't like you because you don't fit in, but I'm not sure why. You don't look like them or act like them. You act bossy but you are also shy. It's weird. You aren't cute and funny like your little sisters, and you are naughty, too. Why can't you stop that? Your mother would be happier if you didn't argue so much. You ruin everything. You could have friends and dance and sing if you were a little better, but you always manage to fall short somehow. What is wrong with you? Why do you bawl so loudly and act so selfishly? Why do you get so angry? You're totally stupid, and*

everyone is embarrassed by you. Why can't you be a peacemaker like Marcy or funny like Alice? Why is your hair so weird, and why are your clothes so ugly? You act like a total dingbat. Just calm down and grow up. Be mature. You will never amount to much because you will always get in your own way. You've ruined my life, and I knew you would. I just knew it.

Just writing that down and reading it again hits me hard because I don't have those thoughts or feelings toward that precious little girl anymore. Since that time, I have learned to adore that child, and she is finally safe inside me. But in 2014, when I wrote my first letter to her, I felt nothing but disgust.

Next, we were supposed to use our opposite hand and write a letter back from that little person. This is what little Natalie wrote to me in her big, scrawling handwriting:

Dear Big Natalie,

I am sorry. I try to be good. I am scared nobody likes me or ever will. I try but I am always wrong. I don't want you to be mad, and I will get as good as I can so you will be okay.

I can't read those words without weeping. I had been spending all these years colluding with others in my life to hate and criticize this child, but she was just a scared, lonely, sad little thing. Not the big, bad, ugly person I had always been led to believe she was.

I had grief work to do. A lot of it. I had been distracting myself with my business, writing, having babies, and homeschooling, but under all that busyness I was in excruciating pain. I also learned that everyone needs an adult ally (there's that empathetic witness!), and when I examined my past and present, I discovered that I did not have one. Well, I had Leslie and a pastoral counselor, but I had to pay them. Did that count? When I think of my childhood as well as my marriage, I was not heard, seen, or understood, and those years made up the bulk of my existence. All of that felt normal to me. It wasn't.

As my friends and I worked our way through the *Ultimate Journey* study, we wrote letters back and forth, to and from our infant self, our toddler self, our grade school self, our middle school self, our high school self, our college self, our young adult self, and our mid-life adult self. We shared our letters with one another in the group, providing that empathetic witness we all desperately needed. Through this experience, I was able to enter into curiosity and compassion for this person who lived in my body in all her stages of development. I was able to connect with her and begin to feel a powerful love for her. I began to see my sacred responsibility to have her back and never let her down if I could help it, and I had the power to do so. I became the adult ally Little Natalie needed, and when I did this, she began to blossom.

One of the journal questions was "What is the difference between a gardener and a critic?" I wrote (and likely learned this from the book): "A critic sees no potential and has no respect for the seed. A critic cannot accept reality. A critic wants everything now. But a gardener sees the future and with wisdom understands what it will take to help the seed grow."

I was a critic. I judged my family of origin, my husband, my children who were struggling and making poor choices, and most of all, I judged myself. I wanted all of the above to change. There was a right and a wrong, dammit, and I wanted everything to be right. I could not accept the truth of where these people were in their own capacity to see, understand, and love. And I could not accept the truth that I had not, so far, ever found wholeness within myself. I had beat on everyone else's door, hoping for their crumbs of love to fill my empty belly, but I had not yet seen that a fountain of unstoppable love was already inside of me. I could see, in a fuzzy sort of way at this point, that I could let go of everyone else at any time, but this truth would come in and out of focus for a while.

One of the last exercises we did that year was to write goodbye letters.

Goodbye to My Old Belief System

On this day, I choose to say goodbye to my belief that I am not worth loving, that I deserve to be mistreated, that I must ignore my own needs and person in order to cater to the demands of others. I say goodbye to the children in grade school and junior high who mocked me and told me I was ugly and stupid. I say goodbye to the fear of being alone and unloved. I say goodbye to perfectionism and the need to be noticed and validated. I say goodbye to the values that tell me I'm not enough. I say goodbye to being a doormat and someone who covers up sin. I say goodbye to expecting others to be like me, agree with me, and to love me. I am totally loved by Christ, and I am never alone. Goodbye to my old belief system. It is time for me to fly free.

Goodbye to John

I loved the boy I thought you were. I had so many hopes for you. I wanted to be the wind beneath your wings, and I believed you would find those wings and soar high one day. But now I am saying goodbye. You didn't want to fly. You seemed content to stay on the ground and kick me around. You didn't want a mutually loving and respectful adult relationship. You only served yourself. I was angry and hurt, but now I'm ready to fly on my own, without you. I can't help you, and now I see that is not my responsibility. But I can help myself, and that is 100 percent my responsibility. I wish we could have done it together, but I will no longer try to force you to do what you do not want to do. Goodbye, John. I will think of you and pray you find the love of Jesus within yourself one day. I will try to remember the times you were kind—the glimpses of what could have been. I learned so much because of my time with you. I found out who I am and who I do not want to be. I found out I am strong and not stuck just because you are. I found out God can open doors and set captives free. I found out you have no power. It was only in my head. Goodbye, John. It is time for me to fly. My True Love is waiting and has been with me all this time. I belong to Him now. It is time for me to fly free.

Goodbye to My Mother

I wanted so badly for you to love me not because I was your daughter, but because you enjoyed hanging out with me just for who I was. I worshipped the ground you walked on and craved to be with you and feel that you were proud of me. I'm sorry you felt everything had to be perfect in order for you to feel happy and safe. There are so many things I have loved about you. Your face, your voice, your generosity, your passion for what you believe in, your devotion to your daughters, your devotion to God. You didn't always see my pain, but I was selfish, too, and I didn't always see yours. When I did, I was at a loss as to how to reach you. You have always been so far away, even when you are close. Goodbye, Mom. Goodbye to the beautiful friendship I always dreamed of having with you. I will always love and admire you. You are a force to be reckoned with, and I know you love God with all your heart. That is something you passed on to me. Goodbye now. It is time for me to fly free.

Goodbye to Past Loves, Potential Mates, and My Dream of a Life Partner

Goodbye to any residual musings of "what ifs." You all had problems. Some worse than John's. None of you really saw me or loved me. You all had your own agendas, and so did I. I never saw or knew you, either. I only wanted to use you, too. I needed someone to satisfy my craving for love and affection. You were all figments of my romantic imagination placed in boxes on display. When you crawled out and presented yourselves in truth, I wanted nothing to do with your reality, nor you with mine.

Goodbye, childhood dreams of knowing and being known. Of growing old with a kindred spirit. Of sharing simple pleasures like a fire, a walk, a book, a verse, a hug. Goodbye, dream of problem-solving together with someone else. Of partnering, collaborating, being better together than apart. Goodbye, dream of making someone happy and being happy in someone else's arms. Of being in a safe, healthy relationship with another adult.

Goodbye, dream of a healthy family of wholeness and blessing. Of walking in unity and peace. Of enjoying the blessings of old age together. Of reaping a bountiful harvest after sowing so many seeds hot day after hot day.

Goodbye to a reputation of honor and respect.

Goodbye to all the things I wanted my whole life. I'm saying goodbye.

It is time for me to fly free.

56
A Record of Wrongs

Covert emotional and spiritual abuse is subtle and hard to pin down unless you know what to look for, and if you're purposefully choosing to ignore it, overlook it, or cover it up, then it's even more difficult to identify. I kept journals, but the Bible verse, "Love keeps no record of wrongs," kept me from writing out specific incidents in my marriage, and after the rare times I did, I ripped out the pages in shame within a couple of days.

I was still meeting with Leslie Vernick, and she encouraged me to begin writing down details so I could start seeing John's patterns of behavior as well as my own. What kinds of things did he do on a regular basis, and in what ways did I typically react? I could not change what he did, but if I knew in advance what his tactics were, I could learn to notice and anticipate them instead of being perpetually thrown off balance. Here were some things that happened when I was in the process of waking up and recognizing patterns:

PATTERN 1

John was going to Walmart, about a two-mile drive from our home, and he asked the little kids if they wanted to go with him. Our eight-year-old daughter, the one who was volatile, had her pajamas on, and he told her she could not go.

Trying to solve the problem, I told her, "Honey, quick, go put on your clothes if you want to go!"

A Record of Wrongs

John still insisted she could not go. He wanted to take our small car, and this meant she would have to ride in the front, but she wasn't tall enough for that. So, I tried to solve *that* problem: "Why not take the van?"

"It's too dangerous," he said, offering his third reason he couldn't take her.

So, I solved *that*. I told John I had just driven the girls home from ballet in the van, and while it was slippery in spots, if you drove slowly, it was fine. "It's two miles to Walmart. You were fine with me driving the kids to church last Sunday in the van on a horrible slippery morning, and that's a long drive. Help me understand why you can't drive two miles to Walmart?"

He had no more reasons not to take her, but he stubbornly said, "No." Our daughter had just come down from getting dressed, and she started to wail, saying, "I just got dressed! I can't go now?"

Rude said, "I guess not. If you go, that means Dad will have to take the van, and you all might die on your way to Walmart, and we can't have that, can we?"

John hated Rude. He shouted, "Why do you always have to make a big deal out of everything?" And turning to the kids, he barked, "Everyone! Get in the van!"

After they left, our oldest son said, "Mom, he didn't want to take all the kids. That was the real issue."

"Why doesn't he just say that, then?" I replied. "I can understand that. He doesn't have to take everyone."

My son said, "He can't admit that. It makes him feel like the bad guy. The way he did it makes *you* look like the bad guy."

Pattern 2

One night John was making a fruit smoothie without putting the blender lid on. He had destroyed the blender tamper a few months prior because he refused to use the protective lid, and I had to buy a new one. Seeing that he was risking the ruin of yet another tamper, our older daughter said, "Dad, don't forget to put the lid on." He did not answer her, and he did not put the lid on. Then he reached for the tamper.

"You need to put the lid on if you are going to use the tamper, so you don't accidentally break the tamper again," I tried to remind him.

He barked, "Why do you have to be so negative?"

There was no good answer for this. If I said, "I'm not being negative," he'd just say, "Yes, you are," and we'd be off to the races. I tried another approach. What if I just leaned into what I knew he believed about me? Rude surfaced again: "Because I'm a bad wife?"

Our daughter jumped to explain, in case he forgot, "Dad, it's because you broke the tamper earlier this year, and she doesn't want you to do it again."

Frustrated that she was now involved in this impossible conversation, I muttered under my breath, "He doesn't care."

John snarled, "Do you think I'm dumb? You're constantly complaining. What is your problem? Why are you on me all the time? I would never harp on you!"

I decided to commit to my prior approach and said, "Because I'm a rotten wife. You, on the other hand, are a wonderful man. That's why you never do anything bad like I do. I can't imagine why you married me. You got the raw end of the deal. I, on the other hand, got God's gift to women when I married you. Lucky me."

John retorted, "You are constantly coming down on me! I would never do that to you!"

It was hopeless. I walked away at that point, but not after realizing I was still taking the bait.

Pattern 3

One day I sent John an email regarding two women's events I wanted to attend. I would sometimes send an email so my requests would be in writing, and he couldn't gaslight me by coming back and saying, "You never told me about that," which he often did. Predictably, he never responded to the email, which was another thing he often did, so I asked him about it a couple days later. He gave a vague answer about how he didn't know his schedule for those two Saturdays off the top of his head.

Our older daughter sensibly suggested, "Check your schedule then."

He said in a helpless tone, "We no longer have a family calendar to check, so how can I know?"

We did have a family calendar, but it wasn't the kind he liked, so he refused to use it. I said, "Check your own calendar then. The family one is clear."

He scowled and whined, "Can't I play with my three-year-old son?" He had been half-heartedly engaging with that child for a brief moment, so he used that to get off topic.

I said, "Of course you can. You could also say, 'Natalie, I'm enjoying some time with our son, but I know this is important to you to have an answer soon. Let me check my schedule and give you an answer in ten minutes.'"

He got angry at such a logical solution and made some disparaging remarks about my impertinence.

When he was finished with his rant, I said, "This is why we have the kind of relationship we have, and we are unable to move forward."

He angrily retorted, "Yes! And it's all because of YOU!"

Indeed.

Pattern 4

One of the areas in my life I wanted to improve was the way I dressed. Because I was afraid to spend money on myself, Leslie encouraged me to learn about what I liked, what I felt good in, and how to take care of myself by investing some resources to gain more experience in this area. I hired a Christian image consultant, Jill Swanson, to come to my home and teach me what kinds of clothing styles would look good on my body shape, as well as what kinds of colors looked best with my skin tone, eyes, and hair.

She looked at my closet full of the same three depressing colors that reflected how I felt about myself but didn't actually complement me in any way, and then she took me shopping. Toward the end of my day with her, John called me. I had left our oldest daughter in charge of the kids, so when John came home, he discovered I was gone without asking his permission. He demanded to know where I was, so I nervously told him I was with an image consultant, and we were shopping. He angrily hung up the phone on me before I could finish explaining.

This situation reminded me of a similar time when my mom took my sisters and me to the Mall of America in 2008 and gave each of us $1,000 to spend on ourselves. I was stunned by that kind of money and felt guilty spending it on myself, but my mom, who was always very generous, insisted. I made sure I kept it practical, and I purchased a winter coat and a pair of boots I needed along with some things we needed for the house. When I got home that night, John wanted to know what we did all day, so I braced myself for his reaction and told him. He demanded to know why I had not kept the money to put in the joint account he controlled. I told him my mom insisted that we spend it on ourselves, and I only used it for practical things I needed. He was not satisfied. He said my mom's behavior was a foolish waste, and I slunk up to our bedroom ashamed and sad. But I realized at that moment *it wasn't about the money* because I wasn't spending any of his money, and my mom's gift to me was none of his business. This, for him, was about my being happy. My having something nice. My having a lovely experience. *My happiness caused his unhappiness and was, therefore, unacceptable.*

The day I wrote this story down, I realized that we were still in the exact same place several years later. Nothing had changed. That night he demanded that I put him on my business bank account, so he could monitor my business spending for *my* business that I ran, built, and supported on my own. My answer was, "*Hell to the no*." In fact, I never again put money in our joint account, either. I got the silent treatment for a while after that, but now, I welcomed the silence.

Pattern 5

One night I overheard John trying to fix a bandage on our five-year-old daughter's finger. It had been injured, and she had to wear a splint with a bandage until it healed. She was crying and saying, "Daddy, you are hurting my bump! Stop pushing on my bump!"

John barked, "That did *not hurt*! Stop crying!"

This particular child had always been a kind, patient, sweet-natured little girl, and she rarely complained about anything, so I was alarmed at her ongoing outcries and his dogged insistence that she should not be allowed to express pain or cry about what he was doing. This wasn't new behavior for him. He would often hurt the kids while joking or having fun, and if they cried or asked him to stop, he would get angry and insist he didn't hurt them, accusing them of overreacting. Then he would do it again to "prove" that it couldn't possibly hurt. It was habitual bullying behavior that caused physical and emotional suffering in our family. This particular time he was not doing it to have fun, yet it was similar in that he denied her pain and made her out to be the liar.

I intervened at that point and asked what was going on. He attempted to make it seem like he, the bully, was being patient and sweet, and she, the essence of sweetness itself, was overreacting and uncooperative. I told him I heard exactly what was going on, and he was hurting her. He insisted that wasn't true, so now both his wife *and* daughter were being hysterical and making things up in their heads. At that point our daughter cried out, "*Yes!* He is hurting my bump!"

I took her away and fixed her bandage in twenty seconds with no pain involved. Later, I went in to explain to John why what he did was so hurtful to his daughter. He got angry and accused me of judging him and making false assumptions. I told him I was sick of his behavior, and I was going to start reporting his behavior toward the kids to the church elders. I knew they believed a wife should just suck it up, but *children?* Maybe they would care about the kids. He said in a mocking tone, "Oh, you're going to tattle on me to George every time?"

George was John's biggest and most sympathetic fan at this point, and he and his wife didn't like that Leslie was coaching me. George's wife had gone over to Leslie Vernick's website and read some of the comments left there by abuse victims, and she didn't like them. She insisted they were all "keeping a record of wrongs" instead of submitting properly, as godly women ought to, so she wrote me an email warning me of the danger I was in by putting myself under the influence of someone like Leslie. I tried to explain that Leslie's website was designed to reach out to those who were not getting the support and help they so desperately needed from their local churches, and, therefore, the comments on her blog would naturally reflect that pain and brokenness. But George's wife continued to add to my growing collection of Christian emails lecturing and condemning me with flowery rhetoric, Bible verses, and Christian clichés.

From that day forward, the possibility of divorce danced around the edges of my mind. I believed that divorce would not only mean losing my marriage, but losing everything I loved, including God. But as far as I could tell, I was losing everything anyway.

57

Goo

I struggle not to look at my former self and say, "Ew." When I feel this way toward her, I know it is not God's image in me looking at her. It is another part of me that feels morbidly triumphant whenever it uncovers something disgusting.

"Ew! I found another nasty thing about you! It's all good though. I'll make sure you know just exactly how gross this one is so you can avoid being like this in the future. When you're all gross like this, it disgusts everyone around you, and if they are disgusted, they won't have any room left to find something nice about you to love, and we can't have that. You might get rejected and die. Thank God, you've got me around, eh?"

And thank God I do have Miss Judgy Pants around. She means well, but she doesn't know it's okay to be a caterpillar. Caterpillars have their own beauty if you look closely enough and think about it, and so do women who just want to be loved and don't know they're a butterfly in the making.

One of the fascinating phases a butterfly goes through before she can be a butterfly is the goo phase. She encloses her caterpillar body in a chrysalis and then dissolves into a hidden packet of jelly with no form or identity. She's literally a Nothing. She doesn't know yet what she will be, but her Creator knows. And this phase is not a nothing phase. This is where all the good stuff happens. The transformation. The metamorphosis. This is her Becoming.

Don't sniff at the goo phase. This is the magic.

This next section is just goo everywhere. I didn't know it until later, but I was living with Complex-Post-Traumatic-Stress-Disorder (C-PTSD) and having all the stress responses of freezing, fighting, fleeing, and fawning at different times. During my separation from 2014–2016, I had no time to keep a journal. I scribbled a few things on my calendars, but for the most part, I was focused on surviving, parenting my kids (eight of whom were still at home), and writing emails back and forth to all the people I'm going to be introducing you to next—names changed, as I mentioned earlier.

Rude: I think you should just expose the entire lot of them. Anne Lamott says, "*You own everything that happened to you. Tell your stories. If people wanted you to write warmly about them, they should have behaved better.*"

Rosie: And Jesus says, "*Father, forgive them, for they don't know what they are doing.*"

Thank you for your input, Rude and Rosie. I'm going to tell my story, but I want the reader to know that I believe most (not all) of these people really didn't know what they were doing. We all drank the same Kool-Aid, so what could I expect? One of my core values is grace, and that means giving people the benefit of the doubt. People have to throw a lot of rocks at me before I finally walk (and sometimes run) away. But grace doesn't mean I continue to expose myself to abuse.

As you read the stories in the coming pages, I hope you'll offer everyone, including me, a little forgiveness. I didn't know what I was doing, either. I was, after all, just a little packet of goo.

58
Bible Counseling

In May of 2014, I wrote in my journal:

> *I have been a child my whole life, and I need to grow up. I'm afraid to walk away from people who drag me back to being a child because they are the god-figures in my life. If I rebel against them, I am rebelling against God Himself, and then He won't be with me. See the twisted thinking? Wanting God has kept me playing this child role, but that isn't what God requires or wants, is it? What if I can have all of God and none of the controlling people in my life who would hold me down and wipe me out so they can feel better about their own brokenness?* **If only**. *I've been fighting and clawing to be an adult. It's time to stop. I don't need anyone's approval. God is calling me to freedom and adulthood.*

I was starting to get it, but I still had a couple more years of banging for help on human doors just to make double, triple, quadruple sure God wasn't there.

That summer, I heard about a female member of our church, Carla, who was getting her nouthetic counseling certificate and looking for people to clobber, er—help. I decided to see if she could help me. Nouthetic counselors are trained in a method of counseling that teaches all of the answers to life's problems can be found in the Bible alone, so Carla informed me right up front that she would not be able to offer me her wisdom or support if I was thinking of a divorce. The Bible was clear that divorce was sin, and God hated it. At that point, I should have run, but instead I assured her that divorce was off the table, and I only wanted help dealing with my own sinful reactions to the things my husband was doing and saying. I knew she would like that answer, and she did. I was accepted.

After a couple of sessions, it became apparent she didn't believe I was being abused. She told me that abuse was a "strong word to use," implying that it was *too* strong in my case. She said she had a great deal of experience with "real abuse" that involved physical injuries, implying that my experiences were petty by comparison.

I had emailed some things to my husband, and in an effort to be transparent, I copied both Carla and Pastor Don, who was helping John, so they could monitor our conversation and offer their feedback. These emails between John and me disclosed ongoing behaviors that hurt me, and although I tried to be objective, I let some of my deep frustration of over two decades peek through.

Carla told me in our next meeting that I was rude to my husband in one of the email exchanges, and it shocked her. (*What? She didn't like my Rude?*) I asked her what, specifically, was so shocking, and she gave me an example where I had been sarcastic. Tail between my legs, my Melancholy part woefully admitted that I should have left that one sarcastic comment out of my email to John. *Bad girl.* Interestingly enough, she did *not* express the slightest shock over the twenty-two years of criticism, silent treatment, and dehumanizing behavior my husband had put me through and was continuing to put me through right before her very eyes. She could see that John still wasn't responding to me or my efforts to communicate on a basic level, and he wasn't making any efforts to get his family back. Because it didn't seem to bother her, I began to wonder if perhaps this kind of behavior was *expected* of males in Christian homes. Maybe I really *was* the crazy one who never got the memo.

In one session she told me, "You've gone on and on about this stuff already. Can we move on to something else?" Stunned, I made a mental note to be careful about what I said to her, or she'd get annoyed and scold me like a child. If she got irritated just *talking* about John's repetitive behaviors with me, how did she think it felt to *live* with them for over two decades?

Carla gave me several homework assignments that involved looking up Bible verses and explaining what they meant and how they related to being a good Christian wife. I was pretty sure I had read four or five times the number of books and Bible studies on that subject than she had, but I dutifully completed all the assignments and turned them in on time. I felt like a child in grade school again, hoping my teacher would like me if I did everything she said.

One of the assignments she gave me was to reach out to three people who knew me well and ask them what they liked and didn't like about how I related to them. I suspected she was fishing for evidence that I was a problem child, but I cooperatively asked Marcy, my adult son, and a friend from church. Their replies were short and sweet. They said I was honest, funny, relatable, willing to admit my mistakes, a good listener, easy to talk to, and empathetic. Regarding what they did not like about me, my sister lightheartedly said she didn't always like my advice, but I was her big sister, so she expected advice now and again. My adult son said he thought the assignment was dumb. And my church friend said I was too decisive and used too many words when trying to explain things. Good to know. My kids would probably agree.

Carla also told me to ask John these same questions. John was a classic stonewaller and generally responded to less than 10 percent of anything I wrote to him, so I wasn't sure he would respond, but *lo and behold*, this time he responded in lightning-flash fashion with a lengthy email detailing the myriad ways I failed to relate well. He prefaced his answer by writing that he hoped and prayed God would communicate the truth through him "in grace." God bless his soul.

I will spare the reader *all* the negative details John believed God wanted him to communicate to the Bible counselor, but here are a few: I wasn't able to see my sin. I wasn't able to forgive my husband. I didn't trust God. I expected too much of my husband. I was disrespectful, rude, and demanding. I was also negative, controlling, and selfishly wanted attention. I *always* accused him of things he *never* did. I made assumptions about him and unfairly judged him.

Then he said he was afraid of me, and others were afraid of me as well. First, he said, was my mom. *What?* She would have scoffed if she knew. She wasn't afraid of anything or anyone, let alone dumb old me. The next one on his list was my youngest sister, Alice. I think he was confused; I was terrified of her, not the other way around. She, like Mom, was unflappable and had no problem giving me the stink eye if I so much as looked at her the wrong way. Yes. I was scared of her stink eye. The third person on his list was his favorite elder and personal fan, George. My best guess was that George thought I was "fierce" because I had a vagina, and yet words still came out of my mouth. Fourth was Pastor Luke, who had groomed me in my early twenties. *His* fear made sense; I had some things on him. I would later join a group of women to testify against him in an investigation that would force him to retire from that church, so I could see how I might be scary to Pastor Luke. And finally, John named a woman from church who believed I should homeschool, wear skirts, and not allow my daughters to go to college, and I was rebelling in all those areas. I could *maybe* see how she might be scared of me. To her I was a rebel, and maybe rebels are scary.

But honestly, I was intimidated by *her*. She seemed so perfect by our church's standards, and I was now considered an unsubmissive wife, the worst possible label for any woman to wear.

Looking back on this years later, I'm aware that any licensed therapist worth their salt would see this move on John's part as classic DARVO: Deny, Attack, and Reverse Victim and Offender. But we weren't dealing with a licensed therapist. We were dealing with a woman who was getting a certificate in Nouthetic Bible counseling, and she didn't see a damn thing. When these assignments were completed and turned in, I noticed she wouldn't comment on them. That's how I knew they were useless busywork. As her compassion for my abuser became more apparent, a familiar panic flooded me with shame and an irrational longing to disappear into the ground. I had come to her for help only to get another noose around my neck. I sent her a respectful "break up" email after a few months of going in circles.

During my time with her, Carla recommended another Bible counselor for both John and me to see together as a couple. John didn't want to do more marriage counseling, but George and Pastor Don were pressuring him to do whatever he needed to do to save the marriage, so he agreed to go if I did the work of setting up the appointment. Since I was still feeling responsible to pull the weight in our relationship, I set up the appointment, and we drove separately to meet with the new counselor. Why did I keep making the effort and trying to find a solution? I wasn't a glutton for punishment. I just wasn't giving Rude the credibility she deserved yet. Rosie and Miss Judgy Pants were still running the show, but even they were running out of steam. However, on this particular day, I brought Rude along in my back pocket, and I let her do what she wanted to do.

Right at the very beginning of the session, the Bible counselor invited John and me to share how our sin had contributed to our marriage problems. Ah, yes. I was familiar with this approach. My entire life was one anxious concern about how my sin was contributing to the entire world's demise. My Melancholy and Spiritualizer parts were wired to scour my inner world, locate my sin, and blame everything that was happening in my life on myself and my failures. Melancholy kept insisting that I deserved to suffer and die, but Rude kept raising her snarky head from my back pocket to audaciously declare, "No! I don't want to suffer and die! I want to live!"

In the past, Rosie, Melancholy, and Spiritualizer would sit in the Bible counselor's office or the pastor's office or the elder's office, and they would cooperate. They would dutifully answer the questions, always ready to throw me under the bus. Sometimes Melancholy would offer exaggerated confessions of sin, *Anne of Green Gables* style, *if only* this new person would help me and provide some relief.

But not this time. This time I put Rude in charge, and she sat stubbornly staring at the carpet, refusing to speak up. She would be as silent as John always was. This time I would let John be the first one to "confess." I wanted to see what would happen if I changed the pattern for once.

After a long silence the Bible counselor asked, "Soooo . . . who would like to go first?" More silence. He looked at me questioningly, as if John's silence was normal man stuff, but my silence indicated rebellious stubbornness the counselor was determined to root out.

Feeling uncomfortable by the counselor's silent stares, I caved a little and admitted, "I usually answer questions like this first. I've easily wallowed in my sin my entire life. I can confess to pages and pages of sin—I am so familiar with it. I'm constantly saying I'm sorry and begging for forgiveness and expecting very little in return. I made this appointment because my ability to confess my sin is not the issue in our marriage. His *inability to confess his* is the issue. So, let's start there." And I turned to look expectantly at John.

255

All the Scary Little Gods

Lest you think that I felt confident and in control, let me clarify that I did not. I was shaking like a leaf inside. My body was nauseated and dizzy. At one point the room swayed and darkened, and I thought I was going to black out. I put my head down and sucked in air. The Bible counselor asked me if I was okay, and I sheepishly told him I felt a little sick. I could hear the critical voices of John and Mom in my head saying, "*What a grandstander. Always being dramatic and making a big deal out of nothing. There is no such thing as a panic attack. People are just making that up to get attention.*" I wondered if the counselor was thinking that, too. I took some deep breaths, and my vision normalized, but my heart was still pounding.

John confessed to a couple of vague sins like "I don't always listen very well" and "Sometimes I can get upset when she is hounding me about things." The Bible counselor seemed satisfied. John had confessed. *Good boy.*

Then came my turn, but I wasn't biting. Rude pushed Freaked to the side and said, "Don't you see how general those confessions are? And half of them are about how he is a victim of his wife. He's turning this all around. I'm not doing this anymore. I'm not going to pour out confessions of how terrible I am. *I'm looking for help.* My husband chronically mistreats me, and nobody will help me!" My voice was desperate and forceful. I leaned forward and begged, "I just need someone to see what is going on here! I need someone to believe me! I need you to stop looking at me and all the reasons why I deserve to be treated like this, and I need you to address his issues!"

The counselor leaned forward, too, and his eyes narrowed on mine. "Do you want to know how I feel right now?" And he waited for an answer.

Taken aback, I meekly said, "Okay."

His eyes stared me down as he said, "I feel like running a million miles per hour in the opposite direction. You are like a buzz saw,

Natalie. I can see why your husband doesn't want to be here and why he is running in the opposite direction from you as well. Do you want to talk about this?"

But I had no control over my mouth, my body, or my brain at that point. My insides were utter chaos. White noise. There was a massive food fight on my bus of parts. Loud sobs spontaneously ripped out of my gut, and it was everything I could do to get my arms to cooperate and pick up my purse so I could stand up on my jelly legs and wobble to the door to leave.

I drove our van home in the pouring rain, and all I remember is scanning the sides of the freeway for a good place to drive the van off—a place that would guarantee I wouldn't survive. Little Natalie was howling in agony, begging me to be done. She could. Not. Do. It. Anymore. *Please, dear God, let the pain end.*

I don't know how I got home.

I found out later that John was telling people, "Natalie quit on two counselors in one year!" At that point, I decided to give it a year, pray for a miracle, and then file for divorce if nothing changed. I stopped going to our church and began visiting a different church. I also found a new "pastoral" counselor who seemed to understand my situation better. I say "seemed" to because eventually I'd have to quit on that one, too.

59
Balls

Over the course of the next two years, people who knew nothing about emotional abuse and had never experienced it themselves would ask me to explain it. This is what I'd tell them.

Let's pretend for a minute that your relationship is like a game of tennis. Can you visualize you and your partner on the tennis court? The game has just begun, and the ball is going back and forth. Back and forth.

Once in a while, the ball drops.

This represents relationship conflict. Sometimes the ball drops on your side, and sometimes it drops on the other side. When it drops on your side, you take the initiative to resolve the conflict. You pick up the ball and try again.

But when the ball falls on the other side, and you ask your partner to pick up the ball and lob it back, he responds with, "Well, it fell because of how you hit the ball. Not my problem. Not my responsibility."

Hmmmm. That's odd. Not really how you've experienced other relationships, but whatever. You want to be cooperative and make this game work, so you walk around to his side of the net *and pick up the ball for him*. Then, you go back to your position to get the ball going again because the game matters to you. The relationship is important, and you take your vows seriously.

But life happens. The ball drops again on his side of the court, and once again, he makes no move to pick it up. You make the logical point that if he doesn't pick up the ball, you won't be able to continue the game. He scowls at you and tells you it's your fault and your problem, and if you care about the game, you'd figure it out. You argue with him because this logic does not make sense. You wait longer, but he refuses to pick up the ball. So, you sadly walk over to his side and pick it up. Again. You have made a commitment for better or for worse, right? Well, this must be what "worse" means. Bummer.

And this goes on for an entire year. Two years. Five years. You pick up all the balls on your side, and you pick up all the balls on his side. You feel resentful because the entire game is up to you. The responsibility to keep the game going falls completely on your shoulders, and that's a heavy weight to bear. The books you read, your church, and your spiritual friends all tell you that if your partner won't do it, the godly thing is to *do it yourself!* You can keep your relationship alive! Don't let bitterness creep in. Do it with a cheerful heart. Let him off the hook. He's a guy, and guys are not like girls. Be okay with the differences! Get over there and *pick up the balls*! God will give you the power you need to make that man happy! Fulfilling your duty as a female will eventually be rewarded with an awesome game.

Besides, your partner is always so happy—smiling and waving at everyone who passes by. Such a friendly, sweet man. If someone outside the court needs help, he interrupts your game to help them out. He is an incredible human being with a magnanimous heart. Johnny-on-the-spot for everyone.

Then, he returns to you and requests that you get the balls going because he is oh, so very tired. Ten years. Fifteen years. Utter exhaustion sets in for you. Panic, even, as you contemplate doing this with gray hair and crispy bones. The future looks grim.

Now you are stomping around. Complaining. Frantically waving your hands. Frowning. Yelling. Your eyes are bloodshot, and your hair is a tangled rat's nest. You look and sound like hell while he looks happy and rested and helpful to everyone who passes by.

And then an idea hits you. You'll stop picking up the balls on his side of the court. Why not? Everyone already thinks you're a lunatic. Why not see what would happen if you didn't cooperate?

The first ball drops on his side. He looks at you like, "Well, aren't you going to get your tushy over here to pick up the ball?" You stare at him triumphantly, crazily, almost drunk on this strange sense of power, and you say, "NO!" He waits. Surely you are bluffing.

But you're not.

Time passes. He looks around uncomfortably and waves at people. The ball remains at his feet. Someone passes by and yells at him, "Hey! The ball is at your feet!"

He waves back. "Yup! Got it covered!" They walk away, assuming the problem is taken care of. But it's not. The ball remains quietly lying there.

You sit down on the tennis court pavement and wait. He gets an idea and goes to the back of the court where a huge bin of balls sits. He grabs a brand-new ball and lobs it at you. You aren't expecting that, and the ball drops. But at least the game is moving again, so ever (if not insanely) hopeful, you haul yourself up, grab the ball, and lob it back.

It falls. You wait.

He leaves that ball on the ground along with the other one, and he grabs a second new one from the bin and starts the game again. You play like this for another "pull-your-hair-out-in-frustration" five years until the entire court floor is covered with balls because you've decided that if he doesn't want to pick up any balls, you're not going to pick them up either.

The game grinds to a halt as you both trip and stumble around all the balls with no conflict ever resolved. Stupefyingly enough, it doesn't seem to bother him. He's fine with the ball-covered pavement as long as everyone that passes by thinks *he's amazeballs*. And they do. After all, look at his long-suffering patience in the face of utter negligence on the part of his wife. He smiles sadly, almost pathetically, and waves a friendly hand at all who pass by.

Meanwhile, you are thinking. Thinking. Thinking. Thinking about how this game never changes. Thinking about the fact that your head hurts from banging it on the same damn wall over and over and over again. Thinking about the fact that this man has never picked up a ball in twenty years, and the chances that he will pick one up now are dismally low.

You are thinking. And then you decide.

You're done. You don't want to be the one who is done. You've invested twenty years of your life picking up this guy's balls, and you really *really* want it to be worth something. But you know now that you could pick them up for the rest of your life and die an early death, or you could walk off the tennis court and find something else to do with the last remaining days of your life.

So, you do. But before you go, you stand by the fence of the court and yell at your partner, "Hey! I'm leaving now! But if you want to pick up your own balls and try again, I'm still open to coming back!"

He looks angrily at you because you talked about his balls that way, and he sullenly chokes out, "What? Look around me! I'm doing my best, but you can't possibly expect me to clean this whole thing up by myself! You made this mess too! Why should I be the one to have to clean it up?!"

You walk away.

Your spiritual friends grab you and tell you you're crazy to leave such an amazing man, and what is your freaking problem, anyway? What a *quitter*! You must not know God, and now your kids will go to hell.

So, you hesitate, worrying about these things. You look back at the court where some men are talking in hushed whispers to your partner. Suddenly, you see some movement. What? Is he going to pick up a ball? Seriously? Why, YES! HE DOES PICK UP A BALL! It's a miracle!

You stare with your mouth gaping open as he walks toward you with the ball. He's actually going to take responsibility for something! Maybe there is hope, after all! They must have convinced him that to play this game, you need to be willing to pick up some balls!

He gets to where you are standing, looks compassionately at you, and says, "See this ball here? It's a real problem. I see that now. I'd like to get rid of it, *but I'm pretty sure it's yours.*"

And that, dear friend, is how you know it's game over.

60

Separation

I had enough, but it couldn't have come at a worse time. Not that any time would be a great time to leave your marriage of twenty-two years when you still had eight kids at home. Our oldest son, who was engaged, had moved into an apartment by himself that summer, and I was planning his groom's dinner and my separation at the same time. There were a few church friends who could see that a separation was necessary, and I asked if they would come over to our home one night so I could read a letter out loud to John. I had decided a letter would be appropriate since John was good at gaslighting and saying, "You never said that." I also knew he would tell others that I said things I never said, and I still believed I had to be able to prove what I said with a written document. So, I decided to clearly spell it out, and John could do with it whatever he chose. A couple of weeks before our son's wedding, a handful of church friends gathered in our living room and listened as I read my letter to John. A song that perfectly captured my sense of hopelessness over our relationship was "Say Something" by A Great Big World.

John said nothing.

Our son's wedding was beautiful. Despite our impending separation, I intentionally focused on the celebration of the day, and it was one of the happiest of my life. When September 1 came, John packed his things and tearfully said goodbye to the kids. He told them that Mom was kicking him out, and he had to go live in our camper at a local campground. This was not true, of course. I had offered to pay for an apartment for him with my soap earnings, but he would live in the camper and tell everyone his sad story until they closed the campground for the winter, and he found an apartment. At one point, he scared some of the kids with the news that he might be moving to Wisconsin or Colorado. I confronted him about this. "Are you seriously considering moving out of state?"

He angrily responded, "Quit being snarky. I was only trying to make a point."

I said, "Asking a clarifying question is not snarky. Were you telling the kids the truth when you said you might be moving away? Or was that a lie?"

He wouldn't answer. I asked him if he realized the kids had been crying and were scared he would move away from them. I told him it wasn't a kind or thoughtful thing for a father to say unless it was true. He said, "I wasn't trying to scare them."

"Well, you did," I told him. "Were you thinking about how they might process that kind of information?"

Then he lectured me about how I was unbiblically forcing him to leave, this was against his wishes, I was refusing to work on our marriage, and I never took responsibility for anything.

When he was finished, I said, "The reason we aren't together anymore is because you've insisted on believing those lies for twenty-two years instead of working on your own side of the street."

He walked out.

John's sister and brother-in-law had come in from out of town to stay with us for the wedding. We had some time alone when John wasn't around, so I had told them John would be moving out soon and why. They were Christians, and I had a tremendous amount of respect for them, but after they left, I felt uneasy. I could tell they were skeptical about the things I shared, and I began to question the wisdom of telling them anything. Sure enough, they sent me an email exhorting me to respect and submit to my husband. They included all the applicable Bible verses to back up this view and reminded me that I should obey Matthew 18:15–16 and tell my problems to the church. They wanted me to remember that the church leaders were my authority, and I needed to obey whatever they recommended. They believed I was trying to find people who would agree with me rather than people who would actually get me back on track, beside my husband in a submissive role. The church elders in authority over me had been through trials and overcame them, so they would be the best ones to guide me toward my proper place. They added that it was wrong for me to separate myself from John. They threw in a few last Bible verses and closed by telling me they loved me very, very much.

That was the last time I ever heard from them.

61

BRAVE

The next few months passed in a blur. The balls I had been proudly juggling for so many years began falling, one by one. One of those balls was homeschooling. Our daughter was increasingly volatile, and just asking her to complete a page in a workbook would trigger a three-hour screaming session where everyone in the house would shut down and hide, so I decided to put some of the children in school. I was still afraid of the public school system, but there was a little neighborhood church school that was reasonably priced, so in the fall of 2014, I enrolled four of the kids. Three of those children loved it, including our troubled daughter, and it gave me a chance to breathe and homeschool my first-grader and take care of my two preschool kids in peace. One child hated it, so after three months I decided to homeschool him for two more years and then put him in public high school where he would ultimately thrive.

Even with three of the kids in school, I still had too many balls in the air, and my stress level was skyrocketing. John was still living in his own apartment and not taking any responsibility for the kids, their education, or their mental and emotional health. He would pick them up one night a week to go swimming at his apartment, but they were my responsibility the rest of the time. I remember doing a lot of crying as soon as I could get the kids to bed and retreat to my own room at night. One night stands out to me in my memory because it created a deep inner shift inside that changed the course of my life. I don't remember how, but I stumbled on a music video by Sara Bareilles called "Brave." I was mesmerized by all the human beings of different colors and shapes and sizes dancing with freedom and joy and love. No shame. No fear. Just being themselves. I had a visceral reaction in my body, and I shook with sobs. This was what I had been looking for my whole life. To be alive without fear and shame. To be able to dance and sing and exist in the open regardless of what human beings thought or said. I knew that this was why God created me. Not to hide in fear. Not to pretend to make the "cool kids" like me. And by "cool kids" I didn't only mean my junior high peers who bullied me. I meant the man I once lived with who despised me. The religious pastors and counselors who wouldn't see or believe me. The family members who didn't know me. Watching that video, I realized that this was how my Creator saw me. Beautiful. Free. Good. Exactly the way I was. I didn't have to hide. I desperately wanted to show up for my life in this way, and I felt my Creator stirring in me, gently waking me up.

"*Precious One, you can walk away from all of that. The door is open. You are free. Come and simply BE with Me.*"

But Religion yanked me back into the ring for another round, and once again, I turned to humans, hoping to find redemption in their sandbox. Ultimately, I did. Only not in the way I expected. Because during this round, I had decided to try something new. I was going to start saying what I wanted to say. I was going to be BRAVE.

62

My Voice

I was on my own now. I would need to grow up and rescue myself if I wanted any kind of future free from abuse, but right as I was poised to flex my wings and fly, Pastor Justin came on as the new lead pastor of our church, and he was keen on exposing and eradicating abuse. I was no longer attending church there, but someone told Pastor Justin about me and one of my friends who was also living in an emotionally abusive marriage. Pastor Justin invited us to his home to meet with him and his wife, another pastor and his wife, the chairman of the elder board and his wife, and two counselors. They seemed sincere, and while I was skeptical that they could do anything to help me, I thought it could be a good opportunity to use my voice, and maybe it would help other women who would come after me. Before we met, they asked if we would send the group a summary of how we had already tried and failed to get help through our church. They promised to read these summaries in preparation for our in-person meeting.

The meeting was a warm and welcoming gathering, and they opened by saying they believed us and were dismayed by how our husbands and our church had chronically mistreated us. We each had a chance to share more details about our story if we wanted to, but instead of talking more about my story, I grabbed the opportunity to offer some suggestions for how they could better help women in the future, based on my experience and what would have been helpful to me.

The most important thing I wanted them to understand involved the ways our church was programming men to be entitled, self-centered abusers while also programming women to be victims. I knew dozens of women who had given up their careers and died to their own desires and needs in order to serve a man and spend exhausting, sometimes physically debilitating, years bearing and raising children with "God's glory" in mind. Many of the ones in my circles also homeschooled their children, which was a draining, thankless, and unseen task in and of itself. Contrary to the picture the leaders in the church wanted to paint, many of these women were not loved, protected, listened to, appreciated, cherished, or supported by their husbands. Instead, they were blamed, shamed, verbally maligned, ignored, lied to, and burdened with the responsibility to fix everyone's "sin." These faithful women had to keep up appearances so "God's Word would not be blasphemed," and they did it believing it was how they could please God, set a good example for their children, and imitate Christ.

I wanted these leaders to notice how they were using the Bible to train survivors to cover up abuse by accusing women of "tearing down their houses" if they dared say anything about what was happening inside those four walls. They were using the Bible to gaslight victims when leaders told them to "overlook a multitude of sins," "forgive and forget," "wait patiently for God to change your husband," "esteem others higher than yourself," "submit," "never get angry," and "win your husband without a word," whenever a victim alluded to any type of marital mistreatment.

These leaders had an opportunity to recognize how women were being forced to choose between their experience of reality and "Christian" rules. This was an impossible double bind because if a Christian woman didn't obey the rules, there could be serious consequences, including excommunication. That left the woman with only one other option, which was to gaslight herself about what was happening. A Christian woman in an abusive marriage had to split herself in half: one half knowing the truth, and the other half obeying the rules in spite of the truth. Was this what Christianity was all about? Creating anxious, shame-driven gaslighters? That's what happens when we don't walk in the truth.

When I was finished, the group of church leaders and their wives reassured us that they had our backs, and they expressed appreciation for our willingness to take a risk and trust them after what we had already been through. One of the pastors made a special point of telling me that even though John had already gained several allies at church who believed him, this pastor believed *me*, and he was not going to be ashamed to say it. "If it came to people leaving the church over taking sides, I would side with you. I believe you," he reassured me. I felt like I had been on the battlefield for twenty-three years, and someone came on the field and said, "I'm taking over for you now," and then carried me off. I didn't have to fight anymore. *I was no longer alone.*

The leadership team promised to talk with John and exercise church discipline if necessary. They also flew in a professional counselor experienced with domestic abuse to do some staff training on the subject. I gave this man several documents I had written along with some of John's letters and accusations, and he read these documents and told the church elders he believed I was telling the truth. I was beginning to notice my own tendency to rely on the opinions of others regarding my own personal experience, but part of me still wanted to be validated. Around this time, I found out some members of the church were spreading negative rumors about me, and I felt pain and even panic. But I had some hope that the leaders of our church would set everything straight. The truth would come out, and I would be vindicated. It couldn't come soon enough.

63

George

I had stopped attending church prior to meeting with Pastor Justin and his team, but now I tentatively returned even though I felt uncomfortable knowing people were talking negatively about me. I still believed that going to church was part of having a healthy relationship with God. The church was the Body of Christ, and I wanted to be part of that.

Justin and his team were calling themselves DART (Domestic Abuse Response Team), and one of the first things they did was address how George had handled my case and my friend's case. George was the elder put in charge of doing marriage counseling for both couples, and after realizing that George had been duped by John's grooming, I put an end to meeting with him when I asked John to move out. However, a few months later, George reached out to me with an invitation to get more marriage counseling from him. I told him I didn't see any evidence that John was interested in relating to me in healthy, responsible ways, and until I could see that, I would decline any further marriage counseling.

George disagreed, gave me his reasons why, and then asked if I would reconsider. Again, I declined, but George persisted by sending a lengthy email accusing me of judging John, not trusting John, airing John's faults, and killing John's spirit. He said that even if John was hurting me and the children, I had no right to assume what his intentions or motives were, and that I needed to be a better communicator. Then he told me I was not a gentle woman, I was disrespectful, and I was discouraging to John. He talked about how critical women like me devastate their husbands. He threw in several Bible verses. He said he was sad to hear I could have a life without John, and that John loved me even if I was unable to believe that. He added several flowery Christian clichés like, "God grants us new mercies every day and pours out an abundance of grace on us so that we can do His will," and "God knew that we could not stand if He sent His Son into the world to condemn the world; that is why He sent Jesus in order that we may be saved," and "My prayer for you is that you would be able to extend God's grace to each other, share the steadfast love of the Lord with each other, help each other grow in the likeness of His precious Son Jesus Christ, to walk humbly with the Lord, and finally—but primarily—fear the Lord and delight in His ways."

There were many things I found wrong about his email, not the least of which was how a person could shred another person to pieces while simultaneously quoting Scripture. I decided to respond with an email carefully addressing the items he brought up one by one, and I concluded with this:

> *I don't think it is unreasonable for me to ask that John show a change of heart in some small ways, consistently, before we enter back into mutual counseling. I think he needs to figure out why he gives up so easily if he truly wants to love me or have a better marriage or be a better dad. When he can show me that it is not just talk, but walk, then I would be willing to work on rebuilding our relationship. What I'm not willing to do is push, prod, or plead anymore. He has to want to and then actually start to do it. A good starting place would be for him to go back to the emails I've sent over the past two months and answer them.*

George could not take "no" for an answer. He sent yet another letter saying he did not want to email back and forth because "it is not a good way to communicate," and then he proceeded to extensively argue every single one of my points, badgering me further about how terribly I was treating poor John. He closed by asking me to read the scriptures he sent, meditate on them, and get back to him with my thoughts about them.

I sent one last email attempting to explain where I was coming from:

> *George, I don't feel like you've heard anything I've tried to say for the past six months. I am trying to put the pieces of my life back together after my final, failed attempts to connect with John, and all I'm hearing is how broken and paralyzed John is and how it is somehow my responsibility to put him together again. Do you honestly think that is what God is requiring?* ***Or is this what you are requiring?*** *I'm also feeling that you somehow think it is a negative thing for me to move forward. I know that I don't have to buckle under those kinds of messages because God says differently; nevertheless, they feel hurtful, as if you want John's happiness but not mine or the children's. Restoration and work come after repentance, not before. And please do not tell me that his heart is repentant and that I am misunderstanding or misjudging him. The evidence is not there, and several of us who actually live with him have tried to tell you, but you've refused to listen.*

Incredibly, George wrote back again, this time requesting to talk to me on the phone. I briefly answered by letting him know I was tired of going around in circles with him, and I asked him to please leave me alone. I never heard from him again. I finally learned that when our "no" is ignored or disrespected, we can stop being polite and just shut the door in someone's face.

64
Confrontation

The DART team met with John twice that spring. After the first meeting, one of the team members, who was a psychologist, told me that both Pastor Justin and the head of the elder board wanted me to know emphatically (she emphasized that word twice) that they believed me before, but after this meeting, they believed me *more*. There was that tremendous sense of relief again—as if a mountain-sized boulder had rolled off my chest. This was what I wanted: to know what was real and what was not. I was still looking for validation that I wasn't crazy. I didn't want to be crazy. John had pulled the wool over everyone else's eyes for over two decades, including two professional counselors and multiple pastors and elders from two different churches, but this was finally the end of the ruse for him.

After they met with John, the team told me he came across as a very nice guy who was polite and easy to talk to, but he wouldn't directly answer any of their questions. He made excuses, spoke in generalities, and shifted blame. When they repeated the questions, he continued to evade them. One of the elders said John insisted everything was my responsibility. John wanted to talk mostly about my anger, but he seemed clueless about why I might be angry. They reminded John about all the things I had done to get help for our marriage and asked him if he could articulate what he had done. He had no answer. He blamed our problems on communication issues. The psychologist pointed out later that John's relationships were all transactional, but there was no empathy, connection, or intimacy. At one point John brought up the fact that he had seen books "laying around the house" that had "put ideas in Natalie's head" about our relationship. The psychologist said she had read all of Leslie Vernick's books, for example, and never once did she get the idea that her marriage was destructive from reading those books. The information was separate from her experience. Moving forward, they recommended psychiatric therapy to John so he could deal with his childhood trauma, and they told me they supported our separation and even a future divorce should John decide not to get ongoing help or not apply himself to do the necessary work to gain self-awareness and change.

A few weeks went by as they waited for John to process their recommendations. During that time, the DART team decided to turn our case over to two elders from the south campus location. Our church had three campuses at the time, and most of the DART team regularly attended the other two, so they felt it made sense for elders from our own campus to manage the rest of the separation process. In light of this upcoming transition, they arranged to have these two new elders join them in meeting with John together for one final meeting where everyone who had been involved up to that point would be present.

When that meeting was over, they told me John seemed dead and unresponsive. They concluded that he had a pattern of leaving things unresolved, and there was no empathy, repentance, or conviction. They told me they did not think John was a believer. He was clueless about his sin and demonstrated a complete lack of ownership for the breakdown of our marriage.

The DART team was starting to get it, but they were about to make a classic mistake. They were going to give my husband some hoops to jump through. I could have told them that emotional and

Confrontation

spiritual abusers are excellent hoop-jumpers and can pass with flying colors once they figure out the rules of the game.

But they never asked.

65

Hoops and Masks

In May of 2015, John had three months to show the DART team that he could change. The team would meet with him once a month to discuss his homework and his progress, and after three months, they would reassess the situation and decide how to proceed from there. They told him to get psychiatric help (he got "Bible counseling" instead), and he was assigned an accountability partner: another father of a large family in our church who didn't know me and didn't know about our situation. This man never once reached out to meet me, but from this time on, he regularly met with and supported John. John was also given a checklist of things to do to show he was changing, but it was just a series of hoops that John would be able to successfully jump through with a little effort and a lot of smoke and mirrors. John was back to figuring out what mask would work best with this new group of people, and I was back on the treadmill going nowhere.

With this new pressure on him, John was suddenly answering every single one of my emails in a timely manner. Some of the emails I sent to John were simple updates to keep him informed of what was going on with the kids, and they didn't require an answer, but now he was uncharacteristically (and unnecessarily) responding to all of them. His responses were robotic and insincere, but the fact that he was responding proved to me that he was capable of doing this in spite of two decades of non-responsiveness, as long as he had someone holding his hand and saying "jump" with a treat at the other end.

Hoops and Masks

The team didn't give me any direction at this point other than to tell me to sit back and wait. I asked them to give me updates in writing, and they responded by telling me about their more recent meeting and the homework they gave John to complete. They wanted to identify the things John did that "drove Natalie crazy." I thought their choice of words was odd. Things that drove me crazy? Did they see me as a petty, easily annoyed wife who kept complaining about socks on the floor or squashed toothpaste tubes? I could feel my hope crumbling at the edges. John was being nice and helpful, per their instructions, but it was just the same old abuse cycle. If the past was any indicator of the present, he was only being nice to get himself off the hook. I was angry for being put in the same position of having to help him and make things easy on him or else looking like an ungrateful, unforgiving, bitter wife.

The women on the DART team recommended that I sit back and let the elders work with John on their own. They wanted me to leave the past behind and focus only on what was going on at present. They wanted me to get out of the way, stop interacting with John, and avoid triggering John to be abusive. *They wanted to see if John was abusive without me being involved.*

They didn't get it. They didn't understand how abuse worked. Toddlers are amazing little creatures when they are at the fair with cotton candy in their sticky fists, and abusers do well when they are not being provoked by everyday life with a human wife and a bunch of human kids. The DART team wanted to see if John could be a good man without any provocations to determine if he was abusive, and that made no sense to me. I wrote to the women:

> *I understand that you are trying to help some of the other elders see John's sin. The idea is that as long as I'm not triggering John to be abusive and manipulative then they*

will be able to see that John does it all by himself. His sin is his responsibility, and they won't be able to pin John's sin on me. But that is not helping them understand abuse at all. That's perpetuating a lie about abuse. The lie is this: Abuse is the woman's fault.

If John's abuse could be miraculously turned into visible bruises and cuts on the outside, would you ask me to avoid triggering my husband as much as possible so that if he hit me, the others could see that it wasn't really my fault? Would you say, "Natalie, when you talk to John, pretend he's never hit you. Let him off the hook as much as possible so he isn't triggered by your fear, anger, and emotion. That way when he hits you, the others can see that you didn't do anything to make him do it. We want them to see you were a good girl with no emotion and no expectations, so they know John just did it because he wanted to be mean. Then we can discipline him for that." This tells me I need to be a perfect little robot wife to avoid getting swung at.

You can tell me everything I'm doing wrong and how I can change. I will work my butt off to change and cooperate. BUT DON'T TELL JOHN. This is John's biggest loophole. His biggest excuse. As long as this is a marriage issue and not an abuse issue, John will continue to lay all responsibility at my feet. Of course, on the outside he will say all the things you want to hear him say. He wants you off his back. But once you are all gone, he will turn to me and stab me in the back with the weapon that you gave to him. So, don't give it to him, OK? Because while nobody can see the gaping wound in my back, I can feel it, and it hurts like hell.

They did not address my concerns but instead reiterated my need to get out of the way. At the end of June, I was still not optimistic about how well John was clearing all the hoops, and I continued making hopeless attempts to show them the more nuanced issues going on. They finally straight out asked me what it would take for me to say, "Yes! John has *changed!*" And that's when I realized John had found the mask that worked best with this group. The only problem was that John's mask didn't work for *me*.

Which then made me the problem.

66
Burn the Ships

John continued being John to the kids and me, but to the team he was "repentant" and "sad and sorry," and "why couldn't Natalie see that?" At the end of three months, the elders believed he was making progress, and they wanted to go for another three months, but they wanted me to "back off." They said I had John "under a microscope," and I needed to "stop testing John" or interacting with him unless they gave me permission. They treated me like a child in their little change experiment, but I wanted to be an adult, like all the other adults. When I appealed to them along those lines, they told me they were concerned I was no longer humbly acknowledging my own sinful contributions to our marriage. I found myself in the familiar double bind that seemed to plague my entire existence, but *that's when I had an epiphany that changed my life.* I was running on a never-ending hamster wheel expecting all these people to see me, hear me, and believe me. As long as I kept looking outside of myself for the things I needed, I would keep going in circles and getting nowhere. But what was I expecting of myself? Was I seeing myself? Hearing myself? Believing in myself? Did I have my own back?

One night I looked in the mirror at my bloodshot eyes and swollen, snot-covered nose, and I saw fire in the sad eyes that looked back at me. I looked deeply into those eyes for the first time in my life, and I saw a human being named Natalie. I saw that *she mattered*, and I chose to fiercely love her. I said with conviction, "Natalie, it's going to be okay. They have no skin in the game of your life. They

Burn the Ships

are irrelevant to your future. Their opinions don't matter. Their games don't matter. *You* matter. And I've got you. From here onward, I'm making a commitment to you. I promise I will never throw you under the bus again. I will never gaslight you, betray you, disbelieve you, tell you that you have no value, or say you are a worthless piece of crap compared to everyone else. From now on, you are my priority. My most important responsibility. Nobody else has to take care of you anymore because guess what? *I'm* going to take care of you."

And I believed her. I also knew that it wasn't just her within me, seeing me, hearing me, and knowing me. It was the essence of the Creator resonating deep within me. God was this protective, encompassing, *knowing* Love. I had a powerful entity who was intertwined with my person, and together, we were One. I would never again feel alone because all the light came flooding in, and in that moment of connection with myself, *I experienced God.*

I instinctively knew my next order of business was to let go of everyone else. If I was going to radically accept and respect my own self, my own choices, my own experiences, and my own unique, God-given perspective, I needed to radically accept and respect the choices, experiences, and perspectives of others. And sometimes, when you respect both yourself and others, you need to part ways.

I sent a grateful, sorrowful, and heart-felt breakup email to everyone on the DART team. Nobody responded. I stood alone on that shore and watched the ships burn, and then I turned around to survey the damage on this island of my life.

67
Mental Health

Having a counselor (unless it was a *Bible* counselor) was a cop-out. It meant you didn't trust God and were not obeying His rulebook. All of the answers you needed for anything were found in the Good Book. This was my programming. Then, children with mental health issues came into my life, and the Good Book didn't have the answers for what ailed them. It didn't have the answers for what ailed my marriage. It didn't have the answers for what ailed my church. I had drilled Scripture into my own heart and life, played Scripture on audio tapes for my kids to fall asleep to, listened to Scripture set to music throughout the day, read the entire Scriptures through every year, filled over twenty journals with Scripture verses, had my older kids memorize large chunks of Scripture, studied Scripture in big and small groups as well as on my own, and heard Scripture preached in church and on the radio and at conferences. Scripture, Scripture, Scripture. I could rattle off the perfect verse that was applicable to absolutely any subject that might come up. My entire existence revolved around God and His Rule Book, making sure I obeyed every jot and tittle, and feeling guilty when I didn't.

In spite of my obsession with the Bible, my marriage was falling apart, my daughter was falling apart, and my toddler had just been diagnosed with ASD (autism spectrum disorder) and would need more than a Bible verse to help him gain the skills he needed in this world. John and I had three children with Tourette's syndrome, one with a speech disfluency, several with attention deficit hyperactivity disorder (ADHD), and we would add ASD and eventually emerging borderline personality disorder (BPD) to the list. I loved the Bible, but it was time to get some scientific help for all these capital letters. I figured since the Creator created science, brains, and bodies, it was probably okay to learn more about all of that, even if that meant learning information found in places other than the Bible. Was God a genie in a little black book? Or was God bigger than that?

While I was juggling my husband's issues, the church folks, my daughter's violent episodes, a home business, and the rest of my kids, I decided to start by focusing my non-biblical energies on my youngest son. This involved reading, phone calls, and paperwork, but eventually I got him into our local school district's program for preschoolers with ASD as well as working with a private Applied Behavior Analysis (ABA) therapist who would come into our home for several hours every day for a year to teach our son speech, language, and social skills.

After our son's testing and diagnosis, I decided to have our emotionally volatile daughter tested as well. She was diagnosed with a variety of things, but she did not fall on the spectrum. She would go on to see multiple counselors, therapists, and psychologists, and we would try various medications and therapies, including spending eighteen months in a day treatment center. After being hospitalized at one point during a manic episode, public mental health resources also got involved. During this time, I put several of my other children in therapy to help them deal with and process the separation of their parents and the trauma of living with an emotionally dysregulated and violent sibling.

If you had told me ten years prior to this that I would be relying on medication, therapists, and the government for help, I would have wept in my tea. But now? I was grasping at any and every opportunity to gain knowledge, insight, and help for my kids anywhere I could get it—except the church. I gave the church over two decades of my life to equip me for the tough stuff, and all they offered was "read your Bible, pray every day, and you'll grow, grow, grow." It was a nice ditty for five-year-olds, but it didn't work for adults in the thick of complicated issues.

Because of my new interactions with licensed therapists, psychologists, and mental health professionals, as well as my extensive reading and research in this field of knowledge, I began to grow in my confidence when it came to understanding the dynamic in my marriage. I met a widening world of people who loved to listen and learn and who didn't treat me like a child but instead treated me with respect as an intelligent, contributing adult. My brain was beginning to believe God viewed me that way, and *I could start viewing myself that way, too.*

After being a member at a large Baptist church for ten years, volunteering, being involved in small groups, and having all of our kids active and engaged with youth activities, I stopped going, and nobody reached out to find out where I was or why. I take that back. One of my very good church friends stopped by one day, unannounced, and nervously told me I was making a big mistake, and I needed to get back under the authority of the elders in the church. I politely but firmly told her where I stood, and I was going to stay standing there. She left, and I never saw her again.

68

Another Hotel Room

On April 1, 2016, I checked into another hotel. This time I was alone and armed with twenty-four journals I had kept throughout the course of my marriage. I was going to spend the next forty-eight hours giving my full attention to what the past versions of me were trying to say, and then I was going to make a final decision about whether or not I should file for divorce.

I played instrumental music on Spotify and began reading. When I came to something I believed was significant, I typed it out on my laptop along with my thoughts, and as I read, I noticed the patterns showing up. Subtle patterns. More obvious patterns. Patterns not just in my relationship with my husband, but in my relationships with my family of origin and some of my church friends. I read about what happened and how I filtered my circumstances through my programming. How those programmed beliefs flooded my body with fear and shame, and how I subsequently responded and showed up for my life in the same ways over and over again. I saw clearly how my beliefs had created a never-ending loop I would never be able to escape unless I interrupted it.

I completed an exercise where I imagined what divorcing John might be like the first year and then five and ten years later. I wrote that I would probably spend much of my time crying. I would be lonely and experience feelings of isolation and sadness. I would grieve for my kids and the loss of the family I had dreamed of and tried so hard to build. But then things would settle down, and we'd all find our new normal. I would get therapy for the kids, and we'd work through it. We'd get stronger. We would heal. I would not have financial stability at first, and we would go back to pinching pennies for a while. Maybe I would have to move. In five years, I would look back on everything like a bad dream. I would be proud I finally went through with it, and I would wonder why I waited for so long. I might grieve the years I wasted. I might be remarried to a healthy man and discover what marriage was intended to be. My kids would be able to see it, too, and might have a better chance of recognizing and marrying a healthy partner. In ten years, I would have sold my soap business, and I'd be helping Christian women just like me while also providing for my family. I would be able to help my kids go through college and discover their own life goals. I would be happy and free.

Then I wrote down what my life would look like if I stayed with John. I would continue to experience emotional turmoil, frustration, and confusion. I would continue to live with foggy thinking, emotional and physical stress, and instability. I would continue to deal with gaslighting, criticism, and the inability to solve problems or find closure. I would have no hope of anything changing or being different, and I would continue to wonder if death would be better than life. Basically, all I could see in one year, five years, ten years, and all the way up to my death was suffering and darkness.

On April 3, 2016, before I checked out, I fell to my knees on that hotel room floor and promised the Creator that I would do whatever I needed to do for this woman who had poured out her heart to me through her journals all weekend. I would be "bad" in the eyes of everyone else in order to be *kind and good* to this precious human named Natalie. I promised I would be God's agent of rescue in her life. *It was me all along. I* was the one called to do This Thing. This Big Scary Thing.

I was going to divorce John's ass.

Part Four

"I've decided that if I had my life to live over again, I would not only climb more mountains, swim more rivers, and watch more sunsets; I wouldn't only jettison my hot water bottles, raincoat, umbrella, parachute, and raft; I would not only go barefoot earlier in the spring and stay out later in the fall; but I would devote not one more minute to monitoring my spiritual growth. No, not one."

—Brennan Manning, *The Furious Longing of God*

I got divorced and lived happily ever after.
The End.

Yeah, that's not how this works. I did get divorced. I divorced the man I worshipped simply because he was my husband. I also divorced the god my religious community worshipped. A scary little god who didn't even exist. That meant I got to discover a Bigger God. That meant I got to actually live my own life—a life the Creator gifted me to live.

But that life still takes place on a planet swirling with a lot of pain, shame, and fear. If abuse is like living in a home filling up with gasoline fumes, divorce is like lighting a match. There's going to be an explosion, and people are going to get hurt. This is why so many women hide the matches. It's easier to silently suffocate while smiling and waving to passersby.

But I figured that our family was dying either way, and if the toxic home blew up, maybe we'd have a chance to build something different in its place. In the aftermath of an explosion, only rubble remains. Where do you even begin to start over? It looks and feels impossible, but communities do it. They start by picking up one thing. And then another. They clear away what no longer works. What no longer carries meaning. When that's finished, they survey the landscape and begin to dream about what could be. They decide what to build on the new, blank canvas of their home. They can rebuild things they loved and want to keep, and they can add new things that were not part of the picture before the explosion.

It's a long, messy process, this rebuilding. This starting over. And we will do it again and again, continuously evolving into the next version of ourselves until our time on this planet is done. What a privilege. What an opportunity. I'm all in. Let's do it together.

69
You Don't Know God

The following week I retained an attorney, completed the paperwork, and filed for divorce. All the sweet, panicked, sad, angry, judgy, shame-filled parts on my bus were exploding with protests, but there was a calmer, stabilizing Presence there as well, and I was tuning into that voice more and more. "*Of course, this feels uncomfortable. You've never done this before. Anyone in your shoes would feel this way. We can understand why. Just let these feelings wash over you like a wave. They won't kill you. Wait and see what happens. They will flood you and then dissipate. See? It's going to be okay. I'm with you, and you've got this.*"

I was getting braver, but old patterns of thinking don't go away overnight. Little Natalie, feeling the fear of change on the horizon, shrilly insisted on letting her "daddies" know her plans. So even though I hadn't had contact with them for over six months, I wrote to the two elders who had been helping John the summer before to let them know I had filed for divorce and—wait for it—*to ask if they had any final thoughts or insights to offer.* (Can you see Rude's eyes rolling?) Sometimes unhooking embedded programming takes years, and I was on a desperate quest for something I would never get—*closure*.

The elders responded by ignoring my question, but they asked if I would give them permission to talk to the pastoral counselor I had been seeing. I said no. They asked if I might be willing to meet with them, and I agreed as long as I could bring my sister Marcy. I wanted to make sure I had a witness in case they tried to gaslight me again.

All the Scary Little Gods

On the day of the meeting, Marcy and I drove to the church office and sat down at a table with one of the elders and the woman in charge of DART. The elder kicked off the meeting with a flowery prayer asking God to allow him to be a "blessing" to me, and then he told me the DART team had concluded that there were two sinners in this situation—John and I—and neither one of us was willing to look outside of our own narrative.

Curious, I asked the elder what I would need to do to see things from outside of my own narrative, and he said, "You don't know God, Natalie. God is absent from your narrative."

The room spun. This man didn't know me. He didn't know my children. He knew nothing about my life other than what John had told him, and from that "reliable" source of information he had decided *I didn't know God?*

I choked out, "God is the *very center* of my narrative." Even while I said it, I knew I wasn't talking to this man anymore. I was talking to a Dead Thing inside of him that could not hear, see, or understand, making this conversation a Dead End.

I reached for my phone and said, "I need to record the rest of this conversation." The DART leader jumped up from her chair and lunged at me saying, "*No!* You will *not* record this!" I was startled at this aggressive show of emotion, and it hit me that this Dead Thing was in her, too, and it could tell I saw it. It didn't want to be seen.

I said, "Why not? Is there something you need to hide?"

She repeated, "You will *not* record this."

"Then we can't continue the conversation," I said evenly.

She leveled her own voice and glared at me, "You are making sad decisions."

Marcy and I gathered up our things to leave as I replied, "I'll let God be the judge of that."

"Yes, God will judge that," she spat.

As we exited the door, she hissed a last, "*So sad!*" with an expression that was not sad at all.

This wasn't the first time I had heard the message of the Dead Thing. I had been hearing that message my entire life: *Your experience doesn't count. Your life doesn't count. Your investment in the lives of others doesn't count. And your belief that you are connected to God is all in your head. You are a nothing. A zero. There is no Empathetic Witness for you because you are so unimportant and insignificant; it's like you don't even exist.*

The message of Love sounds different: *You matter. You are valuable. You carry meaning. Your voice counts.* If the message we are hearing doesn't sound like that, then it is not coming from Love, no matter how many Bible verses are piously woven into the sentences.

I went home and curled up in a ball of frozen pain. I couldn't sleep. I couldn't even cry, which was highly unusual for me. I would eventually undergo intense therapy to work through the impact this experience had on my brain and body. It was just as destructive as if they had put me in the middle of a football stadium to stone me.

The following week, the DART Team asked to meet with me again. I declined.

To find the truth within a lie, all I had to do was flip the lie upside down. The lie said, "You don't know God." The truth is that *I am One with God*. The lie said I had a narrative I made up in my head. The truth is that I am a woman with a lived experience. The lie said I would be safe and loved if I obeyed those who wanted to control me. The truth is that I was never safe with anyone who worshipped a scary little god. They were wrong about many things, but they were ultimately right about one thing:

I didn't know their god.

70
Drugs and Therapy

I had been poised on top of a cliff for years, afraid to jump. Afraid to fall. The Big Question that had plagued me for the past three years, "*Should I stay, or should I go?*" had been answered: I should go. And the relief in my brain was real.

What I wasn't expecting was the way my body reacted. Instead of relaxing into an abuse-free future, I started having mysterious blackouts. Out of the blue, my heart would start racing, the oxygen around me would get sucked away, and the world would get tinier and tinier until it disappeared into darkness. I could sit down and breathe through it, but when it started happening in the car with my kids in the back seat, I knew I needed to figure out what was wrong. I couldn't pull over on the freeway every time I started to feel like I was suffocating.

There were accumulating stressors in my life all at once. I was getting divorced. My dad, who was a quiet pillar of all that was stable, predictable, and reliable in life, was diagnosed with cancer and going through chemotherapy. My daughter was verbally and physically violent for hours at a time on a daily basis. My youngest son was in two different therapy settings every day, and I was driving children to school, homeschool co-op, music lessons, and therapy. I was running a home business, managing several contracted workers, taking care of the house repairs and upkeep, going to individualized education program (IEP) meetings for two children, and taking care of dozens of other big and small daily responsibilities. Instead of getting casseroles, cards, and coffees from family and church friends, I was getting the silent treatment I had grown up dreading. I was completely and utterly alone. I look back at that woman, and I have no idea how she did it, but it wasn't without consequences.

I talked to my regular doctor, and she told me I was likely having anxiety attacks, and would I like to go on Lexapro? Why yes, I would. If it could keep my kids and me safe on the freeway, I'll take some, thank you very much. I felt like everyone already hated me, so how much would it matter if I disappointed them by relying on medication instead of Bible verses to keep us all alive? That was the main (and maybe only) perk about losing everyone. I had nothing else left to lose, so I could do whatever the hell I wanted, which made no difference either way toward garnering the approval of others.

I had already stopped associating Christians with love. The Christians in my life had consistently behaved in unloving and controlling ways, and while I had let go of a lot of what I believed about God, there was one thing I hung onto, and that was my belief that God was the essence of Love. The two were one and the same. I was done with the scary little god who lived in the imaginations of scary little men. They needed everyone to believe in that god so they could justify their lust for sex and power, but that didn't mean I had to believe in that god anymore.

I got on Lexapro, and Love winked at me. The panic attacks stopped, and I could think clearly. It reminded me of when I got my first pair of glasses in the third grade. I could see the tiny branches on the trees outside for the first time in my life, and I didn't even know my vision was a problem until it wasn't anymore. All the responsibilities were still there waiting for me, but now I was able to sleep at night and stay focused during the day. Lexapro was a friend when friends were hard to come by.

All the Scary Little Gods

That summer I started seeing my very first licensed therapist. No more "Bible" or "pastoral" counselors for me. Sheila offered Eye Movement Desensitization and Reprocessing (EMDR) therapy, and we worked through a handful of childhood and adult experiences. It was emotionally draining, and I would shake and sob through most of it, but when a session was over, I would always feel a new lightness I had never known before. Just working through a few of those experiences seemed to unhook me from other experiences that were repeated versions of the original one. I had given Christian Bible counselors years of my life and thousands of my dollars in exchange for deeper trauma. I spent a few months and less than a thousand dollars on EMDR therapy, and by late fall I felt like myself and was able to discontinue therapy.

Despite their dad's protests, I made sure my kids were seeing a licensed therapist as well. My youngest daughter was only eight at the time, but she had been experiencing chronic stomach pain and was uncharacteristically weepy. It eventually came out in therapy that she felt responsible for her dad's emotions. She blamed herself for her dad lying on his apartment couch all the time. The therapist told her that he was an adult who could get help for himself, take a walk, go out with friends, listen to music, talk to a therapist, or read a book. It wasn't a little girl's responsibility to manage her daddy's emotions. That's all it took for her. She transformed back into her happy self, and her stomach pain went away. To this day, she has healthy boundaries and says no without guilt when she decides she doesn't want to do something or see someone. She is also one of the most thoughtful, caring, empathetic human beings I know. Having boundaries doesn't make us mean. They make us healthy.

My fourteen-year-old son hated therapy, so I let him quit. I was in uncharted territory, making decisions on my own, learning to trust my intuition and understanding of my own children instead of looking to the "experts" for the answers. I made some mistakes, but I was starting to be okay with that, too. Maybe God created me to be a human? If that was good enough for God, maybe it could be good enough for me. And maybe I could allow my kids to be humans as well. Maybe none of us had to be perfect little Christian robots sitting in a row in the church pew.

71

Stalkers

Speaking of church pews, we were sitting in a new one at another large Baptist church across town. One day the head of the elder board at this second Baptist church called to let me know the elders from my former church met with them to warn them about me and my refusal to obey them. I knew I had unhooked from their abusive theology because when I heard this, I wasn't triggered—I was amused. I imagined all these little boys playing in their sandbox, throwing sand at the little girl who dared to say no to them. And when she left to go play in a different sandbox, they stalked her all the way to the new sandbox to instruct the kids over there about how much fun it is to throw sand at the girl, and they really ought to try it out. But the boys in the new sandbox had better things to do. They told the girl who said no that she could play in their sandbox in peace. So, she did.

My former church had already sent me an official letter saying they would only "give me permission" to divorce if John had been in continuous, unrepentant sexual sin, chronically beat me up, or physically deserted me. Since he had dutifully obeyed their three gold standards for men, I was now the one in sin by filing for divorce without biblical grounds per their interpretation of the Bible. I was now the one refusing to follow the rules of the membership contract I had signed. According to their sandbox rules, they were right. I wasn't cooperating. I had sent a letter to withdraw my membership two years prior to this, but they would not allow that. In their imaginations, I belonged to them until they decided to let me go.

A woman would one day tell me how she overheard our church elders cracking jokes in the church parking lot about how John was stalking me on Easter of 2017. Before I tell you more about the stalking, however, I want to share something that happened in the late summer of 2016 after I jumped off the divorce cliff. Something I never saw coming. This thing would really stir the pot and give the religious folks something to talk about, and it would change my life and the lives of my children forever.

72
Redemption Stories

Between fourth and eighth grade, I was verbally and sometimes physically bullied almost daily. Somehow, I came out of it and still managed to build a vibrant social life in high school and college, but I had scars of insecurity, fear, and shame, and I often wondered if and how God would bring closure and healing to that chapter of my life. I didn't want the bullies to burn forever in hell. Maybe some people got comfort and joy out of that ending, but it didn't seem like a happy ending to me. That story felt more like the history of human war to me: The bad guys do something horrible, and then the good guys come in and destroy everyone, and then everyone walks away and buries their dead. It's a bad story, and nobody really wins. It's not even all that interesting. If most of the people on earth are destined to be tortured in fire forever and ever, that doesn't make God the winner. That makes the devil the winner. It also repeats the cycle of shame, hate, and war, and who needs faith for that? All we have to do is look around us.

I don't believe that story anymore. The best redemption story I can imagine is one where the bad guys are sad and sorry for the ways they hurt the good guys. They give everything back that they stole. Death is defeated, all is restored, and everyone lives happily ever after in peace and love. Call me an idealist or naive or unscientific or an ostrich with my head in the sand. I get it. I'm probably all of those. But that's what I consciously, intentionally choose to believe about the Creator. About Love. That this whack job of an existence on earth isn't all there is. That one day there will be a Full Healing. Not just for some, but for everyone. Not just for humans. But for animals. Plants. Oceans. Rivers. Forests. All of it. **Winner takes all**. This does require faith, but hey, we all gotta believe something, right? I want to spend the rest of my life believing something beautifully drenched in a powerful love.

This hopeful faith of mine opened the door to something new when a grade school bully showed up in my Facebook feed one day. I had recently gone to a high school reunion, so Facebook started putting some familiar names and faces in my feed, and I was "friending" some of these people. Most of the time, I had fun seeing these older faces, some of whom I could hardly recognize anymore, but when I saw Tom, I felt viscerally repulsed. He was the bully who bonked me on the head in fourth grade, and I had ripped his shirt or something. The details were a bit fuzzy, but I remembered how I felt in my body at the time: scared, angry, and helpless. And yet now, here he was, grinning up at me from my phone while I waited for my son to get out of his preschool class.

Despite my disgust reflex, I felt a morbid fascination to scroll through his feed. It was full of Bible verses, pictures of himself in different parts of the world, pictures of himself with an older woman (his mom?), and pictures of himself with friends. He looked like he might be gay, but the Bible verses threw me off a bit. Could you be gay and a Christian? In the circles where I'd spent my life, this wasn't even imaginable. A former bully publicly quotes the Bible? Was this a redemption story? Was Love giving me a glimpse of Healing? Feeling both curious and cautious, I sent him a message to see if he remembered who I was and what he had done to me in fourth grade. I told him I found it interesting that he seemed to respect and appreciate the Bible, and if that was the case, I was happy he had made his peace with God after being such a creep in grade school. I left out my question about the gay thing and half expected he would never respond, but within minutes he messaged back. He said he didn't remember the incident, but he was sorry for causing me pain. We became Facebook friends—the kind you "friend" and never think about again—and that was that.

Several months later, in mid-August of 2016, about four months into the divorce process with John, Tom-the-bully sent me a Facebook message: "Good morning! One of my New Year's resolutions this year is to let those around me know they are special and loved. You are on my list for today. Continue to just be you. No one does it better. Enjoy the beautiful day." There was a cute little meme attached. I thought it was dumb. "New Year's resolutions? It's August, for crying out loud," Rude muttered. "What a sap." I didn't trust him. I didn't trust anyone at that point in my life. But I minded my manners and thanked him.

After that exchange, I heard nothing for a while, and then a few weeks later he reached out again to recommend a movie he had just seen and enjoyed called *Sing Street*. Again, I thought it was weird and politely thanked him. A couple of weeks later, I watched the movie with my daughter, my sister, and my niece. It was a musical. I thought it was strange that a man would like that movie. The men I had known would not have enjoyed it. This confirmed my suspicions that he was probably gay, and if he was gay, that meant he wasn't trying to make any moves. He had no agenda. He wasn't going to judge me or try to get into my pants. He was just being genuinely kind, and at that point in my life, I really needed some genuine kindness. I was vaguely aware of the way I was stereotyping him, but I didn't care. Just let me have a gay friend, okay?

I told him we loved the movie, and we struck up a conversation on Facebook Messenger. He thought it was bizarre that I had nine kids, and I thought it was bizarre that he had never been married and had none. Our stories were so opposite from one another, and I think that's what kept us in an ongoing text exchange after that. Plus, we were clicking. There was something that felt comfortable and normal about this budding friendship, like putting on an old, familiar pair of tennis shoes I had rediscovered in the back of a closet.

One day we agreed to meet at a local park for a walk. On the way there, "When He Sees Me" by Sara Bareilles was playing on Spotify, and I was nervous. Tom was waiting for me in the parking lot with casual-preppy clothing and *long hair*. A gay, preppy hippy? What was my paradigm for *that*? He was obviously very comfortable with who he was, and I liked that. I, on the other hand, wore sunglasses and never took them off. I had decided he would *not* see me until I wanted him to.

He greeted me with a big smile, and we started walking the trails of what we would later call our Magic Forest. We talked about hard things. Fun things. Personal failures. Ways we had changed since high school and why. There was such an openness and honesty in our conversation. It was easy. Like we had known each other our entire lives, which was so ridiculously cliché, and yet, there it was. The connection was natural and authentic. I asked him if he was gay, which he found amusing, and I found myself surprisingly euphoric to hear him say he wasn't. Because now, I had to admit, I liked him. I liked his energy and personality. I liked the look of his athletic build and toned body. And I wanted to see him again. And again. And again. "Brighter Than the Sun" by Colbie Caillat came on the radio as I drove away, and I could not stop smiling.

We couldn't meet in person very often due to kids and responsibilities, but we began to talk on the phone every night. I would put the kids to bed, and we'd talk until I was almost asleep. I loved the sound of his voice, and we shared a lifetime in those conversations.

In every cell of my body, I had a feeling of "coming home" with this man, something I hadn't experienced with any man before. When Tom told me he was a practicing Catholic, I knew Love was winking at me again.

Eventually, I confided in my sixteen-year-old daughter, and she agreed to watch the kids for me on Saturday nights so I could go out with Tom. This became our weekly ritual until my divorce was final over a year later. He was my friend and confidant all throughout the divorce process. At the time, we had no idea the divorce would drag on for so long. There was a settlement conference scheduled for November 28, 2016, to finalize everything, and I anticipated the divorce to be over before the end of the year. Unfortunately, John canceled the hearing a couple of days before. He had decided to file for 50 percent custody even though he had never tried to spend more than a couple of days a week with our kids prior to that.

Since we weren't sure when the divorce would be over, Tom and I decided to step back from the relationship, but when we realized we were only stepping back out of fear of what others might think, we changed our minds. I was done living my life like that. If people didn't like my decisions, that was okay. I was still going to make them for *me*.

The following Easter in 2017, John wanted to use my van to take the kids somewhere on Good Friday. We sometimes exchanged vehicles for this purpose, so John picked up the kids and my van, and I drove John's Prius to meet Tom for a Good Friday service. I parked John's Prius in Tom's apartment parking lot, and we took Tom's car to the church service. What I didn't know was that John had put a tracker on his Prius.

Two days later on Easter afternoon, Tom was coming into his apartment building, and he saw John in his apartment entryway writing down the names on the mailboxes. Tom took a couple of pictures and sent them to me in a text saying, "Is this your ex?" Yes, it was John. We were a year into the divorce process, but John had told me at one point that we were still married in the eyes of God, and divorce was never going to change that. To John, I was property by biblical law, and now it appeared that I was also his prey to stalk.

I was ready to tell my family about Tom. I had already informed my attorney several months before, and he had advised me to keep my relationship with Tom my own personal business until the divorce was over. I knew John was going to spill the beans if I didn't, so I sent the older kids an email, and I set up a playdate at the park to introduce Tom to my younger kids. The five younger kids enjoyed meeting Tom, but the three oldest boys struggled with the news. One of them sent me a scathing email and walked out of my life for two and a half agonizing years.

But God worked through Tom-the-bully to help Little Natalie heal. She had been hiding from bullies and hoping nobody would see her for far too long, but now she uncurled and came out singing and dancing. I always thought she was an ugly little nerd I had to keep under wraps. I was wrong. She is sparkly and fun. And when she feels safe, Little Natalie can look at childhood bullies and their own painful stories and feel God's Love for all of them because this girl is inextricably and forever connected to the One who writes all the redemption stories.

And now she believes them.

73

Love Just Is

I hadn't been sexually molested. I hadn't been beaten. I didn't grow up in poverty. Nobody close to me had ever died. I lived in a safe, warm, clean, healthy home with a mom who had warm cookies and a listening ear waiting for her kids when they got home from school. I went to camp, swam with cousins, rode horses and bikes and golf carts. I had a church family I loved and relatives I loved even more. If you asked me about my life growing up, I would say, "I lived a charmed life. I had a happy childhood. My family is amazing." Even as I write all of that, I find my body sliding into deep grief, and I have to stop to let my body cry and process.

Everything I wrote is true. And also, I have layers of trauma for the lack of one simple thing: an empathetic witness. An empathetic witness is someone who sees you. They believe you. They hold space for your experience and your inner world even if they, themselves, have never experienced anything like it. They honor and respect your perspective even if they have a different perspective. They are healthy enough within themselves and wise and mature enough to know the world is best seen and understood through many eyes, not just their own.

We all need one such wise soul in our lives to see and know and love us. In my religious culture and upbringing, this wasn't possible. The worldview taught within that frame of reference rejects differing perspectives. They are right, and everyone else is wrong. End of story. There is so much collective trauma within religious cultures brought on by the very beliefs that we are told are the Ultimate Answers.

People who are curled up in fetal positions of fear, grief, and rage aren't able to see or offer love to anyone else. They are too occupied with the survival of the fittest and best. In trying to be like God, they become little adversarial balls of shame and pain, and they pass along these dead messages to everyone around them. They, themselves, become scary little gods.

Sometimes I'll send an email to my mailing list and talk about Love. What Love is. What it isn't. I am fascinated when the most hate-filled emails I receive are responses from Christians to emails about Love. They venomously spit out, "You are evil and will burn in hell forever." "You write gobbledygook." "You don't know God."

Yeah, well, I've heard that one before.

How did Love become gobbledygook? Maybe when we believe in scary little gods made in the image of power-thirsty men, we run any new information through our trauma, fear, and shame, and it gets all garbled up so we can't understand what would set us free.

I used to think I was the problem. If someone opened their mouth and offered an opinion, I had to give that opinion the full weight of credibility. I still believe in holding space for the perspectives of others, but I use a different filter to determine what is wholesome and life-giving and what is coming from a dark place of pain. It's the Love filter. If someone looks at someone else and says with a snarl, "You are evil and will burn in hell forever," that message is not coming from God or from Love. I can let that message slide off my brain and into the ocean of peace I choose to float in. I can say, "May the loving Creator God find you and scoop you up and hold you forever, bringing your shredded heart to wholeness and healing and giving you back everything that has ever been taken from you." And then I can give them over to that Love and know they are safe. If not today, then tomorrow. If not Here, then There. Because Love transcends time and space. And I don't have to control it or force it. Love just is.

74

Connecting the Dots

I hate to torment the reader with even one more word about my church, but it keeps showing up in my story like a bad case of acne. In August of 2016, the elders asked me to come to one of their meetings to *discuss* my request to withdraw membership. Dear God, have mercy on all the living souls of the planet. Will this ever be over?

I wrote: "Thank you, but I will decline."

They wrote back that they were sad I felt this way. They held their meeting about me the following month and sent a follow-up email expressing that, after careful deliberation, they had decided not to grant my request to withdraw membership. Instead, they told me for the umpteenth time that I needed to reconcile with John and submit myself to their authority for my own good and for the sake of my children. They said they were writing with tears. (Can anyone say crocodile?)

Two months later, they sent me a copy of the letter they intended to publicly read to the congregation at the quarterly meeting. "It is not our policy to grant a dismissal of membership to a member who is pursuing a direction that we consider to be sinful. Rather, it is our normal policy to pursue such a member in the process of church discipline." They asked me to confirm receipt, to which I responded with the following:

> I did receive the letter today. It appears that what the elders believe God wants and what I believe God wants are at odds. Since I am responsible before God for the

> life He gave me, I am obligated to obey Him rather than men. You have been grossly deceived, and for that I am sorry; however, I need to stay the course that God has set in front of me. If that means you choose to excommunicate me, so be it. It is a false excommunication that will go unrecognized by God, for I belong to Him, and I will always be part of His Church regardless of whether or not an earthly church organization led by fallible men chooses to treat me otherwise.

Then I wrote in my journal:

> "It's either jump into the unknown or let Pharaoh drag me back to Egypt where I will be given food and shelter in exchange for my voice and wings. They tell us it's a sin to have voices and wings, so they keep us in gilded cages of our own choosing. I could not see this from my Cage View. But from my Sky View, it's crystal clear. I'm never going back. I'm flying free!"

I didn't want simply to enjoy my own flight, though. I knew there were caged survivors longing to fly, and I wanted them to have an empathetic witness to their experience. I wanted them to know they, too, were seen and heard. They, too, had an empathetic witness *within themselves*. I wanted to help them see their cage doors were actually wide open, and they only stayed because they believed they had no choice. But who taught them this? And why?

I changed the name of my website from *Visionary Womanhood* to *Flying Free* and started writing articles for Christian women about emotional and spiritual abuse. The summer of 2018, I wrote a book called *Is It Me? Making Sense of Your Confusing Marriage: A Christian Woman's Guide to Hidden Emotional and Spiritual Abuse*. This book

309

All the Scary Little Gods

would be a necessary and healing empathetic witness for thousands of Christian women, and I would go on to write a companion workbook, teach classes, coach women in groups, and start a private forum so these women could connect and empathetically witness one another. At the end of 2018, the *Flying Free* podcast was born. It was like Love said, "Hey, Sweet Pea, do you want to use your voice? Here's a mic. Start talking." So, I did.

I had spent decades looking for an empathetic witness outside of myself, but the Great Empathetic Witness had been within me all along. I had finally stopped confusing God with controlling religious people, and this cleared the smoke and enabled me to experience God more authentically for who God was. Once I experienced the Great Empathetic Witness, the trauma began to resolve and dissipate, and I was then free to *be* an empathetic witness for women like me as well as show them how to be the same for others.

This is how we change the world—not through power and control, but through empathetic witnessing. Another word for it is Love. And another word for Love is God. And another word for God is Creator. I hope you're starting to connect the dots.

75
Wedding Day

On November 7, 2017, I celebrated my fifty-first birthday. On November 8, 2017, my divorce was final, and I moved out of my past marital home and into Tom's, which was no small feat since I had a soap business with thousands of curing soap bars and hundreds of products. I remember nothing about that day except that it happened. On November 9, 2017, Tom and I were married in a Lutheran church with six of my nine children in attendance. One of my closest high school friends, a female Lutheran pastor, officiated over the marriage of Tom the Catholic and Natalie the Baptist, right there in her own Lutheran church. It was one of the most fantastic God-winks I had ever experienced.

After the ceremony, we had our own mini reception at the local Baker's Square restaurant with pies and fries. We cracked jokes about the latest juicy church gossip circulating at the time. Apparently, I had rebelliously kept a long-time secret lover, and that's why I divorced a godly man. It was an exciting story, but it wasn't mine. We went home, put the kids to bed, and consummated our relationship for the first time, despite what the salacious stories about us said.

My first wedding had been huge with lots of fanfare and Glory to God in the Highest. The marriage that followed was problematic on multiple levels. Glory to God? Not so much. My second wedding was a small, private blip on the screen. The marriage that followed has been a safe place for peace and love to flourish. Glory to God? I believe so. But only God knows about it, which is maybe what giving glory to God is all about in the first place.

76

Soap and Vodka

It was time to sell my soap business. Apple Valley Natural Soap was ten years old and ready to move into a new phase of growth, and so was I. The only problem was we were moving in two completely different directions. My brand-new business educating and coaching Christian women in emotionally and spiritually abusive marriages was taking off. I had no idea so many women like me existed, but I guess when a religious environment encourages men to be entitled assholes and women to be their sex slaves, you'll get that kind of result.

So, I sold the soap business in January of 2018 and began to pour my life into the growing *Flying Free* community. I thought I would feel more emotional about saying goodbye to my soap business baby, but as the movers took the last of the equipment out the door, all I could feel was relief. There was only one thing I regretted. I was also, in a way, losing my sister. Marcy had been working in my home with me almost every day for several years, and I felt close to her. She had been around when my youngest son got diagnosed and went through in-home therapy. She had witnessed my daughter's incessant screaming and rage. She had listened to all the details as they unfolded about John, the divorce, and the church. She seemed excited when I met and fell in love with Tom. I used to call her my "in-house therapist." She was the peacemaker in our family of origin, and she consistently offered support and validation.

But when the soap went out the door, so did she, and I missed her. I considered her to be one of my closest friends, but now I worried that she hadn't felt the same way. Maybe she only loved me because I employed her? We humans tend toward loving and placating the hand that feeds us. She did Snapchat me every day. Marcy is hilariously funny, and she always knew exactly what would make me laugh. I decided this was as good as our relationship was going to get. We were both busy, and it was fine to Snapchat, but I longed for a deeper connection. She was the only family member who seemed to really understand me and what I had gone through. But as the weeks turned into months, and our dad's cancer worsened, I could feel the distance between us growing, and I didn't know why.

I have two final, bittersweet memories with Marcy. One was meeting her at a restaurant our dad enjoyed. We reminisced and grieved his impending death together. It was the one time I truly felt connected in mutual grief with anyone in my family. The other happy memory was going to see *Elf* at the Ordway in St. Paul the following Christmas. We gave each other tickets to celebrate our birthdays that year. We had cranberry vodkas, took our pictures with the big cardboard *Elf*, and did a lot of laughing. I didn't know it would be the last thing we did together. The last time we celebrated each other's birthdays. I couldn't imagine that one day Marcy would join my mom and Alice, and they would all step out of my life.

If I had known, I would have had a lot more cranberry vodka.

77

Funerals

The first funeral I remember attending was for a high school friend's mother. We were in college when she died suddenly of a brain aneurysm while turning up the volume of her stereo in the living room. Her death startled me. She was young. She had kids. She played the piano for us when we practiced for the school pop concert. She was real and warm and hilariously funny. And also, dead. It made no sense.

I had never seen a dead body before, and I nervously walked up to the casket to peek in. Her body looked like a wax figure—a decent rendition, but not really her. I remember wondering how her daughters and husband could be so composed during the wake. They even smiled while they visited with people! If this was my mother, I would be on the floor, utterly undone. A spectacle. A bawl-baby writ large. People would whisper about how ridiculous and self-centered I was to be thinking only about my grief instead of about whether or not the visitors were comfortable. But thank God, this was not my mother, and my funeral manners would not be tested yet.

The next funeral was my infant daughter's. I was beside myself with grief, and yet, despite the stupid comments people made about how she was a little angel in heaven, and how God needed her more than I did, and thank goodness I was young and could try again, I smiled and thought a great deal about whether or not the visitors were comfortable.

I fell apart after they left.

After that, it seemed like everyone lost babies and kids. I collected the funeral programs. Children's cancer. Detached placenta. A rare brain disease. Another baby simply didn't have a brain. I don't know how I did it, but I showed up, I gave hugs, and I even sang at some of their funerals.

And then my grandparents began to die. One by one they came to the end of their earthly roads and passed on to the other side, all of them looking like a wax version of the people I remembered and loved. My dad's spunky mother hung on the longest and died just a few months before he did. Dad's cancer had gone into remission for almost a year, but it had returned, and I remember watching him at my grandma's funeral, knowing his turn was next. But then I looked around at everyone and realized that *we were all next*. Every last one of us. Today was Grandma's day. But one day in the not-too-distant future, it would be our day. It was the oddest feeling to look at that room from the perspective of a hundred years in the future.

As it turned out, Tom's fifty-two-year-old brother was the next one. A heart attack took him one night when he was sleeping in his house alone, and someone found his body a few days later. This was a shocking blow to my new husband, and I saw Tom from a different angle as he handled all the responsibilities of getting the body back to Minnesota, packing up his brother's things, selling his house out of state, and managing all the legalities. He retreated into himself with his grief, and I was left on the outside, unsure of my role. Two months after that, my own dad died, and we both floundered for a while, trying to find our equilibrium. We tried to find our way back to each other through a thick fog of mourning. Once again, life felt fragile, like walking in a minefield, never knowing if the next step would blow up in our faces regardless of how gingerly we placed them. We were getting older. This was going to keep happening. Friends and family were going to start popping off into eternity like popcorn.

I recently read *Fortune* by Lisa Sharon Harper, a book that tells the story of three generations of her relatives and their horrific suffering

All the Scary Little Gods

under America's racist laws and customs. As I listened to her crack open stories that otherwise would be lost to history, I was struck by how precious every human life is and how they come like a surprise from nowhere and then go just as swiftly and mysteriously. Forgotten. Like fragile flowers. One day, alive and full of love and fear and anger and terror and hope and passion. And then the next day, just . . . *gone*.

Gone where?

I look at my little boys tucked in their beds and feel so much love it hurts. Where did that love come from, and when I die, where does all that love go? Will they be surrounded and kept by love when I am gone? Our bodies may be mostly made of water. But our spirits? What are they made of?

The older I get, the more I wonder about death. In my fundamentalist Christian days, I had all the answers, but I still wondered. I think that's because even when we think we know, we really know that we don't know. We simply pick something to believe, swiftly gloss over our death thoughts with our chosen belief, and then move on to picking out what we want to eat at Taco Bell.

But after a funeral, we tend to lie awake in bed at night and feel terror tug at the edges of our not knowing. It's been in those dark moments thinking about death that I've learned to live. In those dark places my faith has been forged. I've gone down into that rabbit hole, and here's where I've landed—for now, anyway. What if Creator, the essence of Love itself, made our essence out of Love, too? And what if Love never ends? Never dies? Is unstoppable and unbreakable? Restores what is gone? Redeems what is stolen? Heals what is broken? What if Love never fails?

I can live with that.

78

Flying Away

"Wake up!" Someone called from far away. "It's time! He's leaving!" I struggled to pull myself out of the vortex of sleep after thirty-two hours of waiting vigil over Dad. The faraway voice was close now. "Natalie! Hurry!" I yanked my body out of the bed and ran to the room where my dad had been dying all weekend. The hymn "I'll Fly Away" was softly playing somewhere.

Marcy was sitting with him when he flew away. The rest of us ran in as soon as she called, but he was already gone. We cried and kissed him. My mom and sisters hugged each other. I stood alone and looked at them and then at his body, my brain still trying to comprehend what had just happened. He wasn't there anymore, and it seemed the oddest thing. I had been afraid that when the coroner came to take him away forever, I would fall apart; instead, I watched them wheel out an empty body. It was not my dad.

He had gone into hospice at home the week before. My mom and two aunts got him all set up in the back room where Marcy and Alice had slept in bunk beds growing up. The doctors were thinking he had about three months left and would be able to enjoy one last summer. My uncle built a ramp in the garage to get his wheelchair up and down the stairs so Mom could take him for walks outside.

But within a few days, he began a rapid decline. I remember asking if I could come see him the Saturday before Memorial Day, but I was told to wait until Sunday. He already had too many guests coming on Saturday, and he was tired. I suspected it had less to do

All the Scary Little Gods

with my dad being tired and more to do with Alice, who didn't want to be in my presence since I got divorced and remarried. I never felt warmth from her direction, but the divorce and remarriage appeared to be her permission from her scary little god to shun me with biblical approval.

Her determination to deny my existence was confirmed the next day when I at last had the family's permission to visit, and she was sitting on the living room floor as I walked in. I nervously attempted a quiet, insecure "hi" and, unsurprisingly, got nothing in return. I went back to Dad's room to find him grabbing at the air and repeating nonsensical sentences. I was unprepared for the shock of this, and I burst into panicked tears. My dad was gone, out of his right mind, and *my family had not told me or allowed me to see him on his last coherent day?* How could they do this to me? I was filled with grief and rage that had nowhere to go but inward, where it pummeled and pounded at my stomach and my head.

My mom and sisters left me alone with him. I wasn't sure if they were being coolly polite or if my presence repulsed them, but either way, I was grateful for the space. I sat and sobbed while he contentedly babbled and batted at invisible things. After a while, I was able to calm down enough to be curious. He was in his own little world. Maybe his brain was reliving memories. Maybe it was just glitching around, neurons randomly firing nonsense. At least he seemed peaceful even though his brain was obviously active. That was so like him, to just accept whatever came. To Surrender. To Succumb.

That was so *un*like me. Every fiber of my being was protesting this whole thing. That it had to be here, in this home, in this room. That it had to be with these people who seemed to be annoyed and upset with me. I felt, once again, like the problem child—the reason their world was not as perfect as it should be. I had spent my entire life trying to find the mysterious code to belonging here, but it kept changing, like a tease. Something inside me was clawing and scratching to get out and away, but I could not find a way out of this. I would have to sit here, make myself as small as possible, hold my breath, close my eyes, and wait it out. How could an adult walk into a house and suddenly be seven years old again?

I spent the next thirty-six hours being violently yanked between grief and shame. *My dad is dying.* The voice inside kept repeating like a robot. Throughout the process, various people came and went. Alice's son, his wife, and new baby stopped by. I had that familiar and irresistible urge to hold the baby, but I resisted. It belonged to Alice. I knew my place.

My dad is dying.

My own eldest son and his wife stopped by as well, and while they had not spoken to me for months, they politely said hello as if I were a stranger in my own childhood home. Maybe I had always been a stranger.

And my dad kept on dying.

At one point I went to the basement where I could be alone. Breathe. Let some of this pressure attacking at my insides out. It was dark and cool down there, and it smelled like home. This was the place Dad spent a good deal of time watching sports and TV shows. *All in the Family, M*A*S*H, Hawaii 5–0, Hee Haw.* His desk was still there in the corner, the wall covered with pictures grandchildren had made for him over the years. My family did not seem to know me, but these walls did, and the realization of being seen by walls created just enough compassion to prick a hole in the dam of my heart and let out the waters in a powerful gush of howling pain. Thankfully, I was skilled at howling in silence, and I lost track of time in the deluge. I'd think the storm was done, and another cloud would burst open within, and I'd be a mess again.

I was spent and must have looked like shit by the time I went back upstairs, but nobody noticed I had been gone, and nobody said anything about my appearance. I was invisible, but I remembered that being invisible had its advantages. I could observe others from my invisible place, so I watched my mom bustle about, expertly changing my dad's diapers and talking with visitors. She had a job to do, and she was going to do it, by God. She cracked little jokes here and there to lighten the mood, but I thought I could see panic behind her eyes. This man was her universe, and he was leaving too soon.

They had purchased a brand-new retirement condominium with plans to move in another year and be done with shoveling snow, lawn care, and the relentless upkeep of owning a home. They were going to grow old in peace together, but cancer had come along and stolen all of that from them. From *her*. I wondered if she had to keep telling herself to keep going, that she would have time to deal with the loss later, that now there were diapers to change and people to greet. She had always been so stoic, trusting that God would only do her good and not evil all the days of her life. I wondered if she wrestled with her faith now. Even just a little bit. Wasn't Jesus supposed to come back before all this death and old age ruined everything? Did she ever question, "Where the hell are you?"

I didn't know. But I felt such a desolation of sadness for her, and I didn't know what to do with it. I couldn't offer it. I felt they would all think I was faking it or pretending to be a good girl when everyone already knew I was a fraud. So, I shyly watched my mom from my invisible distance, a tangled knot of confusion and sadness.

This is what it's like to watch your dad die. This is it.

We thought he was going to die that first night. He almost did. We could feel him wanting to go, but something caused him to hesitate. He rallied and came back. At one point when all of us were in the room with him, his eyes fluttered open, and he said as clear as day, "Goodbye, girls!" Of course, we all burst into tears. All I could think was, "This only happens in the movies." But then, under his quiet demeanor, my dad always had a theatrical flair. It made sense that he would milk his death for all it was worth and leave us with a dramatic, film-worthy goodbye.

A man after my own heart.

So, I played epic movie soundtracks on my phone whenever I had time alone with him, and while I'm fairly certain it annoyed the hell out of my mom and sisters, I'm just as certain it delighted him, providing the perfect background music for his grand exit from this life and entrance into the next one.

When the hospice nurse checked in the following morning, he was surprised to see my dad was still alive. He said sometimes this happens, and that Dad would likely go another day and then leave us the following night. His prediction was correct. In the wee hours of the morning on May 29, 2018, my beautiful father slipped away from us into the Oneness of Love.

The next day, all the cottonwood trees were shedding their white seed puffs into the air, and they floated like thousands of slow-motion angels through the atmosphere.

79
Dad

My family did not invite me to join them in planning Dad's funeral. When I asked Marcy if I could help, she waved her hand as if it were a trifle and said, "We don't need any help."

"But this is Dad's funeral. I want to be part of it," I said, confused.

"We just figured you were too busy. We've already done everything. If you want to bring some paper and pencils and put them in the middle of the tables for people to write their memories at the reception, you can do that." Her voice had a tone of finality in it. As if to say, *"Don't make this into something."*

I purchased golf pencils in honor of my dad's love of golfing and solemnly placed them on each table along with note cards. It was my only contribution, and all the little friends on my bus, especially Rosie, took it seriously. On the day of his funeral, I took a Xanax (sorry, Spiritualizer) and watched the ceremony unfold like a dream in which I was a silent, invisible, somewhat numb observer. When it was over, my youngest sister, Alice, invited immediate family over to her home, and her husband invited my ex-husband and our older boys to go golfing in honor of my dad. Tom and I were not invited. I asked Marcy if she knew why, and I confessed to her that it hurt to be left out. Once again, she dismissed my thoughts, saying, "It's no big deal. You don't have to make it something it isn't." The unspoken message was, *"Don't make waves. Walk away."* So, I did. But not without having feelings. Sadness. Indignation. Shame. Fear. I allowed all of it.

Even as I try to write this chapter, a critical part of me hisses much of what I heard growing up: *"You don't have to pout about it. It's been five years now. Do you really have to put something about it in your book? It was your dad's funeral, for God's sake, but must you make everything in the universe about you all the time? Fine. Whatever. Have it out. Be a bawl baby. Get some violins going. I hope it makes you feel better."*

I want to honor the little girl who went home that day and both raged and cried. I want her to say what she wants to say—what she wasn't allowed to say before. Little Natalie is usually afraid to be vulnerable. Afraid of rejection. So, what if I leaned into her fears and invited you, the reader, to join me in a little eulogy of my own for my dad? It's nothing all that profound. My dad was a simple man with a simple life, and I would like to meander around in my memories for a couple of minutes, the way we do at funerals. If you would like to be an empathetic witness to my final thoughts about my dad, then come along. Sit with me in this sacred place that exists outside of time or space. It's like my own little funeral for my dad, right here in the pages of a book.

Let me tell you about my dad.

My dad was a quiet mountain. Emotions would sometimes rage around him, but he, himself, was immovable. He watched and listened and simply *was*. Perhaps he learned early on that this was the safest way to navigate an emotionally fragile and chaotic world.

One of my earliest memories with him was walking through a gas station holding his hand. I noticed a man who looked older, like my dad, but he was my size. Fascinated, I pointed and said, "Daddy, look at that little man over there!" Dad glanced over to where I was pointing, then looked away and said nothing, but I felt his big hand slowly, gently, and powerfully squeezing my own, and somehow, I knew I was to mind my own beeswax. That was how he corrected me. A look. A squeeze. Quiet strength.

My dad rarely raised his voice. He could get exasperated, such as when we giggled too much during family game night or slurped the last of our chocolate malts through the straw even though there was nothing left to slurp. "That's enough," he would say sternly. As I recall, we might do one last slurp, but with the giggling, we simply could not stop, and then he would say game night was over, and that was that. I do remember one incident in one of our long car rides up to see all the grandparents in northern Minnesota. My sisters and I were fighting, and he got upset enough to pull the car over and spank us by the side of the road. I only remember it because I don't remember him ever doing that before or after. It was such a shocking anomaly.

It must have been challenging for him to live with three teenage daughters. We would nitpick, argue, and fight, and he would quietly refuse to participate. While we woke up crabby, he woke up pleasant, and he patiently put up with our annoyed remarks. I felt guilty because he'd drive me early in the morning to my high school jazz group practice at school and ask me questions, trying to get into my world, and I would answer shortly because I wanted to be silent when I was feeling out of sorts and not quite ready to go into another school day. I used to worry that he would die, and I'd be riddled with guilt for the rest of my life about how I squandered my time with him feeling irritated. And now he is gone. I don't feel guilty. I was an angsty teenager, and having raised a few of them myself, I get it. But I do feel profound sadness, and I would give anything to go back for one last car ride with him. But then again, if I had it, I would probably spend it weeping hysterically, begging him to stay, and it would not be a good experience for either of us.

One of the most painful realities of life on this planet is that nothing lasts. My dad often said, with each passing season, "It's the end of another era." And we would feel the weight of that grief. The miracle hiding in that truth is that even as one moment is making its exit, another one is making an entrance. Once we figure this out, we can revel in each *now* and let the warm sands slip through our fingers in delight, knowing that there is an infinite world of ocean and beach to experience.

Dad always looked like a million bucks. He wore suits to work every day until he retired. He'd walk past me in the hall, and I could smell his aftershave. I'd hear him kiss my mom before he left. It wasn't just a peck. It was a sweet and lingering kiss. Maybe a little too juicy for my liking as a teenager. I knew he loved my mom with an eternal love. Nothing she could do or say would stop that love from always being present and available for her. I hoped that one day I would be loved like that, and I think my dad hoped that for his daughters as well.

The summer before he died, I met him at a coffee shop and told him about Tom. I was still in the middle of the divorce, which had dragged on and was in its fifteenth month of going nowhere. My family did not look kindly on divorce, and certainly not dating while getting divorced, but my dad didn't flinch. Maybe cancer had given him perspective. Maybe watching me suffer in my marriage for so many years had opened up his mind to other realities than one narrow belief about divorce that held so many in oppression and sorrow for their entire lives. Or maybe he had simply learned that the women in his life were going to do whatever the hell they wanted to do whether he agreed with it or not. Whatever the reason, he expressed warmth and joy when he found out I was dating Tom and that it was serious. He did ask, somewhat apologetically, as if he was obligated to ask but didn't really want to go there, "Is he a Christian?"

"Yes, he is a Catholic Christian," I replied. He flinched almost imperceptibly. It was so subtle that I might have imagined it based on my knowledge of our family convictions and beliefs, such as the one about Catholics burning in hell for torturing the Protestants and worshipping Mary. But Dad said nothing, and when he finally met Tom several months later at Christmas, after we were married, he welcomed Tom warmly. Tom only remembers feeling loved in spite of Mom seating him in the corner of the long table as far away from herself as possible.

Dad came to every single concert, theater performance, and special event that involved his daughters. Once he had acquired eighteen grandchildren, he wasn't able to make every event but only because he could not be in two places at once. If he could, he would have, but sometimes the grandkids had to take turns. When he was there watching, the kids could feel it, and I'm pretty sure they played and sang and recited and acted better for it. Since his departure, I still find myself scanning the seats for his presence, and sometimes I will spot the back of a head that looks like his, and my heart will both leap with hope and sink in pain in less than a second. Then I have to remind myself that he is here in my heart.

Dad tried to teach me how to golf at one point, but I was a hopeless and disinterested student. I did love to drive the golf cart, though, so on occasion, when we could use my grandpa's cart, I would come along to be the caddy. I loved our summers up north. My mom's folks had a cabin on Big Cormorant Lake in central Minnesota, and we would spend two weeks every summer hanging out with cousins and aunts and uncles shooting off fireworks, smoking candy cigarettes, and swimming for endless hours in the algae-filled waters. Dad loved movies, and it became our little tradition to go to one, just the two of us, each summer. We saw *Raiders of the Lost Ark*, *Jaws*, and *Twilight Zone: The Movie*, to name a few. He also loved food and treats, and he would take all of us to the Dairy Queen for ice cream cones while we were on vacation or after any big event. On the way home from the cabin, he would make one last vacation stop at Tasty's Pizza in

Columbia Heights, where we had lived until I was seven. He would buy two large pepperoni pizzas and a pitcher of Pepsi. I remember watching his eyes as he looked longingly at the pizza while it quickly disappeared. I wanted the last piece, but he always seemed so sad when it was over, so we all let him have it. Most of the time. We may have left that neighborhood when we moved, but we never left our love of Tasty's Pizza. To this day, I still go back periodically to have the best pizza in the world. And to remember.

When I was young, Dad played on a city softball team with several of my extended relatives, which meant we got to play in different parks all over the Twin Cities with all my cousins. I never wanted those moments to end. Dad got along with anyone and everyone. He was quiet, but he had a dry sense of humor and an impeccable sense of timing. He would listen to the conversation and then, at just the right moment, softly drop a hilarious little twist to whatever was being talked about. He wasn't the life of the party, but he was someone you definitely wanted at the party. You also definitely wanted his financial prowess. As a comptroller for a large commercial real estate company as well as the church treasurer for many years, he was good with money. He saved and paid for all three of his daughters' big weddings as well as most of their college. He never lied or said anything mean about anyone. You could trust him with everything. And we all did.

He loved his grandkids. When I lost baby Elizabeth, he had a hard time getting over her death. He cried. He wrote about it. He wanted to talk about it all the time. He had his heart set on doing all the things he had done with his little girls all over again with this first little granddaughter. At the time, his grief over a child he never knew seemed over the top and a bit odd, but looking back, I now believe he was grieving the loss of his own little girls and their childhoods, and losing Elizabeth gave him permission to fall into that sadness and grieve about all of it. Within a few years, he had numerous grandchildren, and he entered grandfather-hood with gusto. He generously rented cabins for us every summer so we could replicate with our own children the cabin memories we had grown up with. For one week out of the summer, he'd hang out with his grandkids swimming, fishing, golfing, and pulling skiers and tubers over the lake waters while they screamed with glee.

After he got cancer, Dad couldn't read books anymore because of his failing eyesight. Being a book lover myself, I couldn't imagine what a loss he must be feeling, so I introduced him to Audible and got him started with some books. He fell in love and ultimately listened to hundreds of them before he died. It made me happy that he didn't have to lie in bed doing nothing. He could still get lost in historical biographies, mysteries, and crime dramas.

About a week and a half before Dad died, he was in the hospital, and I brought him his favorite chocolate-covered cherries from Abdallah's, a chocolatier not far from where we lived. He was so composed. So at peace. He was still *so him*. He said to me, "I had a good life, and I lived it to the fullest. I got to experience many memorable things, including watching my children and grandchildren grow up. I watched many eras come and go, and now it is the end of my last era, and I'm ready to go. You keep going. You still have life to live and love. We will be together again someday."

When I looked at the emaciated and discolored shell of my dad, I saw Creator God. And Creator in me connected with Creator in him, and there was a Knowing. How do I know this? Because when I am aware of Creator in me, I am flooded with peace and love, and everything else disappears. I can see with Creator eyes, and things look very different. And that is what I saw and felt when he said those words to me.

Dad

I gave him one last chocolate-covered cherry and a hug and then walked to my car, struggling to see the sidewalk in front of me through the tears, and I knew I had just experienced the end of an era. Goodbye, Dad. I love you.

80

Tsunami

Some people come into your life out of nowhere, yet their comfortable familiarity feels as if they have always been there. This is how I felt when an amazing young man came into my oldest daughter's life. In a world of small, controlling men throwing fits about who is better than whom, this boy was an angel. I admit, I wasn't quite sure he fit into our family. We were still shattered and awkwardly limping toward healing, and he entered our recovery space smiling and full of life and love. But he came from a hurting family as well: a missing father and a surviving mother. I suspected my family might not recognize what a treasure he was. Not at the beginning. But as he spent time with us on vacation and holidays, he became a trusted brother and friend to my children, and he became a son to me.

In the summer of 2020, he dropped by to visit me with flowers, and on our warm, sunny deck, he asked me for my oldest daughter's hand in marriage. She didn't know. He wanted to surprise her. I was ecstatic. This young man was really and truly going to be my son! Somehow, I had always known his destiny belonged in our family's future bloodline. I offered him the wedding ring from my former marriage so he could use the diamonds to make a new ring; we took pictures to commemorate this moment; and I floated on air the rest of the day.

I did not yet see the tsunami on the far horizon.

My daughter was a camp counselor that summer for a few weeks, but she would be returning in time for our upcoming cabin vacation.

Tsunami

The adult kids were all joining us that year, and I happily planned the activities for our time together. We would make memories horseback riding, biking, boating, and swimming.

And then she called. She wasn't coming home. She wanted to stay at camp. She met someone there, and she was questioning her relationship with her boyfriend. If it were a "forever" relationship, why was she pulled in by this other person? She didn't know. She was in knots, crying and unsure of what to do, but one thing she did know. She did not believe it was fair to let this boy believe she was all in when clearly her heart had been distracted by someone else. She wasn't even sure the "someone else" was worth pursuing long-term, but just the fact that she was drawn in a new direction left her confused and miserable. She was only going to come back for the weekend in between camp sessions, long enough to break the news to her boyfriend in person. It was only fair. But the day of her return was also the Saturday when we were leaving for the cabin.

I completely fell apart. All I could imagine was this exquisite soul on a serene beach, innocently and joyfully enjoying the beauty all around him, anticipating a future of promise, but in the distance, I could see the wave of destruction heading toward him. He wouldn't see until the tsunami was upon him, picking him up, consuming him, and spitting him out as if he were of no more consequence than the rocks, crabs, and sand around him. And that would be the end of the loveliest young man I had now come to think of as my own son.

I could hardly sleep the next two nights and cried off and on as I miserably packed up suitcases, grocery bags, and dreams. At one point, a desperate thought momentarily flicked at the edge of my brain. Perhaps he might marry one of my younger daughters? (Seriously, Rosie? This isn't *Fiddler on the Roof*.) But, of course, he was only meant for one. He would never come with us now. He would never

331

be part of our family. He would leave my world forever, and I knew I would grieve his loss as if he had died.

The tsunami slammed into his world that Saturday and did everything I knew it would. I allowed myself to enter fully into the grief of it. When the tears came, I succumbed to their force. On the second day of the vacation, I injured my back while horseback riding and could not walk for several days. I lay in the cabin on a hard bed, writhing in agony of heart, soul, and body, and I had no energy to fight or resist it. I was undone. Toward the end of the week, when I could slowly and gingerly walk a few paces, I hobbled outside to sit on a tree stump where I could get a satellite connection, and I could talk to this young man on my phone. He was as shredded and raw with pain as I imagined he would be. I could hear the bitter questions pounding from his heart. Where was God in all of this? Why was this happening? It made no sense.

I had no answers. Some things cannot be explained, only endured. I was relieved when the week was over, and we returned to a hollow normal. My daughter came back from camp, but she was not herself. A few days later, the boy she had met at summer camp drove three hours to see her at our home. When he arrived, my daughter walked him into the kitchen to meet me. He offered a vague smile and limp handshake, which I took vaguely and limply in return. I asked him if he wanted anything to drink. "I don't know," he replied with an utter absence of personality.

Annoyed, I responded, "Well, if you decide you would like something later, let me know." I abruptly turned away, disgusted with this unsatisfactory replacement and disappointed in my own failure to like him. He didn't have a chance in the world with me.

My daughter led him upstairs to talk, and twenty minutes later they came back down. He quietly went out the front door without saying goodbye. She came into the kitchen sobbing. "I sent him away. I don't like him. I've made a horrible mistake. I don't know what I was thinking, and now I've lost the man I love. *What have I done?*" What had she done, indeed. I hugged her, but there was nothing to be done about it. Tsunamis like this leave no survivors.

But we didn't account for Love. How could we? What had we seen of Love so far? We had only known a love conditioned on our perfection and pleasing those around us. Even in the home and church, places where Love should have thrived and nourished and led by example, we had only encountered Love's imposter.

But the extraordinary young man who loved my daughter had tapped into Something most people can't see and, therefore, don't believe. After the tsunami had triumphantly spent its rage and left him for dead, this boy slowly lifted himself to his feet and made his way back over to the girl. He wisely understood something. She had been swallowed up by the same powerful waters that had tried to destroy him. He bent over her, and with a heart full of love, understanding, and forgiveness, he brushed the sand and seaweed off, turned her over, and kissed her. She woke up, and one year later, they said, "I do," at the bottom of a bright green ski slope in July.

Love. Tsunamis don't stand a chance in the face of the real thing.

81

Mom

As of this publication, my mom and two sisters have not talked to me for almost five years. Breaking the silence would be simple. All I would need to do is apologize and beg forgiveness for breaking my marriage vows and getting remarried to a Catholic. For having the audacity to exist and take up space in the universe as my own person with separate thoughts, feelings, and experiences from her and her other daughters. I would need to quietly cooperate with several unspoken expectations as well as tolerate disrespect and manipulation. In the past, when I've curiously waited to see if Mom would break the silence if I did *not* say I was sorry, I discovered she was stronger than I was. Our relationship was like a game of Don't Blink. I always blinked first. I couldn't live without Mom. But in 2019, I stopped waiting for her to blink. I simply tapped out and walked away from the game entirely. When I was younger, I preferred pretending that, if push came to shove, my family would ultimately have my back. But this newer, older version of me knew better and was more interested in the truth than pretending, even if it hurt.

During the first two years of the Silent Treatment, the grief weighed so heavy that when the rage bubbled up to cover and numb that pain, I allowed it, even welcomed it. I was angry at the lies those churches taught about God. I was angry at the collective hate and vitriol their theology produced in the hearts of those who believed the lies. I was angry at how these lies shredded families and caused comparisons, competitions, and a lust for power and control. And I was angry at how covert abuse had permission to run rampant because victims were scared to speak up for fear of losing the ones they loved. I was *sick to death* of being scared to lose the ones I loved. Fuck it. I lost them all anyway.

After a couple years of losing sleep and perseverating and ranting about it, I decided I didn't want to feel that much anger anymore. Rage is exhausting. But this meant I had to move into sadness. Under all that anger hid Little Natalie, lost in the desolate darkness of believing she was unloved and abandoned. During this stage, my brain continued to search for ways to make sense of everything and get some closure, but I was intentionally moving toward the pain and allowing it to hang out with me, like a sad friend. When Freaked said, "This shouldn't be happening," I would answer back with, "But it is, and we're going to be okay." I was learning how to listen to myself with compassion, and this helped me move toward acceptance.

In spite of having made progress in my grief, there was still something raw and festering deep inside. I couldn't figure out what was lingering until June of 2022 when I listened to the book *No Bad Parts* by Richard Schwartz, the founder of the Internal Family Systems (IFS) model, on Audible.[6] An exercise in the book asked the reader to think of a person in their life who triggered them, and I picked my mother. Next, the exercise instructed me to put my mom in a room by herself, so she stayed contained but still visible through a window. Then, I had to imagine my mom doing or saying something that would typically trigger me and notice what happened in my body and mind as a protector part of me jumped in to save me.

I didn't take long coming up with a triggering memory, and upon the thought of it, I noticed a protector part showed up. This protector part was an angry ball of Tasmanian Devil Fire, and my heart began to pound in my chest. I decided to call this ball of fire "Mad Mama." Just then, Spiritualizer popped up, "What is your problem, Mad Mama? Ever heard of this thing called *forgiveness*?"

And Freaked said, "Yeah! Stop with the fire thing! You're freaking me out!"

And Melancholy moaned, "You are going to *ruin my life with your anger!*"

And then, from a deep, compassionate place within me, I quietly asked Mad Mama, "Why are you so angry?"

She roared, "Can't you see that gigantic, immovable rock in there? That's your mother, and she won't look at you! She has her back to you, and she refuses to turn around and see you! It's not fair! I need to go into that room and bang and pound on that rock! I need that rock to turn around *right now* and see Little Natalie!"

"Why do you need my mother to see Little Natalie so badly?" I asked Mad Mama.

"So Little Natalie will be *loved!* So Little Natalie will know *it's going to be okay!* So Little Natalie will *belong* somewhere!" Mad Mama raged mournfully.

Mad Mama was trying to get my own mom to love the little girl part of me who still needed her mother, and the only way Mad Mama could think to do this was to bang on the big, cold, hard boulder and try to get its attention. Because it never worked, Mad Mama's rage continued to increase over the years until it became out of control, and then other protector parts had to jump in and judge her, shame her, and push her away, so I could go through life without murdering anyone.

But during this time, my core Self, intertwined with my Creator, looked without shame at Mad Mama and said, "*Thank you.* Thank you for loving Little Natalie so much that you would try to help her in this way. *I see you, and I see what you are trying to do.*"

Then, I looked at Freaked and Melancholy and Spiritualizer and all the other parts of me on my bus, and I said, "Mad Mama isn't bad. She is only frantic. Frantic because she loves Little Natalie and wants to protect her and give her what she needs. What every human needs: a mother's love. Isn't Mad Mama amazing?"

I could sense my parts calming down. They attentively watched me as I continued to talk to Mad Mama. "What would you do, Mad Mama, if you no longer had to protect Little Natalie from the big rock that won't look at her or love her?"

Mad Mama's fire had gone down significantly once she knew I was really seeing her. *Really* listening to her. She said, "If I didn't have to get the mother-rock to love Little Natalie, I would have time and energy to love Little Natalie myself. *I would be her Mama.*"

I burst into tears. In that moment, I finally saw what was going on. I had always known this raging ball of fire inside of me existed, and I feared and judged this part of me. I was ashamed of her. I even blamed her rage for why I couldn't find Love. I thought she was bad. But once I connected with her and found out about the exhausting responsibility she carried inside of me, I felt compassion toward her and gratitude for the painful role she had been forced to play in my life all those years.

I told Mad Mama that she was released from her duty to protect Little Natalie from the mother-rock who wouldn't turn to look at Little Natalie, and instead, Mad Mama could be Little Natalie's mother. Essentially, *I made a decision deep inside my core to be the mother I needed.* I was the one to bring the healing. Not my mom. *Me.* Or, I should say, *God within me*, because God within me was able to hold love and space for all the people in the story.

Through new eyes, this Mad Mama part looked different to me. She no longer looked like a raging ball of angry fire. She looked like a *star*. This part of me experienced deep healing. And this is who she is inside of me now. She is Star, Little Natalie's mother, and she is full of energy and fire and warmth and regeneration.

But the exercise wasn't over. I turned my focus to the woman in the room, and I no longer saw my mother as a boulder with its back to me. Instead, through these same eyes of compassion and love, I saw a tiny, elderly woman, and all I felt was compassion for her. I realized that she, too, had parts, and her parts were just doing their best to protect her little self.

I love Natalie, and I love her mom. (Rude says, "Most of the time.") When fear and shame flood my body, I disconnect from myself and others. I will only have the capacity to truly enter into love for others when I have entered into the fullness of love for all the parts of myself. If I keep doing this work of learning to know and love my Self—and that includes all of my parts—I can fly free in peace. When one person finds this healing, it creates a ripple effect that impacts the world in ways we will never know about, and that means my inner work matters. So does yours.

I wish I could wrap up this part of my story in a pretty bow, offer a path for others to follow, and call it a productive day. I can't. My story isn't over. My family of origin's story isn't over. But even if there is no connection on this side of death, connection is waiting for my mom and me on the other side. Because remember? Love.

82
Letting Go

What happens when you believe it's your job to make sure everyone is happy, and you are a failure if they aren't? You work hard and eventually fall apart. I found out the key to putting myself back together was letting go of everyone else. Letting other people have their own human emotions. Letting myself be a human who isn't perfect. My daughter—the one who struggled with emotional regulation—taught me this.

I had tried everything to help her, including medication, psychotherapy, day treatment, family therapy, DBT therapy, group therapy, the police, the county's mental health services, parent coaching, days of reading and researching, hospitalization, a local troubled teen club, taking her out for lunch every week, hiding, begging, praying, and weeping, and *nothing changed*. The older she got, the bigger she got, and the more frightening, exhausting, and hopeless the entire thing became. My four younger children had C-PTSD symptoms from the trauma of living in a violent home they could not escape, and I was responsible to somehow provide safety and healing for them while still meeting the needs of this child who was plagued with the unsolvable problem of how to make sense of life inside her chaotic body.

When Tom and I were dating, I told him what was going on. I warned him that if he married me, he would inherit our problems as well as our preciousness, and most of the time our family felt more problematic than precious. Sometimes he could hear her screaming in the background when we were on the phone, but he was not prepared for the shock of reality once it inhabited his space. At first, she was on her best behavior. We were in a new home, life held new interest, and she had her own room. But in a matter of a few weeks, the novelty wore off, and she was back at it with just as much fervor and force as ever. Who knew that I would become familiar with two cities' worth of police officers? They popped in regularly several times a month whenever I needed some extra protection from my own daughter's rage.

I begged John to cooperate with a plan where I would take her when the other kids were with him at his place, and he would take her when they were with Tom and me. I reasoned that this would give the other kids some space to relax and heal, and it would give our daughter the undivided attention she needed. All the therapists agreed, but John did not. He argued that she had no issues when she was with him, so I should figure out what I was doing wrong to cause her violence. He believed the kids should stay together, and I was ridiculous to think the kids were traumatized.

She was only sixteen when we found out she had been participating in a variety of risky behaviors, and I was terrified something would happen to her before I could stop it, so I tried a different solution. I begged John to sign papers to get in-home occupational therapy provided through the county. This would provide us with therapists who would come into our home and help her learn emotional regulation skills when real-life triggers happened in real time. He refused to sign the papers.

On the morning of March 29, 2019, she chased my seven-year-old son and me upstairs, and I locked us in my bedroom. She stood by the door yelling that I neglected my responsibilities as a mother, that Dad did a lot more than I did, and that I was "a fucking bitch." My son eventually got thirsty, and I needed to take some medication, so when we thought she had gone to her room, I quietly stepped out and went to the kitchen to get some water. She must have heard me because she came down and pushed me while I was holding the full glass of water, and it sloshed all over me. Startled and angry, I reacted instantly by splashing the remainder of the water in the glass at her and fled to my room. There, I discovered she had broken the lock to the bedroom door, so I grabbed the seven-year-old, and we locked ourselves in the bathroom. He cried, terrified, and asked me if she would try to run us through with his big brother's sword replica.

When things had calmed down, I came out, made coffee, and was planning to take the two little boys to the grocery store like we were having a normal day in an American suburb. My daughter defiantly stood between the coffee on the counter and me, refusing to let me get some, and I was afraid she would push me if I tried, in the same way she had pushed me with the glass full of water earlier. Not wanting hot coffee all over me, I left it on the countertop, put the boys in the car, and drove away. While we were gone, she salted my coffee and poured out the rest of the coffee in the carafe so I wouldn't have any. When we got home, she was sleeping on the couch, and we tiptoed around her, hoping she would sleep all day so we could have a reprieve.

That evening, Tom installed three new locks on our bedroom door, which also had a huge crack in it from her kicking. She wanted to go out for a bike ride, but her bike was broken, so she screamed at Tom for not fixing it that day. We locked ourselves in the bedroom, and she demanded that we allow her to walk to a friend's house. At first, I said no. It was a cold night, and I never agreed to her doing anything that would put her at risk. But she stood quietly outside our door, and every ten to fifteen minutes she would bang on it so loudly that we would jump out of our skin, hearts pounding. I finally relented and told her she could go. I had spent years trying to keep her safe, trying to help her, and at that moment all I wanted was relief.

She packed a few things and left around 8:45 PM. I don't think she knew where she was going or what she was doing. I was awake all night, my heart pounding, sweat dripping off my body, afraid of what was happening to her, afraid of what was happening to my other kids, afraid of what was happening to me. And when the night was over, I knew what I had to do.

The next morning, I found her on our back porch. She didn't give me any details about what she had done all night, but she seemed subdued and spent. I told her to pack all her things. Tom would be dropping her off at her dad's house, and she was not allowed to live with me. I loved her with all my heart, and this was breaking me to pieces, but I could not allow her to terrorize us anymore. She must have been exhausted herself, because she quietly packed her things, and Tom dropped her off at John's house. Next to divorcing John, it was the most painful decision of my life.

Later that day, I sat my four younger children down and told them I was going to protect them from now on. Their childhoods would no longer revolve around their sister's childhood. Their lives would no longer be marked by terror and fear as long as they lived under my roof. I would do everything in my power to provide peace and safety and healing. But what about the daughter I just abandoned at her dad's house? What kind of mother does that? How was I offering her protection and love? I laid in bed listening to "Satellite Call" by Sara Bareilles and completely fell apart. I loved my daughter so much, but I would have to love her "from the ground" now.

There was that grief again, and on top of that was a thick frosting of shame. All the Christian programming kicked into high gear and did its best to scream platitudes and clichés in my brain, but now I could more clearly hear that Stable Voice, and it reminded me that Love always wins, but sometimes it looks like losing first.

Letting Go

I loved all my children. It was not perfect love by a long shot, but it was love in the capacity I had at that point. Love for my younger children looked like protection and healing, while love for this daughter looked like letting go. To use another biblical metaphor, the father in the story of the Prodigal Son did not desperately cling to his son when that boy announced that he wanted to take his inheritance and skip town. The father did not beg or plead. He simply gave the boy his inheritance and sadly said goodbye. Did he not love the boy? He knew what the boy would do with the money and with his life. Why didn't he stop the young man?

Because he loved him.

Today's version of Christianity wants to control the son. Threaten the son with eternal torture. Force the son to stay and do his duty. And when the son leaves, many Christians will turn back to their warm homes in disgust and say, "Good riddance. He was never one of us to begin with." But in the story, Jesus communicates a profound truth. God is not like people. God is not a control freak. God honors His creation and gives us freedom to choose. Why? Because God knows that Love wins in the end. Not at the beginning of the story. Not in the middle of the story. But at the end of the story. Love wins. *This* is the purest of Love. And we are like Love when we offer the same to one another.

In my messy way, I let my daughter go. It appeared that I was pushing her out, and in one way, I was. I had given her countless warnings, years of therapy and support, and many opportunities to make different choices, but there was one thing I had never tried, and that was to let her go. This didn't mean I lost contact with her. To the contrary, I kept in touch via text and phone. I regularly took her out to spend one-on-one time with her, away from the other kids. At first, she was cold to me, but in a surprisingly short time, she warmed up, and we began to develop a relationship that no longer involved triggers and fear and violence. She was enfolded back into our family on holidays and vacations and other gatherings where she had a better chance at creating successful connections with her siblings that were healing for everyone.

Several years have passed since this happened, and my daughter graduated high school summa cum laude, held down a job, bought her own car, and moved into her own studio apartment with her therapy cat. I have the honor of regularly spending time with her, and I consider her my beloved friend and child. I hope the reader sees that relationships can heal, not because the people in the relationships are all prettied up and perfect, but because they are willing to love in spite of how imperfect and problematic we can all be.

Sometimes love means letting someone go so they can find their own wings to fly free. And sometimes those wings will bring them back to us in a full circle of love.

83
The Art of Grief

Babies are my drug of choice, and I've felt this way since I was practically a baby myself. Dolls were my first babies, and they were as real to me as any person in my early childhood. I would get a new doll for Christmas and take her with me to Grandpa and Grandma's house and everywhere else I went for the first few months of her life with me. After that initial bonding period, my new baby would be assimilated into the growing family of assorted dolls on my bed.

I always wanted five children. My friends thought I was crazy, but I would pencil in potential names on the covers of my notebooks and dream of how many girls and boys there would be to love. Looking back, I still get caught in wonder that I ended up with nine of them. Each one was the most exquisite treasure. The first twenty-four hours in the hospital with my newborn was like being in a warm, golden haze of drunken love. This little person was a living, moving *being* and *all mine*. Part of me and yet separate. Perfect. A blank slate only in need of my love, and my love was so overwhelmingly powerful within me, I thought it was everything and all this child would need.

I would meet my child's needs as quickly as I could, most of the time anticipating them before the child had a chance to voice them. I'd pop a breath mint in my mouth before nursing, or I'd make sure not to breathe in their face so they wouldn't be uncomfortable with the terrible scent coming from some unknown origin above them. I made sure they were immediately changed so they wouldn't suffer

1. I was meticulous about being sanitary so they wouldn't ...eyond the essential, practical things, my entire purpose in life was to give them what I had always dreamed of having. Powerful, unstoppable, unflappable Love. What could happen in a child's life if they bathed in this resource while growing up? I was determined to find out.

But baby after baby grew up, and to my utter despair at times, I realized my love was actually not powerful, unstoppable, or unflappable. My love was not enough. I got impatient when they refused to read the words on the page or eat the food on their plate. Why did they make so much noise? Why did they demand more when I had already given everything I could and needed some sleep? My love was not enough to protect them. I would watch them, as if from outside of my body, get reprimanded, and my heart would break seeing their young hands nervously twitching by their sides and the embarrassment and sadness in their eyes. All I wanted in those moments was to sink into the earth and spare them the pain of having a human life with a human mother. Why could I not be the perfect mother they deserved? One by one I had determined to give them the moon and stars, and one by one I failed.

I eventually realized that in trying to be a goddess mother, I had failed to be a normal, human mother. Which is, at the end of the day, all a human child requires. I learned this late in the game after young brains had been programmed and cement had been hardened. And then I blew up their worlds by disregarding all the rules that I, myself, had taught them: "Never give up. Forgive and forget. Die to yourself. Make everyone happy. Always smile. Pretend you've got it together even if you're dying inside. This is how you'll bring glory to God."

Now they had a divorced mom who had given up on her marriage. Who refused to forget what it was like to live in hell. Who wanted to live and have a voice. Who was making everyone unhappy by leaving her husband. Who was no longer smiling but crying. Who most assuredly did *not* have it all together. And who had been kicked out of God's church because all she could do was bring shame to God.

Now what? How would I pick up those pieces? What would I have to offer these beloved human lives I had the brazen, selfish audacity to bring into this chaotic world that only threatened to overwhelm them with eventual grief and loss?

All of this came to the surface when one of my children went under the deep waters of depression, and I wondered if he would die there—both figuratively and literally. Any grief or panic I had ever experienced so far in my entire existence paled in comparison with the dark horror of the possibility that my darling boy would be in so much pain that he might take his own life. I knew he was taking risks with drugs, and his health was poor. He lived several hours away, and I was helpless to change or fix any of it. I was watching *Stranger Things* with some of my kids, and I felt like I was living in a similar dark and demonic upside-down place where there was no control—only terror, pain, and sadness. I grasped for God in that darkness. Where was Love now? Where was Love when children decided life was so dark that they had to end it? And what kind of monster was I to have brought an innocent child into this world only to live in such despair? There were no answers in this darkness. Only thick, black-as-tar grief.

During this time, I learned the art of grief work. I would slip into a hot bath in a dark bathroom, play sad music, and let my body shake with sobs. "*Don't fight the grief, Natalie. Enter into it. I'm not only in the upside-right world of life in the sun, but I'm also and especially in the upside-down world of life in the dark.*" The Empathetic Witness within me quietly held me in those dark waters while I let out all the shrieking screams of my shredded heart. Then, my body would calm

I would get out and go to bed, exhausted and spent, but also with a deep sense of peace that I was not alone. Because I wasn't. I used to pace the kitchen floor speaking all my prayer requests out loud to that Great Bubblegum Machine in the sky, waiting in faith for my sugarplum answer. With this grief, I sat in water and cried, my entire being a prayer of Oneness with my Creator who embodied all of it from the blazing sun to the cold rock moon to the woman huddled in her bathtub to the children tossing and turning alone in dark apartments.

I am still learning this art of grieving as well as the art of letting go—which is the same thing, I guess. Those babies were never mine. They were always meant to have their own trajectory. Their own destiny. And it didn't involve me at all. It was never supposed to. I thought if I did it right, our big family would be all enmeshed with one another, relying on each other, counting on each other, supporting one another, and controlling one another—everyone's future hanging on the balance of everyone else's.

Now I know this mindset is dysfunctional. Of course, I wanted to keep the support and the love, but I needed to release the control and the enmeshment. Once I let go of my dream, I was able to enter into God's dream for our family. In this dream, every person is precious, unique, and free, and everyone else holds space for that person to be all he or she was created to be. We also hold space for that person to figure out who that is. To make mistakes. To fail. To suffer. To try again. To break things and to repair what gets broken.

I could not offer this to these nine incredible human beings until I learned how to offer it to all my own little parts within me. They, too, needed someone to hold space for them to make mistakes, fail, suffer, break things, and repair. These lovely dark parts were only trying to help me and doing it the best way they knew how. Creator God within me taught me how to love them, which ended up being easy. All I had to do was enter into Creator Love, and suddenly I could see them through Creator Love Eyes. When they were seen, known, heard, and understood, they relaxed and came to rest within me. And then, from that place of rest, I could turn my gaze to my babies and offer them the same Creator Love I had already practiced on my own little parts.

I didn't need to be a goddess mother, and my children didn't need to be perfect little specimens in my religious experiment. Instead, we only needed to be who we were: a human mom with human children doing our human thing of feeling all the brilliant joy of holding a newborn child and all the anguished lament of letting the child go.

84
What a Son Needs

"I have seen him climbing a tree while she stood beneath him in unutterable anguish; she had to let him climb, for boys must be brave, but I am sure that, as she watched him, she fell from every branch."

—J.M. Barrie, *The Little White Bird*

I was walking through Target and saw a younger teenaged boy who looked just like my oldest son when he was that age. I had to put my head down to hide the tears. My son hadn't been speaking to me since I filed for divorce, and I missed him like hell. I was bone-weary with grieving the loss of so many people who had never died. When was the pain ever going to end? Was I ever going to get my son back?

I was. Two and a half years after losing him, this boy and I broke the ice one weekend at a small family gathering in a little cabin in northern Minnesota, and we began to tentatively rebuild our fragile relationship. A few months later, we had lunch, and he shared some painful things he remembered about his childhood. I wanted to hold space for him and his reality, but some of the things he shared didn't match up with my own memories. I had spent so many years discounting my own memories and experiences, and I wasn't yet in a space where I could do that again even for the sake of helping my son feel better. And was it even necessary? Was it my job to make him feel better? I desperately wanted him to feel heard and loved. That's how good relationships work. I also desperately wanted to have a relationship with him. Would he only want a relationship with me if

I discounted myself? Would I have to let him go again because I wasn't willing to gaslight myself to manage his pain? He genuinely believed what he had experienced was unjust and wrong, so I had to figure out how to acknowledge the reality of his painful experience without lying to myself. I wanted to show up and honor *both* of us. I'm not sure I pulled it off well that day. I sensed he walked away not feeling as heard as he wanted to feel, and so did I.

But here's the amazing thing: We both loved each other enough to hold that tension and let it be what it was and still come back and continue to do repair work. And that has made all the difference. It has been several years now, and we once again have a good relationship. We have both worked hard on our own side of the street. We have both changed and grown, and I know we will always have our own backs, and ironically, this is how we will also be able to have one another's backs.

Many years ago, I wrote down a quote in my journal from something I must have read somewhere: "A son needs a mother who understands she is a sinner and in constant need of forgiveness. Such a mother will be patient with her son's failures and extend grace instead of anger." Now, years later, I no longer believe that's true. I was a mother who believed I was the most wretched of sinners, and this belief created extreme shame in my body. When we have shame in our bodies, we don't show up in our lives with patience and grace. We have flight/fight/freeze/fawn responses instead. This means when our kids misbehave or trigger us, we either shut down, yell, hide, or placate. These are all human responses. I know how this works because I have lived it my entire life.

Here's how I would change this quote: "A son needs a mother who understands that she is human and makes mistakes just like he is human and makes mistakes. Such a mother will be patient with her own failures and her son's failures. She will keep trying again and again, and she will encourage him to do the same since making mistakes is one of the best ways humans learn and grow. Such a mother will model what it means to truly love because such a mother knows that we can only love when we know we are fully loved ourselves."

85
COVID

I had already worked through and healed huge chunks of trauma when COVID hit, but I was unprepared for how COVID would trigger my fragility and fear again. I didn't only fear losing a loved one. I was watching the *entire world* emotionally fall apart. I was observing collective trauma surfacing and bubbling over into vitriol on Facebook and riots on the streets. For a highly sensitive Myers Briggs INFJ, the reactions to COVID were overwhelming, and I was struggling with existential thoughts like: "*We are insignificant little ants. We live and die. We are irrelevant.*" I had been lied to and betrayed by almost every religious person in my life. Was *everything* I believed my whole life a lie? What about the existence of God? I began to spiral down the dark hole of doubt, but it was a hole I needed to explore. COVID gave me the gift of time to do that.

I had been running around playing Whack-a-Mole for decades, and I was emotionally exhausted, but that game was all I knew. Getting out of my abusive marriage and church was helpful, but I had only traded moles. My new set of moles included all the responsibilities of running a business that was suddenly helping thousands of Christian women all over the world, and I had so much whacking momentum, I didn't know how to put the club down and just *be*. I wasn't even sure I wanted to. If everything slowed down, I might have to feel my grief, and that would hurt too much. Plus, if I dug down deeper, I was afraid I didn't deserve to take up space in the universe unless I was making myself useful. But all of this meant I was also too busy to enjoy life. To enjoy the simple things, like bike rides with my kids. Picnics. Painting rocks. Watercolors. Sitting on the deck doing nothing. Walking with Tom.

Until COVID. Suddenly my kids were all home. Tom was home. We had three new puppies and nowhere to go. I will never forget the long "rock walks" we would take with the kids, planting newly painted rocks along a woodsy path, adding to the growing collection as other families did the same. Rocks that said things like "You Matter," "Be Brave," and "Just Breathe." It was lovely, until someone came along and took all of them. We were sad, but then we decided to believe that someone collected them in their basement, and one day they would be on display in a COVID museum, and that story made us feel much better.

During this time, I also went back into mediation with my ex in hopes of getting him to comply with the divorce agreement he signed almost three years prior, but it didn't go as I had hoped. I had to let go of insisting on what was just and fair in order to be content with *what was*. Also, several of my kids were still struggling in different ways, dealing with anxiety, depression, shame, and fear. I would remember the years of pacing the floor of my kitchen, praying God would make my children "strong and mighty in spirit," so they would grow up to change the world. Were those prayers a wasted effort? Was I a fool to think Someone was listening? That Someone cared? And is that what gives us meaning—changing the world? What if our kids are too sick to change the world? Too depressed? Too lost? And what does changing the world mean, anyway? And do only people who are world changers deserve to be here? Are they the only ones who matter? Who have value?

I loved my kids so much it hurt. I needed to believe Someone bigger than me loved them, too, because I was getting older and was going to die one day, and I never wanted them to feel alone. I never wanted them to think they were floating around like an insignificant cottonwood seed puff in spring, waiting to get grounded into the dirt with the next rain. I wanted them to know they mattered. They were my entire world. But if I was also just a Nothing in the universe who didn't matter, then none of us mattered. Leisurely walks, music, ice cream, mountains, satellites, art, language, stories, and Love? They were just universal neurons randomly glitching around without meaning anything, and one day the lights would go out, and the whole thing would power down into eternal silence.

No wonder some of my kids were depressed. I was depressed, too, and I didn't like it. Even if God didn't exist, that belief was shutting me down, and I didn't want to live what was left of my short life that way. I had been taught a lot of information about God my entire life, which became the foundation of my faith. But what if that information was wrong?

I wasn't ready to give up my faith because it was more than just information to me. I had too many encounters with Something beyond myself that I could not explain. For example, one morning I woke up with so much despair in my body that I was crying and praying, "*I need to know! I need to know if You are personal! I need to know if You exist, yes, but mostly, I need to know ARE YOU CONNECTED TO ME? Are we together? Do You see me?*"

An hour later, I sat down at my computer and received a message from a random stranger in a forum for an SEO (search engine optimization) course I was taking. The message was a simple Bible verse. And no, this was not a Christian SEO course, and I never heard from this person again, and I had no idea why this person sent the message to me. The verse was Jeremiah 29:12–14: "Then you will call upon Me and come and pray to Me, and I will listen to you. You will seek

Me and find Me when you search for Me with all your heart. I will be found by you, declares the LORD."

The verse seemed to be God answering me, "Yes, Natalie. I am connected to you. You'll never be able to prove it to anyone else, and that's okay. You only need to know for yourself. Let Me do all the connecting of all the dots for your kids and the rest of the universe. You be content with the fact that I am connecting the dots for you in your own universe."

Nobody can take that away from me. My relationship with the Creator is mine. What kind of life did I want to live? How did I want to show up in this world? I would need to figure that out and then intentionally choose beliefs that would enable me to live that life. I needed to figure out what I wanted to believe about God because at the end of the day, nobody really knows anything for sure about God. Everyone is just making guesses, and some of those guesses are creating better things in the world than others. Even for those who believe the Bible, that book has been used and twisted to promote all kinds of horrible things in the world, including genocide, sexual abuse, slavery, and misogyny. People aren't building churches and communities on what the Bible teaches. They are building churches and communities on their own interpretations of the Bible—their own personal guesses about what the Bible is saying. Hence all the different kinds of churches.

The Bible had been used to justify so much abuse in my own life and the lives of thousands of Christian women, so I wasn't about to build my faith on a book that could be used like a weapon. I didn't want a book. I wanted the Spirit. I didn't want a map. I wanted the Place. I didn't want a religion. I wanted a Relationship. I wanted what Jesus promised when He said in John 14:16–17, 26: "And I will ask the Father, and He will give you another Advocate to be with you forever—the Spirit of truth. The world cannot receive Him, because it neither sees Him nor knows Him. But you do know Him, for He abides with you and will be in you. But the Advocate, the Holy Spirit, whom the Father will send in My name, will teach you all things and will remind you of everything I have told you." Jesus didn't say He was sending us a book to teach us all things. He said He was sending us the Advocate. The Spirit of God, Love, living and breathing and moving inside of my core being. That's what I wanted. And by the time we were no longer wearing face masks, I was no longer in the hole of doubt.

86

Sin

A common theme throughout my life has been an incessant fascination with sin. I don't think children naturally think about what horrible wretches they are, nor do I think that is mentally or spiritually healthy, but that's what I obsessed about my entire life. That's what I was taught. I was that spider in Jonathan Edwards's essay "Sinners in the Hands of an Angry God," and it terrified me. If love casts out fear, then there was definitely a lack of love in my life.

I believed a humble and God-fearing soul should navel gaze into the depths of one's depravity, and not only that, but a responsible person would point out the depravity of others. I was respectful of others, sensitive to their feelings, and deeply empathetic, thank God, which helped curb my propensity to judge the hell out of everyone to their faces, but I still judged people in my heart. I remember going to church after I had done some deconstruction in this area, and I saw some teenagers wearing what I used to believe were questionable clothes. I noticed that I didn't care even the tiniest bit, and I felt euphorically free. I noticed this about other things, too. (Freaked is begging me not to tell you about this example because Melancholy is so ashamed of it, but I think it's a miraculous demonstration of what's possible even for the most Judgy Pants parts of us. Rude wants me to say, "Try not to puke.")

After the 2003 Academy Awards, I wrote this in my journal:

> *I watched the Academy Awards last night and caught a glimpse of what I think God sees when He sees those self-centered, misinformed, ignorant snobs. I saw fear. I saw deep within each self-absorbed man and woman a depth of fear and suffering like I will never know as a child of God. This is why their heads are in the sand when it comes to reality. They can't look at it with any hope of anything greater than themselves. I felt sad for them. They've never really lived. They've never truly known love or peace or joy. They've never learned that life is found by dying. It's tragic.*

When I rediscovered and read that old journal entry two decades later, my body flooded with both shame and gratitude because here's the bizarre thing: I happened to read that journal entry **the very day after** watching the 2023 Academy Awards exactly twenty years later. The thoughts and feelings I had after watching the 2023 Academy Awards were so profoundly different that I decided to write a follow-up blurb to see how much I had changed in twenty years:

> *I watched the Academy Awards last night and caught a glimpse of what I think God sees when Love embodies those vibrant, talented human beings who have put their hearts and souls into their art. I saw deep within each brave man and woman a depth of love and connection like I have known as a child of God. This is why their heads and hearts and hands are immersed in their craft of attempting to reveal what is transcendent and real. They can see small glimpses, through their work, of something Greater than themselves, and this is what gives their lives meaning—to be able to offer this hope to*

> *others through art. I felt love for them. They are living with freedom and courage, willing to try, to fail, and to try again. They are willing to edit, practice, and rework it, and they are willing to have conversations. They have learned that life is found by living it to the fullest, in all its joys, sorrows, and unanswered questions. It's miraculous.*

The fact that we can evolve into brand-new versions of ourselves is also miraculous, but God doesn't change anyone without their desire, permission, and cooperation. I want to clarify this for anyone who might be looping on the thought, "See! People change! My abusive partner can change! I just know it!" No, abusers don't often change, simply because they don't think anything is wrong with them, and no amount of telling them is going to change their minds.

Which brings us back to sin. I have observed and personally experienced being on the receiving end of Christians who point out the sins of others using carefully selected Bible verses dotted with syrupy Christian clichés, and it's ugly and painful. I know many of them *mean well*. They're just scared. "If people aren't perfect, they will suffer, so let's help everyone be perfect."

That never works, and sometimes it turns into a tit for tat. "Well, now, *wait a minute*. What about your own sin? Take the log out of your own eye, and I'll worry about the speck in mine."

"But you need to focus on your own sin!"

"And you need to focus on yours!"

And on and on it goes.

If we try to tell our adult children what they are doing wrong, we can kiss their asses goodbye because most adults don't like that. If we want healthy adult relationships, we have to learn how to mind our own beeswax. I've tried doing this in my own little parenting experiment to see if it works. My adult kids appreciate the space and opportunity to make their own choices and mistakes, even if they are "sinful" according to some people. *But wait a minute, what if they are sinful according to God?* What if they are? I no longer worship an anxious little god in the corner wringing his hands over how the world is going to hell in a handbasket. This means I don't have to be afraid, either. I worship a Big Creator God who can handle hard stuff, including my kids and their issues. God loves them more than I ever could. Does this mean I have to experience the heartache of watching them suffer in pain from some of their poor decisions? Yes. Bossing kids around *does* have its perks. If they listen, then you get to feel better about yourself. You get to be in control of all the people, and that feels powerful. But that will also come back to bite you in the butt down the road because, like I said, adults don't like bossy pants, and they will eventually set you aside so they can live their own lives. Don't worry, though! You've still got a life to control. *Your own.*

I read an amazing book a few years ago called *A Failure of Nerve* by Edwin Friedman, and I learned the truth that we will never be able to influence anyone who is in movement away from us.[7] To try to do that is a wasted effort, and yet this is what many of us tend to do. We chase, argue, shame, strong-arm, and threaten people into the kingdom of heaven, but we are only deluding ourselves. *"Woe to you, teachers of the law and Pharisees, you hypocrites! You travel over land and sea to win a single convert, and when you have succeeded, you make them twice as much a child of hell as you are"* (Matthew 23:15).

So how do we change the world? By now, you know what I'm going to say, right? Love. The love that says "buh-bye" to fear. Love is a huge game changer, and Love will inevitably influence those in movement toward it. Plus, here's the cool thing: *Most people are attracted to love.* Humans are wired to crave it. So, if you want to influence your adult kids or anyone else on the planet, learn how to love. Jesus ate and drank with sinners. He was witness to their thoughts, ideas, hurts, confusion, anger, and shame. He didn't add to the mess by heaping more shame on them. He held space for them and gave them the gift of time and grace. What if we could be like that? What if the same God/Love/Source/Creator who was embedded in the core of Jesus Christ was also embedded in our core? This was the whole point of his story.

We create what we focus on. I don't want to focus on sin anymore. I want to focus on Love. I wonder what will happen. Want to join me?

87
Church and Bible

"[T]he Bible is sacred because it is our introduction to God; it is not the end point of our understanding. The Bible was never intended to create boundaries for God; let us not limit the Creator of the universe with God's own set of Scriptures. When we act as if the expansiveness of God can be contained within sixty-six books, we are shortchanging both God and ourselves."

—Tiffany Yecke Brooks, *Gaslighted by God*

During the course of my life, I have added all kinds of things to my faith. Ideas about how to get to heaven, how to raise godly kids, what to believe about marriage, what the correct male and female roles are, how not to cause men to lust but also how to keep men happy, what denominations and authors and pastors are good and which ones are bad, how to dress, how to talk (or not, as the case may be), how much to give and to whom to give it, for whom to vote, and how to interpret the Bible. My whole life I've felt like I was walking on a path that was twelve inches wide on the edge of a mountainside. On one side was the mountain wall, and on the other side was a drop-off that would lead to going *splat*. Over the past ten years as I've tossed these collected ideas over the cliff, one by one, I've watched that path widen until now I am no longer on a narrow path, but rather in a wide-open field where I can run and dance and *be* without any fear. "*He brought me out into a spacious place; he rescued me because he delighted in me"* (*Psalm 18:19, NIV*).

In Matthew 23, Jesus got pissy at the Pharisees for heaping heavy burdens on the people. I wonder why. Could it be because rules weren't the point of a relationship with God? What if we can have an intimate, thriving, happy, connected relationship with our Creator without all the add-ons?

I wanted to find out.

When COVID hit, many of the churches in our area shut down, and I used that as my excuse to stop going. Church triggered me anyway. I'd walk in and feel my anxiety skyrocket. I'd look at people and wonder if they were frauds preparing to groom and manipulate their next innocent victim. It wasn't going to be me or my kids. No sir. These Christians scared the hell out of me now.

Also, after getting controlling, manipulative emails and messages littered with hundreds of Bible verses (because God agreed with them, after all), I decided to set my Bible aside for a while as well. Would God love me if I didn't go to church *or* read the Bible? Was He a whiny god stomping His feet around heaven when people didn't follow orders, kind of like the Greek and Roman gods or the religious leaders in the Bible or the ones in my church? Or was He different? Bigger? More mature? More confident in His ability to succeed at whatever He set out to accomplish without my help? Maybe more mysterious?

I decided to ask myself, "What does it mean to simply follow Jesus?" Wasn't that a Christian anyway? A Christ follower? I didn't set my Bible down completely. I read through the gospel of John over two dozen times. I would read through it and then go back to the beginning and read through it again. After doing this, I boiled my faith down to one thing: Love.

That's it.

But what does that mean? I wanted to find out without church and without the Bible and without the rules of my particular denomination or any denomination, for that matter. I wanted to find out from the Spirit, whom Jesus said I had within me. But this meant I needed to stop *doing* and start *listening*. I needed to ask more questions instead of thinking I already had all the answers. And I needed to be okay with never having all the answers. Or even a fraction of them. The universe was bigger than that. Could I be okay with the mystery of God? The mystery of Love?

So, when a child used drugs or had sex or mistreated their body, instead of freaking out, I started asking myself, "Where is Love showing up here? And how can I be a conduit of that Love?" When a child was disrespectful and ungrateful, instead of being indignant and taking it personally, I asked the same question, "How is Love showing up here, and how can I be a conduit of that Love?" I decided that Love was always present in every situation, including the messy ones. I needed to be better at *seeing* it.

The key, I discovered, was tapping into that Love within myself *for myself*. If I didn't feel safe and held in that Love, I couldn't offer it to anyone around me. You might think that offering Love means letting people abuse you. I don't think so. Sometimes people *will* abuse us, and we can't control that. They will steal our wallet or our identity. They will drive drunk and kill a loved one. They will spread lies about us. People are messy, and they do egregious things that create all kinds of chaos and heartache for themselves and the world around them. Love might mean calling the police and getting an unsafe person into a place where they can't harm others who need protection. Love might mean holding space for and weeping with someone who has made harmful choices for themselves and letting them know you care, and you understand why they thought they could solve their pain through those choices. Love might mean letting go, like the father of the prodigal son did, but always standing at the door, ready to throw a feast for them when they come home. Sometimes love means crying out in anguish over the grave of a treasured person and raging in agony over how they were lost.

I try to think about how Love shows up for all of the people in the story and not just some. If a daddy is abusing his children, how does Love show up for the abuser, and how does Love show up for the children? I wrestle with questions like this, but I don't ask people for the answers anymore. I look to the Spirit of God within me for help to understand because that Spirit is full of wisdom and ready to offer it to anyone who is seeking. Jesus modeled this best. He broke Sabbath laws to Love. Love over law. Wisdom over words on a page. He didn't throw out the law or the words, but He showed us how Love transforms all of it. Love fulfills all of it.

What would happen if people who followed Jesus delighted in learning new things and thinking in new ways instead of being certain they already have all the answers? Isn't that what Jesus was trying to communicate when He said the kingdom of heaven was made up of children? Children don't think they have all the answers. (At least not until they reach their teen years and suddenly know everything.) Children love to learn, explore, think creatively without inhibitions, and stretch their imaginations beyond the limits of what we know to be reality on this planet. In the Gospels, we learn that the *oh-so-wise* disciples wanted to shoo the children away. What did those pesky kids know? They couldn't possibly appreciate who Jesus was. He was the Messiah who would overthrow those terrible Romans! "Stand back, young 'uns! We've got important business here!" But Jesus wasn't having any of that. The disciples' wisdom was foolish. What might be different in this world if a few people followed in the footsteps of

Jesus? We can, you know. But we'll have to leave our smarty pants behind.

What about suffering? How can God stand by and watch suffering when He could do something about it? We think, "Hey, I'm a Christian! If I play my cards right, I shouldn't have miscarriages or watch my friend die or get diabetes!" Really? Christian or not, if you are human, you are born to trouble (John 16:33). This planet is chaotic, and humans are chaotic. While I was writing this book, a young boy was killed in a boating accident at the little Christian camp my own two boys were attending. A family dropped their child off for a fun week at camp not knowing they would never see him again. It was a senseless accident that will haunt many people for the rest of their lives, and yet, that kind of thing is happening randomly all over the world every second of every day. Nobody is exempt. How do we make sense of it? We can't. All we can do is feel the pain. There are no answers for us today, and maybe we need to let go of our need to have them right now. That's not what we are offered. What we *are* offered is a life, however brief, to live. How do we want to live it? That is the only thing we have any control over. Our own life. Our own Self.

Jesus came right smack dab into the middle of this mess, and people viewed him as a poor bastard baby. The Jews thought their Messiah should overthrow the Roman government and set up peace on earth. Don't we think that? "GOD SHOULD DO THIS AND THAT AND THE OTHER THING AND MAKE EVERYTHING PERFECT AND RIGHT, AND WE CHRISTIANS ARE GOING TO HELP HIM DO IT!"

But God didn't do that, and God doesn't do that. God is doing something different. Jesus tried to explain what God is doing with the analogies of the little mustard seed eventually growing into a great tree and the little grain of yeast eventually leavening the whole lump of dough. Jesus was the seed; Jesus was the grain of Love. And the kingdom of God is the tree and the dough. God isn't planning to "win" by overthrowing power systems, fighting, and trying to gain power over others by setting up little kingdoms with little kings in the world or in our churches or in our homes. When Christians try this, they are using human methods to achieve their goals. That's a sign that they are not listening or tuning in to the Holy Spirit or Love within them because God's way is different. The kingdom of God starts in one individual heart. Love grows there and then spills over into another individual heart and so on and so forth until the world is transformed. This is a slow process. We will never see the end result in our lifetime, but we all play a role. We are all mustard seeds. We are all grains of yeast. Will we grow Love in our own hearts? Will we hold Love for others?

Jesus said He was the vine, and we are the branches. Love is the vine. Are we grafted into it? Connected to it? Allowing its lifeblood to flow through us? *Do you love the person who has your name?* (That's you!) It starts there, yet oddly, many Christians teach self-loathing. No wonder churches are full of anemic Lovers. We are skilled at self-deprecation and flagellation—so much so that when we are done beating ourselves up, we turn to our neighbor to finish the business.

"*Let no one deceive himself. If any of you thinks he is wise in this age, he should become a fool, so that he may become wise. For the wisdom of this world is foolishness in God's sight*" (1 Corinthians 3:18–19).

I'm not currently attending any church and, amazingly, my relationship with God is more real, vibrant, and life-giving than it ever was in the days when I was jumping through all those religious hoops. Jesus never came to set up another world religion. He came to offer something better. Love. It's as simple as that. Gobbledygook to some. Life-changing to others. "*He who has ears to hear, let him hear*" (Matthew 11:15).

Going to church isn't bad. In fact, having a community around our faith can be life-giving and satisfying. But if you've suffered from egregious abuse at the hands of people from churches you've attended, it's not only okay to take a break, but it might be necessary in order to heal. Not going to church doesn't mean you aren't a Christian or that you're a subpar Christian. There are other ways to connect with those who share your faith, and of course, every moment of every day you are connected to your loving Creator. Never forget that connection has nothing to do with what you do or don't do.

In my fifties, I traded an oppressive, man-made religion for the Living Creator God. I left behind my fishing nets and everything else I knew and loved to follow Love. And now that I've written it down for my grandchildren and great-grandchildren and all the children after that, I'm never looking back. I hope they don't, either.

88
Prayer

A woman of faith in an emotionally abusive relationship has likely spent most of her life fervently praying for relief. Praying for help. Praying for hope. Praying for answers. Praying for her children. Praying for a healed marriage. Praying for her husband to wake up and stop hurting their family. Praying to be a better wife. Praying for patience and perseverance. Praying for power and grace. Begging to be seen and heard.

And finally, after years of no change and nothing to show for her investment of time and emotional energy, she stops. God will do what He does, so what's the point of asking for anything different? God becomes an extension of her abusive partner—refusing to hear or see or validate her. Controlling everything. Doling out tokens of kindness here and there simply to string her along. Desiring one thing only: His own glory and fame. She is a pawn in her husband's game and an even smaller, more insignificant pawn in God's game. She is powerless, helpless, and hopeless. It's a dark and desolate place to be.

This was me. I spent thirty to sixty minutes a day pacing my kitchen floor before the family woke up—praying. Just praying. But what if prayer isn't what we think it is? What if the purpose of prayer is totally different? What if the god we were praying to doesn't even exist? What if our Creator is so much more than a gumball machine? What if the point of prayer is simply *Love*?

If we believe the purpose of our life is to go from one tangible victory to another, we will be sorely disappointed. Victories defined by our limited, time-and-space-locked consciousness are almost always things that bring us comfort and joy *now*. Christians love a good testimony. "I once was blind, but now I see." "I once was sick, but now I'm healed." "I once was stuck, but now I'm free." What about the ones who remain blind? Sick? Stuck? We don't like to talk about them. In fact, because that scares us, we push them away and blame them for their problems. If it's their fault, then we can avoid catching their bad luck disease by our own efforts of working hard, being good, and praying right.

If we expected that blindness, sickness, and stuckness would sometimes be companions on our journey, we might resist less. I no longer think of prayer as something I *do*. I think of it as something I *am*. I no longer believe prayer is a simple, single formula for connection to God. I believe prayer is a way of *being*.

When Paul says to "pray without ceasing" in 1 Thessalonians, I think this is what he is talking about. If we think of prayer as being an audible dialogue between us and God with some possible physical rules like making sure eyes are closed, heads are bowed, and knees are bent, we will not be able to pray without ceasing. Someone's got to make dinner. But what if prayer is a posture of simply being aware that we are in the presence of our Creator every moment of every day? Our inner rant while we drive down Highway 35W is a prayer. So is belting out the words to Katy Perry's "Roar" a few minutes later. So, too, are the body-wracked sobs we have that night in our empty bed after we've put the kids to sleep, and the house is quiet and dark and lonely. All of it. Sacred time and space. Prayer.

Consider this: What if the very darkness and feeling of abandonment is your current prayer? And what if the Creator always meets you there even if you don't sense His presence? How would your life change if you knew—really *knew*—this was true?

Praying *can* be pacing your kitchen floor every morning, but it is so much more than that. Prayer is life. Every breath you take in and out is a prayer. Every walk you take, wherever it leads you, is a prayer. Every bite of food you enjoy is a prayer. Every thought you have is a prayer because God is woven into the fabric of your DNA. You are *one* with God. As a beloved creation, your very existence is a prayer simply because you are connected in a mysterious, cosmic way to your Creator. This Source is part of you. As your awareness of this connection grows, you will experience more and more confidence and peace and rest in that Presence. It is there even when you are unaware of it, in the same way an infant's relationship and communication with its mother is very real and sweet and intimate although the infant is not cognizant of the scope of that relationship or communication. Prayer is our intimate, mysterious, and powerful connection with the Lover of our souls. It is our oxygen.

We want so badly for life to be this way. I put in a quarter—I get a big, juicy, colorful gumball. I put in the time—I get a promotion. I put in the right ingredients—I get a delicious apple pie. I put in the homeschooling—I get godly children who will rise up and call me blessed. I put on a jumper that covers my knees—I never get sexually abused by a man. I put in a certain number of hours in prayer—I get all my prayers answered (most of them in my lifetime).

Prayer doesn't work that way. As we've learned, life on planet Earth sucks. Abusers live to a ripe old age without sanctions while victims die young from cancer. Kids rebel. Hurricanes destroy homes and kill people. Daddies molest their children. This is not what God envisioned, but despite the choices humans make, Love is doing a bazillion, trillion things every moment of every day to create beauty out of the ashes of our lives when they collide with the brokenness of Earth. Life on this planet will always be a bouquet of roses and thorns.

God doesn't promise us a gumball for a quarter, but God does promise that Love will always be with us while we are still in the middle of all that is wrong on Earth. And we also know Love's got us when life is over, and God will make everything right in the fullness of time. When we give up our gumball machine idea of God, "we pass from thinking of God as part of our life to the realization that we are part of his life," writes Richard J. Foster in his book *Prayer*.[8] Prayer brings unseen powers into play that change the course of history in ways we will not see until eternity. As we grow into our awareness of how connected we are to our Creator, even when we cannot see or feel it, we will also grow in our confident conviction that God not only hears us, but God goes into action in the world because of us. Greg Boyd preached a sermon called "Why We Can't Know Why," where he said everything every human does all day long has a ripple effect that continues through all of history.[9] Think about that. It's mind-boggling. It reminds me of the movie *The Curious Case of Benjamin Button*, in which a ballerina is hit by a truck. The scene plays backward through all the minute things that happened leading up to the accident. If only the phone hadn't rung. If only a man hadn't taken her taxi. If only the taxi driver hadn't purchased a cup of coffee. If only. If only. If only. But all those things *did* happen, and the result meant the ballerina and the truck were at the same place at the same time, and there was a horrible accident. Now take that scene and multiply it an infinite number of times, and this is what is going on in the world on any given second of any given day. For thousands and thousands of years. And while God doesn't control all these minuscule choices everyone is making, Love does infuse life with a bazillion, trillion stories of redemption. There are hurricanes, yes. And there are also rainbows.

So where does prayer come in? Greg Boyd says that if life is made up of an infinite number of ripples from all our human choices, prayer is like throwing a big boulder in the water. Now we've got a *wave*. Prayer makes a difference, but perhaps not in the ways we always want. We have to remember that we are finite, and we don't know what God knows. When I think of how I might apply this to my own life, I think of how I prayed for my kids all those years, and so many of them are suffering in ways I never wanted them to suffer. Some are confused. Some have turned away from God. How can this be? Can I trust God? Did God not "choose" them to be His own? Were they created for the sole purpose of being lost for all eternity? If God is who I believe God is, I cannot believe that's true. I don't trust my kids to know or understand what is best for them. I don't trust them to make wise choices. I don't trust them to cling to God.

I trust God to save them in Love's own time and in Love's own way. I surrender my fear for them and my love for them to our Creator who loves them and knows them far better than I could ever dream of knowing or loving them. When I pray that Love will restore broken relationships one day, I believe, in faith, that love will do things I'll never know about to bring such a restoration. If not here on Earth, then in eternity. This life is not all there is. The wonderful story God is writing doesn't find its ending in time and space.

How does God answer prayer on this planet? Through us. We are the hands and feet of Jesus in this world. We demonstrate who God is by our actions. When we fight for justice and truth, we are showing the character of God. Imperfect, yes. But *still*. Amazing privilege. You may pray that others will see the truth, but Love may answer by helping *you* to see the truth. You may pray for God to open a door, but Love may turn you around and open a completely different door, a door you didn't know existed before. When we see wrongs that need to be righted, people who need to be cared for, or projects that need to be created, that is the Holy Spirit moving us to be Love's presence in this world.

    God was always going to rescue me from abuse. How? Through a woman named Natalie. But first, Love had to teach me how to be a rescuer. And the first victim I needed to rescue was myself.

89
Surprise

We sat around the Christmas tree opening presents, youngest to oldest. It was the day after Christmas, but what is a day? We were all there, with the exception of one son who had to work, but all the other pieces of Christmas were intact and humming with energy. The music, the smells, the talking and laughing, and the presents. We're big on presents. I got that from my mom, although her wrapped presents were always gorgeous works of art, while mine were wrapped efficiently if not prettily.

One of my daughters handed me a small shirt box. She was expecting her first baby, but the rest of the family didn't know about it yet. Her plan was to have me open a present, and the gift inside would reveal her special secret to everyone else. I feigned ignorance and opened the box. Inside was a cute little onesie with "Baby ____ #1" on the front along with an ultrasound picture. I acted surprised and showed everyone the T-shirt, anticipating their howls of delight. They howled all right, but not for the reason I was thinking. My daughter said, "Mom, look at the name on the T-shirt." I looked. The last name on the shirt was not my daughter's last name. It was my son's. *What?!* My son and *his* wife were having a baby, too?!

Surprise!

They had been trying for a few years with repeated miscarriages, so I was almost crying with happiness for them and for all of us. This meant we would be expecting my first two grandbabies in 2023. Amazing.

Then, my daughter handed me a second small shirt box, and sure enough, inside was her announcement with a "Baby ____#1" onesie inside. The crowd cheered with joy, and it was quite a moment. We commenced with everyone else opening gifts until my turn came around again. My younger, unmarried son handed me a small shirt box that looked just like the first two. I glanced at his girlfriend who was grinning and then nervously opened the box, trying to think about how to react if this was what I was afraid it was.

Inside the box was a onesie that said "Baby ____ #2" with an ultrasound picture. My oldest son and his wife were having *twins*! I was crying, and everyone was screaming with excitement. Unbelievable. What a miracle. I could not wrap my brain around it. I had a lot of kids, but never twins. This was a first for our family, and I was in raptures about it.

After we had calmed down again, we resumed going around the circle opening gifts until everyone finished. I had one last gift, a small box, and I opened it carefully, enjoying this last bit of Christmas surprise. All balled up in a tiny wad was another little onesie with the words "Baby _____ #3" and a third ultrasound picture. There was silence. My brain almost shut down; it was overloaded with shock. And then it hit me. My son and his wife were having *triplets*. "Stop. It," I shouted. "You've got to be kidding me." I felt a combination of exhilaration and profound fear. What if they lost all three of them? This would be a high-risk pregnancy. What if something goes wrong? All the little parts on my bus were throwing food in every direction, and I could feel the chaos inside. Some parts were cheering and celebrating while others were screaming out in terror. In a fog, I hugged my daughter-in-law and spent the next few hours processing this surprise.

"It's a miracle." I had heard those words before. But I had also watched miracles go sour. Were they still miracles if they died? What if the triplets lived and my daughter's baby died? How would she and her husband get through that? The babies were all due within a week of each other. I knew all the things that could go wrong. My serious, cautious, and prepared parts went into full-blown panic, yelling out directions and preparation strategies. "Batten down the hatches! There's a storm brewing! WE SHALL SURVIVE!"

Other parts were bawling: "*No! We will not survive! Might as well jump off the boat now!*"

Other parts were wide-eyed with quiet wonder and hope. And still other parts were dancing on tables in wild, joyous abandon looking for the nearest person to bear hug.

And where was I? I could see me inside, interwoven with Creator God, quietly and lovingly watching all the drama on my bus. All I could feel there in that serene space was pure love. Love for my children. Love for those tiny babies who were already changing the world by just *being* and nothing more. Love for all my own dramatic, wild, and beautiful parts who had their own beliefs and good reasons for reacting in all their various ways. Everything made sense in my core. Where God *was*. Where God ***is***. Where God will *always and forever be*. And guess what? God isn't little or scary.

Surprise.

Epilogue

My four (cutest ever) grandbabies are all here now, beginning their own Grand Adventure. It will be full of disappointment, failures, setbacks, and heartaches. And it will also be full of fun, wins, discoveries, and Love.

Always Love.

Dear Reader,

This was my story, but **what about yours?** If you have struggled with the same questions and relentless anxiety you read about in my story, I want you to know you're not alone. In 2016, I gathered together thirty Christian women, and we called ourselves Flying Free. We met weekly on Zoom, where I taught classes and coached. I invited guest speakers to come in and teach from their areas of expertise. I invited members to share their stories. That little group of women grew into a thriving community of hundreds, and we started a private forum where everyone could connect 24/7. If you're ready to do the same work I've done healing my relationship with God and with myself, **I'd love to have you join us!** You can learn more about our education and coaching community and how you can be part of it by going to joinflyingfree.com. The Flying Free program is specifically for women of faith in emotionally and spiritually destructive marriages, families, and communities.

In 2018, I wrote a bestselling book that is recommended by counselors and therapists throughout the United States. It's called *Is it Me? Making Sense of Your Confusing Marriage: A Christian Woman's Guide to Hidden Emotional and Spiritual Abuse*. You can purchase this book in paperback, Kindle, and Audible formats on Amazon. I also created a comprehensive companion workbook to help you process the things you'll learn in my book and augment your therapy work. I'd love to send you the first chapters of my book and companion workbook when you join my mailing list. Just head over to my website, flyingfreenow.com, to sign up.

Dear Reader

In 2019, I started the Flying Free podcast, and every week I release a new episode to educate, encourage, and inspire Christian women in destructive relationships. You can find the Flying Free podcast on your favorite podcast app.

And finally, if you aren't sure whether or not you are in an emotionally abusive marriage, I've created a quiz to help you figure that out. You can take that quiz by going to emotionalabusequiz.com.

Thank you for spending this time with me. Our time together does not have to end here. Let's stay in touch!

xoxo

Natalie

Notes

1. Schwartz, Richard, PhD. *Introduction to Internal Family Systems, Second Edition.* Colorado, US: Sounds True, 2023.
2. Riemersma, Jenna. *Altogether You: Experiencing Personal and Spiritual Transformation with Internal Family Systems Therapy.* Pivotal Press, 2020.
3. Augustine, St. *Augustine of Hippo, Selected Writings.* New Jersey, US: Paulist Press, 1984.
4. Chambers, Oswald. "February 23: The Determination to Serve." *My Utmost for His Highest.* Grand Rapids, MI: Our Daily Bread Publishing, 2017.
5. Yungen, Ray. *A Time of Departing: How Ancient Mystical Practices Are Uniting Christians with the World's Religions.* Oregon, US: Lighthouse Trails Publishing, 2020.
6. Schwartz, Richard, PhD. *No Bad Parts: Healing Trauma and Restoring Wholeness with the Internal Family Systems Model.* Colorado, US: Sounds True, 2021.
7. Friedman, Edward. *A Failure of Nerve: Leadership in the Age of the Quick Fix.* Seabury Books, 2007.
8. Foster, Richard J. *Prayer: Finding the Heart's True Home, Tenth Anniversary Edition.* New York: HarperOne, 2002.
9. Boyd, Greg. "Why We Can't Know Why." Woodland Hills Church, St. Paul, MN. June 18, 2017. Video, 40:43. https://whchurch.org/sermon/why-we-cant-know-why/.

Made in United States
North Haven, CT
19 March 2024